35

S

HOU

LOCATION

HOUSE OF COMMONS LIBRARY

LOCATION	R DEFENCE
AUTHOR	SMITH
Acc DATE	**26 OCT 2006**

HOUSE OF COMMONS LIBRARY

TO BE
DISPOSED
BY
AUTHORITY

D1580352

House of Commons Library

54056000842143

H. 114

The Defence of the Realm in the 1980s

Dan Smith

CROOM HELM LONDON

© 1980 Dan Smith
Croom Helm Ltd, 2-10 St John's Road, London SW11

British Library Cataloguing in Publication Data

Smith, Dan
    The defence of the realm in the 1980's.
    1. Great Britain – Military policy
    I. Title
    355.03'35'41   UA647
    ISBN 0-85664-873-6

HOUSE OF COMMONS
LIBRARY
CATALOGUED

Printed and bound in Great Britain by
Biddles Ltd, Guildford and King's Lynn

CONTENTS

FIGURES AND TABLES

Figures

Tables

GLOSSARY OF ABBREVIATIONS

Note: Given below are the full forms of abbreviations used in the text and notes; for the meaning of the terms, see the text. It should also be noted that much military equipment is referred to by an assortment of numbers and letters; these are code terms rather than abbreviations and are not included in this glossary.

ABM	Anti-ballistic missile(s)
ACDA	Arms Control and Disarmament Agency
ADM	Atomic demolition munitions
AFV	Armoured fighting vehicle(s)
AFVG	Anglo-French variable geometry aircraft
AGM	Air-to-ground missile(s)
ALCM	Air-launched cruise missile(s)
APC	Armoured personnel-carrier(s)
ASM	Anti-ship missile(s)
AST 403	Air Staff Target 403
ASW	Anti-submarine warfare
ATGW	Anti-tank guided weapon(s)
AWACS	Airborne Warning and Control System
BAC	British Aircraft Corporation
BAOR	British Army of the Rhine
C^3	Command, Control and Communications
CDB	Command data buffer
CIA	Central Intelligence Agency
DoD	Department of Defense
ECCM	Electronic counter-counter measures
ECM	Electronic counter measures
EEC	European Economic Community
EMP	Electromagnetic Pulse
EMS	European Monetary System
ERW	Enhanced Radiation Warhead
FRG	Federal Republic of Germany
GCD	General and Complete Disarmament
GDP	Gross Domestic Product
GLCM	Ground-launched cruise missile(s)
GNP	Gross National Product

ICBM	Inter-continental ballistic missile(s)
IEPG	Independent European Programme Group
IISS	International Institute for Strategic Studies
IRA	Irish Republican Army
JCS	Joint Chiefs of Staff
LRCM	Long range cruise missile(s)
MAD	Mutual assured destruction
MBB	Messerschmidt-Boelkow-Blohm
MBFR	Mutual and Balanced Force Reductions
MBT 80	Main Battle Tank 80
MEASL	Marconi-Elliott Avionics Systems
MFR	Mutual Force Reductions
MIRV	Multiple independently targetted re-entry vehicle(s)
MoD	Ministry of Defence
MoU	Memorandum of Understanding
MP	Member of Parliament
MRCA	Multi-role combat aircraft
MRV	Multiple re-entry vehicle(s)
MUREFAAMCE	Mutual Reductions of Forces and Armaments and Associated Measures in Central Europe
NATO	North Atlantic Treaty Organisation
NPG	Nuclear Planning Group
PGM	Precision-guided munition(s)
RAF	Royal Air Force
RN	Royal Navy
ROF	Royal Ordnance Factory
SAC	Strategic Air Command
SACEUR	Supreme Allied Commander in Europe
SALT	Strategic Arms Limitation Talks
SAM	Surface-to-air missile(s)
SIOP	Single Integrated Operational Plan
SIPRI	Stockholm International Peace Research Institute
SLBM	Submarine-launched ballistic missile(s)
SLCM	Submarine-launched cruise missile(s)
SMS	Stores management system
SSBN	(Nuclear-powered submarine equipped with nuclear missiles)
TEA	Triethyl aluminium
TNW	Tactical nuclear weapon(s)
TOW	Tube-fired, Optically-tracked, Wire-guided
UKVG	United Kingdom variable geometry aircraft

PREFACE

The subject of this book is British defence policy, seen as an aspect of the external relations of the British state; it is a study of the way in which, and the circumstances in which, the state organises armed force in support of its interests and in response to the pressures and challenges of international politics. But it is, or tries to be, a study in a particular sense — a critical study, not simply an outline but a series of questions about the evolution and conditions of policy, about its current form and its possible future trajectory, questions to which the answers are regularly discomforting.

In developing its subject, the book perforce ranges rather widely, discussing the domestic political and economic conditions of defence policy and its international context. Arguments are advanced about, amongst other things, the nature of military power and its limitations and dangers, the evolution of nuclear strategy and military technology, the policy of the USSR and developments within the western alliance, the crisis of the international capitalist system and the possible responses to it, the meaning of military confrontation in Europe and the prospects for measures of disarmament, possible sources for change in defence policy and the barriers to change. It involves both discussion of recent history and speculation on the shape of international politics in the 1980s and beyond. Yet despite this ambitious scope, I am uncomfortably aware of certain limitations, of further issues which might have been raised or treated more fully.

In particular, little space is given to the increasing multi-polarity of world power. The policies and evolution of China and Japan, changes in the international military order as more states procure sophisticated weaponry, and the dangerous potential of the international proliferation of possession of nuclear weapons receive scant attention. One reason for this is simply the need to draw the line somewhere, to present a study of reasonable length in which the main themes are relatively clear; a second reason, which makes this lack excusable, is that British defence policy is largely focussed into the bi-polar East-West confrontation, and it is this arena of rivalry which must be of the highest priority in a discussion of that policy. I should add that a further aspect of growing multi-polarity, the relative decline of the USA and the potential for increased power for Western Europe, is a major theme, especially of the later chapters.

I am also aware that the discussion of the dilemmas and contradictions of British and American policy and strategy is not adequately matched by a similar discussion of Soviet policy. Here I have preferred to sketch the broad outlines of Soviet policy, its weaknesses, dilemmas and dangers, rather than venture into the details of the difficult and murky subject of the nature of Soviet society, the domestic roots of its foreign policy, the history of its development and the ideological and political forms that have been produced.

I have also given only peripheral attention to a crucial problem of defence policy, the reality of and potential for the domestic use of armed force against political and other groups who oppose the state in one form or another. The issue is treated only where it is relevant to the subject of defence policy as an aspect of external relations. I do not want either to understate the importance of this problem or to ignore the evident connections between external and internal aspects of defence policy, but I have deliberately chosen to focus in this work on the external aspects, which I believe are insufficiently studied and understood, even by those who have voiced concern about the domestic dimensions of force. Too often, military preparations against an external threat are seen as a charade or a sideshow; they are not — armed force is a basic reality of international politics, even when it is not actively employed, and of the relations of the British state with both its allies and its adversaries.

That, however, is enough about what the book does not contain. In seeking to analyse British defence policy I have taken a rather function-alist approach: issues outside the strict confines of defence policy as such are included only where an understanding of them is essential to an understanding of the basic subject. Readers will have to decide whether the account is satisfactory, or whether it is too narrow or too wide.

It is always difficult to assess what a book's readership will be. In writing this book, I have had hopes that it will be of interest both to specialists and students of the subject, and to people who are averagely informed about current events and politics, especially to those who have a specific or general sense of unease about parts or all of British defence policy. With these aspirations towards an expert and a general readership, I hope the balance of the language and presentation of arguments will satisfy both: I have tried to avoid boring the expert with long explana-tions of familiar terms and concepts, and to avoid baffling the layperson with esoteric and abbreviated formulations. The subject of military policy has developed its own language; when drawing on its vocabulary I have explained the terms except where they are self-explanatory, and have occasionally jettisoned the specialised terms in favour of others more accessible to a wider readership. One feature of the language is its love of initials and acronyms; when these are used they are explained, and there is also a glossary to refresh the memory in those paragraphs where sets of initials pile up at a dizzying speed. At the same time, I have tried to effect some kind of a balance between generalisations and detailed points, between abstract and concrete analysis, in which both elements are equally necessary.

The book begins with two brief chapters which outline the conceptual basis on which it proceeds. The term *defence* is itself controversial — who or what is being 'defended' and is it a completely reactive process? Chapter 1 discusses this question, while the second chapter seeks to clarify the meaning of *strategy* in the military context. This is followed by a discussion of the main dilemmas of British defence policy via the context of international alliances and super power rivalry (Chapter 3) and military confrontation, especially in Europe (Chapter 4), arriving at its British destination in Chapter 5. The outstanding theme of Chapter 5 is the problems the British state has faced in making adequate resources available to sustain the military capabilities it has desired, problems exacerbated by massive increases in the costs of major weapon systems and the challenges of technological advance. The problem of costs and the momentum of military technology is the subject of Chapter 6, which opens the way for a discussion in Chapter 7 of the possibility of resolving these problems through closer West European or trans-Atlantic co-operation, a discussion necessarily set in the context of intra-alliance relations and possible developments. Chapter 7 deals with the prospects for changes in the process of armament, and is complemented by Chapter 8, a discussion of the prospects for establishing a genuine process of disarmament. Finally, Chapters 9 and 10 draw the threads of the arguments together, to assess both the likely and the desirable options for British defence policy through the 1980s on the basis of the trajectories of Britain, its allies and main adversaries as the decade unfolds. Roughly, the book falls into three parts: the first five chapters outline the conceptual and factual background, the next three assess the impetus for some kind of change, and the last two speculate on the outcome.

I firmly hope that the discussion of options in defence policy in the final chapter does not turn out to be the last word on the question; it is intended to stimulate further thinking, not close the subject off. It would not only be a matter for personal frustration if it were the last word, it would also, more importantly, be a political disaster. The chapter sets out options between which choices can be made, but in the absence of a wide-ranging and challenging debate which breaks the grip of a narrow consensus on the subject, there will be no recognisable choices. Instead, the British state through the forces of inertia and stagnation, will simply edge and slip in one direction or another, whichever direction requires the least change and imagination. The first necessary condition, though it alone is not sufficient, for genuine choices about British defence policy is the development and enrichment of a political process of debate. This book is a small contribution towards it.

ACKNOWLEDGEMENTS

I must take this opportunity of gratefully acknowledging invaluable assistance I have received in the course of writing and researching for this book.

The basic research was conducted in 1976/7 with the support of a grant from the Joseph Rowntree Charitable Trust; I am especially grateful to the Trustees for helping me start on this task, and for appointing a small group to review and discuss my work consisting of Sidney Bailey, Trevor Jepson and Nicholas Sims who have already received my thanks. Further research has been conducted as part of a project on weapons procurement and production in Western Europe, funded by the Deutsche Gesellschaft für Friedens- und Konflictforschung, without which the book would not have been possible. I also want to thank my colleagues in this project for invaluable discussion and intellectual stimulation — Michael Brzoska, Peter Lock and Herbert Wulf in Hamburg and Clare Mundy in London.

My work has been pursued in the hospitable conditions provided by the Richardson Institute for Conflict and Peace Research, under the gentle and pleasant direction of Michael Nicholson, and more recently by the Department of Economics in Birkbeck College. I have also been fortunate enough to have been able to take advantage of the resources of other institutions, particularly: the Berghof-Stiftung in Berlin, and the Arbeitsgruppe Rüstung und Unterentwicklung of the Institut für Sicherheitspolitik und Friedensforschung in Hamburg; the Center for Defense Information and the Military Audit Project in Washington, DC; and the National Action/Research on the Military Industrial Complex project of the American Friends Service Committee in Philadelphia.

Over the period, working and discussing the issues with numerous friends and colleagues has made a crucial contribution to my own thinking; they have been so many that I hope they will take no offence if I do not list them here. But I must mention those who read parts of the manuscript and gave me the benefit of their advice: Harry Dean, Fred Halliday, Jill Lewis, Clare Mundy, Eric Shaw, Nicholas Sims, Ron Smith, Paul Stares and Herbert Wulf — for their comments, criticisms and encouragement I am profoundly grateful.

Naturally, none of these institutions or individuals bears any responsibility for the presentation and interpretation of facts in this book, for

17

the arguments and conclusions; these are all my responsibility, as are any errors or misconceptions.

1 DEFENCE POLICY AND THE STATE

In the financial year 1979/80, the British military budget was £8,558 million, representing about 4.7 per cent of the gross domestic product expected that year, and was responsible for the employment of just over one million people including 330,000 in the armed forces.[1] The budget showed a real increase (i.e., an increase apart from the effects of inflation) of 4.6 per cent over the 1978/9 budget, with a further increase of 3 per cent planned for the following year. The Labour government responsible for this military budget for the last year of the 1970s had, since it was elected in February 1974, overseen a roughly stable pattern of expenditure on military preparations.[2]

British investment of economic resources in the military is but one part of a global process. Figures calculated by the American Arms Control and Disarmament Agency (ACDA) show that world military spending in 1976 was about $380 billion, equivalent to 5.6 per cent of the world's combined gross national products. The total is two and a half times as much as was spent on public health programmes, and just less than was spent on education. Of the total, over 70 per cent is accounted for by the military preparations of the states of the North Atlantic Treaty Organisation (NATO) and the Warsaw Pact (WP), 45 per cent by NATO alone.[3]

These figures provide a rough measure of the scale of military preparations, in Britain and worldwide, viewed as economic phenomena. But it is, of course, inadequate to view them solely in that way. These preparations, especially by NATO and the WP, have resulted in the development, production, and stockpiling of means of destruction on an awesome and quite unprecedented scale. During the 1960s, studies in NATO and the US Defense Department concluded that a tactical nuclear war in Europe would result in between 2 and 20 million deaths, even on the most favourable assumptions, and even before cities were attacked, with a high probability of 100 million dead if cities were attacked.[4] This would be regarded as a limited nuclear war. In 1974, an estimate was produced by the US Defense Department to show that a Soviet attack on ground-based American strategic nuclear missiles would produce about 800,000 casualties; under severe criticism, this estimate was revised upwards, to a range between 5.6 million casualties if the Soviet attack were intended to destroy about 40 per cent of the

19

US missile force, and 18.3 million if the aim was to destroy 80 per cent of the force.[5] It is barely possible to imagine the scale of destruction from a full-scale unlimited nuclear war between the USA and USSR. A study by the US National Security Council places minimum death figures at 140 million in the USA and 113 million in the USSR, while an ACDA study which assumes attacks only on military and industrial targets calculates immediate American fatalities at 105 to 130 million, with 80 to 95 million for the USSR.[6] A 1975 report to the US government concluded that about ten years after a major nuclear war in the northern half of the world, survivors in the *southern* hemisphere would be subject to 'relatively minimal stress'.[7]

So, on the one hand, we can note major economic investment in military preparations, and, on the other, the stockpiling of massive destructive power, recognition of which must serve as the acknowledged backdrop to all discussion of defence policy. The task of this book is to discuss why, and with what consequences, and in what fashion, Britain contributes to this process. The first focus, and the recurring reference point, for any such discussion must be the state which deploys the armed forces and administers the military preparations.

In any modern society, the military establishment is a wing, and evidently an important wing, of the permanent state apparatus. Through the military, a particular type of state power is developed and expressed – the power to coerce, and therefore to threaten coercion and resist it, in both domestic and international relations. As we have already seen, some states have built up a capacity for coercion on a quite spectacular scale. Coercive power may not be used for long periods, may be more implicit than explicit, may lose its sharpness or confront a more powerful adversary, but its existence is a basic political reality. Defence policy is the administration and organisation of this power by a state and, as such, is a fundamental component of state power.

Four basic arenas for military power can be identified. First, it can be used within domestic society; secondly, it can be used in relations between states with different social systems; thirdly, in relations between states with essentially the same social systems; fourthly, it can be used to subjugate and colonise states and nations and resist movements to throw off that subjugation. It is in the last three arenas that the emphasis of this book is placed, on defence policy as an aspect of foreign policy. It should be added that in both the domestic and the international arenas coercion is not limited to military forms – by which I do not just mean to draw attention to para-military forces; there are, for example, economic policies available to some states to use as coercive instruments

— in other words, a study of defence policy does not constitute a complete study of coercion in either domestic or international politics.

The state is more than just the government of the day. Decisions in British defence policy are not the sole prerogative of the Defence Secretary nor of the Cabinet, whatever the formalities, and the policy would hardly be workable if they were. Decisions emerge out of a balance between the elected government, civil servants, the uniformed military, military sectors of industry and other influences. Other NATO states, and especially the USA, not only help shape the international environment within which decisions are taken, but also intervene more or less directly over specific issues and the general direction of policy. Ministers' room for manoeuvre is diminished by these factors and by the effects of decisions taken by previous ministers and governments.

The continuity of policy is assured precisely because it is the state and not just the government which takes the decisions and carries them out. This is aided by the comparative lack of major decisions; there is an incremental succession of relatively minor decisions which make it hard and undesirable for any government to attempt sharp changes in policy as momentum builds up over a period behind a particular course of action. It can now take ten years or more to develop major weapon systems from the drawing-board to their entry into production; a single project may thus have to survive two or three changes of government and several changes of Defence Secretary before it enters service. The continuity which is necessary just to ensure that the armed services get equipped with the tools of their trade can only be provided by a stability in decision-making which derives from the permanence of the state.

This continuity is made politically acceptable by the basic consensus on defence policy between the major British political parties. This does not mean there are no important disagreements on major issues, such as the size of the budget, nuclear weapons and some particular weapons projects, but that between the parliamentary leaderships of the Conservative, Labour and Liberal parties disagreement exists within limits. The basic political and strategic concepts of present defence policy within NATO are accepted even if there may be disputes about how to implement them. As I shall argue in Chapter 5, this continuity means that the long-term failure to resolve the main dilemmas of defence policy cannot be laid at the door of either the Conservative or the Labour party alone.

But if consensus makes continuity politically acceptable, it is the actual state apparatus which is the basis of continuity. It is within this apparatus that the main sources of expert advice and privileged information reside, and there that the capacity exists to administer the military

effort. The very nature of defence policy places a great deal of power
and influence in the hands of certain parts of the state, and to say anything of importance about defence policy it is therefore necessary to
say something about the state and the reasons for which it requires
military force.

For an author with no intention of going deep into an analysis of
the British state, its history and role in society, this means entering a
veritable minefield. But it would be as disreputable to discuss defence
policy without offering some substantive comments about the state
which decides and operates that policy as it would be to treat the subject without mentioning nuclear weapons and their effects (although
both omissions are very common). Moreover, although this minefield
should not detract attention from the main project of the book and the
remarks which follow are necessarily summary in nature, the apparent
detour is relevant to the main project because of the use of concepts
of national security in discussion about defence. I shall argue that the
nature of the state makes the concept of national security as a tool for
analysis problematic and misleading. I shall argue this in relation to the
British state, but it holds true for all the states whose defence policies
are discussed in this book.

It will be generally agreed that the primary task of the British state
is to maintain the stability and ensure the continuity of society. To do
this a large and growing range of activities are undertaken, from economic policy to education, health and welfare policies, from domestic
policing to defence policy, and so on. But the crucial fact about the
nature of these activities and this role is that in ensuring the stability
and viability of British society, the state is ensuring the stability and
viability of a system of class division and inequality. I refer here not to
what are often thought of as British peculiarities — marked differences
of accent, education, 'culture' and other dimensions which superficially
separate one social group from another, nor to the often minute grada-
tions of social rank within groups. Rather, I am referring to those basic
differences of wealth, opportunity, liberty and power which define the
qualitative distinctions between a bourgeois ruling class and the sub-
ordinate classes. I cannot see that it is credible to wish away or ignore
these differences, especially after the excellent empirical study of class
by Westergaard and Resler.[8]

The state's role is often seen as that of arbiter between contending
and unequal classes, acting as a referee of social conflict, itself neutral
and concerned only to guarantee the continuance of basic social values.
This notion has a respectable history and is still vigorously argued, but

it cannot explain how the state can be neutral between classes yet able positively to defend chosen values. If the state is to defend values it cannot be neutral when one class or group calls them in question, and if the society whose basic values are to be defended is based on class division and inequality the state's role in perpetuating those values and the social structures from which they grow must self-evidently be favourable to the powerful at the expense of the weak. As it has been concisely put, 'The class state does not go between the classes in order to separate fighters, but to connect them, in an asymmetric relationship of domination and exploitation.'[9]

'Asymmetry' does not mean the process is all one way; state intervention in the economy and society has on occasion improved the condition of the working class and weaker social groups, such as the elderly, without eliminating the basis of class division and unequal power. Taxation to support this kind of intervention is thought by many of the wealthier to be punitively high and is bitterly resisted. These tactical disagreements between all or part of the ruling class and a state which fundamentally supports it demonstrate the characteristic separation of the state from society which not only provides the space for conflicts of this kind, but also permits other groups to effect social advances and improvements to their conditions by acting upon the state. The state can itself be thought of as an arena of conflict — conflict between classes and conflict within classes, which affects the activities of the state apparatus according to the relative strengths of the contending groups.

The fact that social conflicts can be internalised within the state is evident in defence policy, where the failure to resolve certain long-standing dilemmas over the shape and extent of defence policy can be traced to unresolved conflicts between different groups, each of which can, directly or indirectly, bring some influence to bear on the final decision. The way in which defence decisions are taken reflects not only the state's strategic logic, economic priorities, commitments to allies, and the necessary compromise between them; it reflects also the differing abilities of various groups to affect decisions on particular issues.

One should interject, however, that theories of the class state are still in a process of development and formation. To put it less charitably, they have hitherto failed, in all their infinite variety, to provide convincing explanations of how the power of the class state functions, and particularly of how it gains consent.[10] In fact, development of theories of the state is unlikely to be fruitful if it is confined to the realm of theory — increasingly sophisticated cerebral ballet will probably prove to be unproductive. What is required is a thorough analysis of the state in all its functions, an analysis which should be both factually detailed and theoretically coherent.[11] Part of my intention in this book is to contribute to the groundwork of such analysis by a study of defence policy.

In the domestic arena the state is tasked with maintaining the existing social order; in the international arena, the same task has a different nature, not least because of the existence of other states, both capitalist and non-capitalist, both weaker and stronger. In broad terms, foreign policy continues the support of the interests of the ruling class, but in a very different context. And as an aspect of foreign relations, defence policy is the medium through which the state organises military power in support of its international functions. Some of these functions cannot be usefully supported by military power – for example, participation in trade and tariff agreements or international monetary regulation – but even then, in sorting out which are the powerful states most likely to get something approximating their own way, the military factor is never entirely absent from the equation. For some states, their military power may be trifling compared to some of their partners' or rivals', and this again will be a factor among several which decide how strongly they fulfil their international functions.

Depending upon the international interests of the state and ruling class (and these interests may also conflict on occasion), defence policy may be active or passive, aggressive or purely reactive and defensive. Because of this, some object to the term 'defence policy' at all, but I think this is a purely semantic point as long as one is clear that the object of defence policy is military power.

However, this does raise the need to question the concept of 'defence', to ask who or what is defended by the policy and how. Most discussions of policy omit the question, and when it is asked, the answer tends to be rather confused, demanding further definitional questions. A most useful essay by John Baylis is very specific in defining the term 'policy', yet seems to duck the hard questions when it comes to defining 'defence': by his account, defence policy facilitates 'not only the protection but also the pursuit of the perceived national interests of the state'; it means protecting the homeland and population as well as overseas territories, and safeguarding 'what are seen as the political and economic interests of the state in the world as a whole'; it means marshalling 'a nation's defence resources' for 'ensuring national security, protecting vital interests and furthering the international aims of the state.'[12] This has the merit of focussing attention upon the state, yet refuses to discuss whose 'perceived national interests of the state' are being protected and pursued, or how some perceived interests rather than other perceived interests become the ones to be defended. No definition of 'national security' is offered, either what it does mean or what it ought to mean. It might be thought unfair to expect Baylis to go beyond analysing defence policy, to analyse social and political processes lying behind defence policy, but in the unanswered and unasked questions lie the silent assumptions which form the starting point for analysis and shape much of that analysis.

The literature on defence is certainly capable of offering a definition of national security, one widely acceptable suggestion being that it is the ability of a society to perpetuate its existence and sustain its values in the face of threats and challenges from internal or external sources.[13] Here, the hidden assumption is that society is capable of appearing as a single univocal actor in the field of foreign and defence policy. Yet the argument undermines itself by noting that national security can be threatened from within society. And as soon as the existence of class division and distinctions within society is admitted, the argument cannot be sustained; it becomes impossible to conceive of 'society' as such as an actor in international politics.

It is more useful to reformulate the definition, to suggest that what is at stake is the ability of a state to perpetuate itself and continue its role and functions in the face of domestic and international threats and challenges. There is still a problem here, as it can be difficult to conceive even of the state as a single univocal actor. Disagreements within the state about defence policy are common and often leak into public awareness, with senior officers, for example, complaining about inadequate funds; equally common is finding the state acting contradictorily, especially over the procurement of equipment. These are symptoms of the internalisation of conflict and failure to resolve the main defence dilemmas. Even so, the state is evidently operative in defence policy in a way that an entity such as 'nation' or 'society' cannot be.

In the context of defence policy, then, the concept of national security must be limited to referring to the capacity of the state's armed forces to fulfil its functions. Of course, the state also perpetuates itself by non-military means, and thus the concept can be, and often is, extended beyond the scope of defence policy into other fields. Where state interests are blurred, contradictory or hazily perceived, the capacity of armed force to provide security will not be very high, and force cannot respond effectively to all the challenges a state faces. More important, however, is that defining the concept in this way makes the term *'national* security' very dubious, and similarly the concept of national interest. What is involved is *state* security and the state's interest, which may or may not be the same as a recognisable national security and national interest. Partly because of its partial separation from society, the state is capable on occasion of representing the interests of the whole society, as during World War II in its resistance to Nazi Germany. But that is an exceptional case, incapable of supporting a general rule.

This discussion has evidently brought us some way from the ground of orthodox approaches to defence policy, but such approaches tend to fudge or evade basic issues and cannot be adopted if there is any intention of rigorous analysis. There is common ground here with them, however, in the shared view that defence policy concerns matters at the heart of the life of state and society, which means that discussion of defence policy cannot be regarded as a purely technical affair.

Indeed, the dilemmas of British defence policy are not technical problems. The issue is not one of making choices between options on the basis of criteria established by scientific and technical analysis. Rather, these dilemmas reflect the basic problems attached to the British state's role in the international arena, deriving from the interaction of domestic and international forces. The long-term political and economic decline of Britain places increasing strains upon the ingenuities of British defence planners, strains which are steadily becoming intolerable. Because the military is so crucial to the state, discussing defence policy means discussing those wider problems.

The possibility of resolving those dilemmas on a more or less long-term basis raises the issue of the degree to which social and political change are necessary companions of change in defence policy. Such social and political change might be revolutionary or might be more or less cosmetic, but any attempt to resolve the main dilemmas must be based on an effort to deal with their domestic roots. Problems would still be encountered, since the international determinants of these dilemmas are not susceptible to unilateral solution, and this may also be true of domestic determinants, but there is a clear link between change in defence policy and wider social and political change. Equally, the link holds the other way round — perspectives embracing one degree or another of social and political change must consider defence policy and armed force as an element of society and state. The study of defence policy, then, can expand and strengthen perspectives of a changed social and political order.

Notes

1. *Statement on the Defence Estimates 1979*, Cmnd 7474 (HMSO, London, 1979), paras 145 and 341, and Annex B.

2. *The Government's Expenditure Plans 1979/80 to 1982/3*, Cmnd 7439 (HMSO, London, 1979), pp. 32-3.

3. *World Military Expenditures and Arms Transfers 1967-1976* (US ACDA, Washington, DC, 1978).

4. A.C. Enthoven and K.W. Smith, *How Much is Enough? Shaping the Defense Program 1961-1969* (Harper & Row, New York, 1971), p. 128.

5. See S.D. Drell and F. von Hippel, 'Limited Nuclear War', *Scientific American*, November 1976, vol. 235, no. 5.

6. Both studies cited in *The Defense Monitor*, February 1979, vol. VIII, no. 2.

7. *Long-term Worldwide Effects of Multiple Nuclear Weapons Detonations* (US ACDA, Washington, DC, 1975).

8. J. Westergaard and H. Resler, *Class in a Capitalist Society* (Penguin, Harmondsworth, 1976).

9. G. Therborn, *What Does the Ruling Class Do when it Rules?* (NLB, London, 1978), p. 97.

10. A useful survey of this variety is B. Jessop, 'Recent Theories of the Capitalist State', *Cambridge Journal of Economics*, December 1977, vol. 1, no. 4.

11. Thus, despite definite theoretical shortcomings, the most useful studies of the state are grounded in factual analysis: e.g., C. Ackroyd, K. Margolis, J. Rosenhead and T. Shallice, *The Technology of Political Control* (Penguin, Harmondsworth, 1977); T. Bunyan, *The History and Practice of the Political Police in Britain* (Quartet, London, 1977); R. Miliband, *The State in Capitalist Society* (Weidenfeld & Nicolson, London, 1969).

12. Introduction in J. Baylis (ed.), *British Defence Policy in a Changing World* (Croom Helm, London, 1977), pp. 13-14.

13. As given, for example, by R.N. Cooper, 'National Resources and National Security', in *The Middle East and the International System II: Security and the Energy Crisis*, Adelphi Paper 115 (IISS, London, 1975).

2 STRATEGY: MANAGEMENT AND IDEOLOGY

In discussion of defence policy, the meaning and use of some of the basic terms can themselves cause a deal of confusion. Many who study the subject would agree that 'strategy' is among the most misused words in the language, but it is hard to find any two people in full agreement on the correct meaning and usage. Two particular problems are the history of the terms 'strategy' and 'tactics', which has endowed them with meanings that linger with varying degrees of validity in the modern world, and the arbitrary way in which the labels 'tactical' and 'strategic' get attached to various forces and types of weapons: the dividing line between tactical and strategic weapons is far from clear and blurred further by the same weapons being tactical in one role and strategic in another. But some clarity about the terms is important, because it is through tactical and strategic decisions and doctrines that defence policy is expressed and implemented; they represent important levels at which the problems and dilemmas of policy must be confronted. The purpose of the discussion in this chapter is therefore largely definitional, to introduce the discussions of policy, strategy and tactical doctrines in the following chapters.

Tactics was defined by Field Marshall Wavell as 'the art of handling troops on the battlefield', and strategy as 'the art of bringing troops to the battlefield in a favourable position'; of the two arts, tactics was the higher and the more complex, for strategy was 'to a certain degree mechanical and subject to conventions', its main principles being 'simple and easy to grasp'.[1] As an art, strategy was thus inferior to tactics, and as an activity, it was but a preliminary to battle, the business of tactics, and also the main business of war. In an age of intercontinental nuclear missiles, when troops may be annihilated on their way to a devastated battlefield, the relevance of such axioms is dubious at best; they can be thought to represent a traditionalist view of the matter. But perhaps more important is that Wavell defined strategy not in terms of policy, its objectives and priorities, but in terms of battle which could be seen, to some degree, as a self-enclosed and self-sufficient activity. In contrast to this approach, discussion of strategy must begin with policy and with the state which develops it, with its goals in war or in peacetime military policy, and its capability to fulfil them.

A successful strategy is not simply a good plan: it requires adequately equipped forces to carry it out, and this depends both on the available productive capacities and technological development of industry, and on having people prepared and willing to fight. If industry cannot provide the necessary equipment (and there is no adequate external source), the strategy must obviously be abandoned or fail; problems of morale or commitment to the overall policy, in the forces or in society as a whole, also endanger strategy. The conditions for a successful strategy, then, start with the social and political conditions of the state.

However, starting with the state and policy does not mean one can assume a linear process; this is a problem with many discussions of strategy which tend to assume that policy leads to strategy, which leads to tactics, and the further down the line we are, the closer we are to the actual business of killing people. The temptation to think in this way is rather large given the rigid hierarchies of military organisations where orders proceed down a chain of command, from people with wide responsibilities far from battle to people with successively narrower responsibilities closer to battle. Strong though the temptation is, it should be resisted, for it thoroughly obscures the complexity of the processes which produce strategy, pit strategies against each other, and ultimately decide which will be successful.

The relationship between tactics, strategy and policy is best grasped if tactics is conceived as a part of strategy and strategy as a part of policy. The activities covered under each heading are not sealed off from each other; compartmentalisation between these aspects of military planning and action is incomplete and far from rigid. Tactics and strategy are instruments of policy, but also constituent parts of the whole. Military doctrines not only express how defence policy is to be implemented, but themselves constrain and help shape that policy.

Strategy itself is not a single process: we must, at least, distinguish between strategic objectives and forms of strategy. While in principle the strategic objective is more or less given by policy, the form of strategy which is to attain that objective cannot flow directly from it; it depends on the way military force is structured, equipped and located. The development of a new form of strategy, such as became available with the development of nuclear weapons, can lead to the replacement of old strategic objectives by new ones. For example, in World War II the political goal of securing the unconditional surrender of Japan was to have been reached through the strategic objective of invasion; the nuclear devastation of Hiroshima and Nagasaki in August 1945 led swiftly to unconditional surrender, eliminating any need for invasion. There is much to be said about the morality, politics and historical impact of this momentous event, but here I am simply concerned to use it as a dramatic example of the dynamic relation within strategic planning between objectives and forms.

We can thus think of strategy as a differentiated component of defence policy, through which the means to attain political goals are organised and managed, just as defence policy is the medium through which armed force is organised to support the state's international functions. Strategy is an instrument of management by the state in defence policy. Further, because strategy expresses the relation of one state to others, both hostile and friendly, it is a political instrument in its own right. The rest of this chapter will discuss this dual role of strategy.

The theme of strategy as a form of management is fairly common in modern writings, and able to provide important insights into military functioning.[2] It is, unfortunately, often taken too far, by those who, in trying to draw too many analogies to business management are too intent on seeing soldiers as technicians, and seem to forget that even when the aim is to deter war the major management problem for armed forces even in the modern age is to persuade large numbers of people to be ready to kill and get themselves killed (especially the latter). But the consensus that management is involved is much less stable when it comes to defining the object of management. On the one hand, there is a fairly expansive definition that strategy is 'the art of controlling and utilizing the resources of a nation — or a coalition of nations — including its armed forces.'[3] On the other hand, a more restrictive definition suggests that strategy does not deal with questions such as the administration, structure and financing of armed forces, nor with aspects of recruitment and providing equipment.[4]

The restrictive definition, though perhaps more orderly, is difficult to sustain. It attempts to distinguish policy from strategy on an administrative basis, but this is misleading because it means erecting rigid divisions between inherently connected aspects of the organisation of armed force. The structure of armed forces is crucial to their capacity to carry out given strategic and tactical tasks; especially important is ensuring proper logistic arrangements at each level of the forces' structures. There must be enough people and equipment, properly trained and properly maintained, and there must be enough finances to pay the people well enough to prevent routine gripes becoming major problems of low morale.

It is certainly important to be able to distinguish between policy and strategy, but this should be done in terms of the nature of decisions confronted under the different headings. In abstract terms, defence policy is the medium through which force is organised, while strategy is the instrument with which it is organised. In specific terms, to take an example, a decision to build a new combat aircraft together with other West European states, rather than to produce it independently or buy from the USA, would be a decision of defence policy; the capabilities and roles of the aircraft would be a matter for strategic decision. If West European industry was unable to provide the required capabilities, the priority attached to the strategic considerations might lead to a change of policy and a different source for the aircraft – or the import-ance attached to a policy of West European industrial co-operation might lead to strategic changes, expressed by seeking less demanding roles and thus less sophisticated capabilities more easily within the reach of West European industry. Thus, taking the more inclusive definition of the object of strategic management – 'the resources of a nation' – neither obviates the need nor eliminates the possibility of distinguishing between policy and strategy.

Military organisations are directed by strategic decisions, but they also participate in developing them so that the decisions are strongly shaped by the organisations' existing structures, traditions, precepts and preferences, and perhaps by the social origins, education and general outlook of their leading officers. The result is a strong element of sub-jectivity in strategic planning, often visible in the way different forces confront different decisions. For example, the British and Federal German armies stationed alongside each other in northern Germany face the same supposed enemy on the same terrain with the same strategic objectives within NATO. Yet their tank units, the central component of their forces, are equipped with very different tanks, the British *Chieftain* being much slower and more heavily armoured than the German *Leopard*, with correspondingly different doctrines of tank war-fare.[5] Similar differences can be noted for armoured personnel carriers, revolving around the question of whether infantry should have to leave their vehicles in order to fight or be able to fight while on the move in their vehicles. Although strategic judgement must weigh objective factors, it does so on the basis of the collective institutional subjectivity of the armed forces in question, in which national, cultural and historical particularities are strong constitutive elements.

A characteristic of military organisations is the demand of so many of them for strict discipline and obedience within the framework of a rigid and minutely detailed hierarchy. Although strict discipline can be pragmatically justified as necessary to control people who have to go out and risk getting killed, it is not clear that all the minutiae of ranks and the traditions and rituals around them are necessary for the efficient functioning of armed forces. What is clear is that most military organisations, including all those in NATO, believe that the minutiae are necessary; detailed distinctions of rank and certain forms of behaviour are an important part of the way members of those organisations are educated to see themselves and their role.

In fact, many forces have loosened hierarchical rigidity at points to improve military functioning: for example, the Nelsonian tradition in the British navy under which even fairly junior officers could act on their own initiative without awaiting orders or permission; one of the most effective modern forces, the Israeli army, is characterised by a similar flexibility encouraging initiative (though not unilateral action) from below. But, by and large, inflexibility is the military way, and what is interesting is that this is a virtue of only limited value (for example, in situations demanding die-hard defence and self-sacrifice). Liddell Hart developed a theory of military history essentially based on the view that the characteristic directness of military operations only rarely provided success, and usually only at great cost; the most successful generals were the few who had the imagination to approach tactical and strategic objectives indirectly or those who, as more often happened, were forced by circumstances into taking an indirect approach.[6] Thus, if inflexibility based on rigid hierarchy is the military way, the reasons for this are essentially subjective; there could be, and at times have been, other ways of proceeding.

Subjectivity is present not only in the definition of forms of strategy, but also of strategic objectives, which are set not according to some scientific method, nor as an automatic product of a given policy, but through the interplay of the possibly ambiguous or contradictory objectives of the state, the perceptions it generates of itself and the international scene, its competing domestic and international priorities and the available forms of strategy developed in the armed forces. At the core of it all is the assessment of its objectives and capacities produced in the state through the interaction of its various institutions and influential groups outside the state.

Equally complex is the translation of a strategic objective into a requirement for a particular force. Especially in peacetime, assessing the amount and type of equipment needed to fulfil a particular task is a matter of estimating at best, and of more than a little guesswork.[7] The process would be purely arbitrary, were it not for the past experience of the relevant military institution which provides the basis for many strategic decisions. However, assessing what forces and how much equipment are needed must always have some relationship to what is available if the decision is to be more than wishful thinking. 'The resources of a nation' are finite, and by no means all of them are available for strategic planning in any meaningful sense; other calls on them, for public and private consumption and investment, cannot be wished away. Possibilities are further limited by the technological level of industry and the extent of its productive capacities. This brings us to military industry, the second major organisation that is an object of strategic management.

There may be two immediate objections to this approach, relating first to the definition of military industry, and secondly to the question of whether there is such a process as strategic management of the industry. In the widest sense, military industry would include any company providing any goods to the armed forces — aircraft, tanks, communications, components produced on sub-contracts, uniforms, food, and so on and on. But by no means all the suppliers are wholly or even significantly dependent on military contracts for their business. Further, many firms which always have military orders on their books have a widely fluctuating proportion of their workforces engaged in such work, and this is likely to be especially true for components manufacturers. Military industry is thus rather fluid at the edges, and it is probably stretching the term to call it an 'organisation'. But at the core, there are firms who are totally, or in sectors, specialised for development and production of weapon systems, other military equipment (such as for communications and surveillance) and their components, and these constitute what is normally called military industry.[8]

More complex is the issue of whether or not there is strategic management of this sector of industry, since many would argue that defence policy almost exclusively serves the interests of this sector and is effectively created and dominated by it. This is, however, far too simple and monocausal an explanation of a process which cannot be properly explained in such a way. Like all advanced technologies, military technology and industry have developed a strong momentum, based on the drive constantly to develop improvements in weapon systems' performance. States which are committed to sustaining military industrial capacity are thereby committed to keeping that capacity operating and thus sustaining the costs of the momentum of successive improvements.[9] But if the state needs industry to equip its forces independently, industry needs the state as the main purchaser of its products and, increasingly, as its export agent. The history of state reorganisation of military industry, particularly in Britain and France in the past twenty years, shows states can have plenty of room for manoeuvre against the corporations. In both Britain and France, major sections of military industry have been nationalised and thus included within the state, which means that the image of a 'military industrial complex' of large private corporations, an image largely developed by liberal critics of the USA's armament programmes, cannot be applied without major modifications. What must be perceived is not a one-way channel of influence from either party to the other, but a more complex relationship within which a dilute strategic management of military industry exists.

A further dimension of the relation between military industry and the military itself is that the latter is structured around the deployment of the major weapon systems – tanks, armoured vehicles, artillery, missiles, aircraft, major surface ships and submarines – while the industry is structured around the capability to develop and produce the same systems. This structural pairing between producer and consumer is hardly surprising, and it could be argued that only thus can the military get the equipment it requires and the industry be sure its products will be purchased. But this privileged relation of military industry to its market does provide a further constraint upon the range of options open to strategic planners, and tends to act as a kind of self-sealing mechanism against possibly unfavourable intervention from a third party, such as a newly elected government trying to change strategy.

Thus, in relation to both organisations which are objects of strategic management, forces and industry, the process of management is complex. Strategic decisions are not and cannot be handed down from on high to give shape to hitherto shapeless entities and direct their functioning. The objects of strategic management themselves contribute to decision-making, and constrain the possibilities for strategy which can, as a process of management and planning, be seen as a matter of selecting within a limited range of options. Ultimately that range must be seen as the product of the social and political conditions within which the state operates.

The only test of the efficacy of this process is war; in peacetime there is no objective test of strategy. But it is not only each side's capabilities that are pitted against each other, but also their perceptions, both in particular engagements and in prolonged campaigns or the war as a whole. Liddell Hart commented instructively on an incident in the battle of Leyte Gulf in World War II, when the Japanese admiral misinterpreted intercepted US Navy radio signals and turned away from an engagement, missing a chance to crush elements of the American fleet:

It was one more of the many cases in history which show that battles are apt to be decided more by fancies than by facts. The impression made on the commander's mind often counts much more than any actual blow and its physical effect.[10]

The German invasion of France illustrates the importance of perception in a different way, for, contrary to widespread impressions, the German victory was not due to superior numbers, which the German army did not actually possess. Bennet and Dando have shown that the key lay in the fact that, viewed through French strategic assumptions and concepts, a German offensive through the Ardennes was the least rational, and therefore least likely, German option, but that the German high command was playing a different game which precisely counted on the limitations of French strategy.[11] German perception was superior, and its offensive through the Ardennes both a surprise and a swift success. The importance of strategic perception has long been recognised: the saying, 'Know the enemy and know yourself; in a hundred battles you will never be in peril' has been made famous by Chairman Mao, but like many of his military axioms it is taken from a Chinese strategist, Sun Tzu, who lived some 2,400 years ago.[12]

Clearly, war is more than just a contest between strategic perceptions, but it is important to stress this aspect to understand strategy in peacetime. During war, strategy is a political instrument in its own right, as well as an instrument of management; on its merits depends the state's survival, not to mention millions of lives. In peacetime strategy also has a directly political function, and this is more than ever the case in the era since World War II when NATO states have built their military confrontation with the Warsaw Pact on the basis of deterrence, of avoiding war and dissuading hostile actions.

There is a well known axiom from Clausewitz, to the effect that war is a continuation of policy by other means; the intent of the axiom is directed at arguing the need for continuation of political control of the military in wartime and for keeping a sense of political objectives. But as well as what the nature of war should be, it can be taken to refer to the nature of policy, if by 'policy' we here understand the normal process of inter-state relations. For military preparations are an ever-present part of that process; through them a state says something about itself and its relations with other states, both allies and rivals — to begin with, it says who it regards as allies, who as rivals. The nature of its strategy expresses its power and how it may be used, for what ends and in what parts of the world. Thus, Soviet strategic decisions to expand naval deployment during the 1960s reflected the USSR's assessment of its right and ability to behave as a truly global power. Western concern at Soviet naval and nuclear programmes is largely explicable as concern at the perceptions other states would thereby have of Soviet power, and at the political benefit this would give the USSR.[13] It is possible for war to be a continuation of 'policy' in part because of the nature of 'policy' itself.

The state interprets itself — its objectives, strength and policies — to the world, partly through its strategic decisions. The announcement of strategies is intended to affect perceptions in other states and groups of states. Equally, it thus interprets the world and its role in it to domestic society. In this sense, strategy is both a form of ideology and an ideological weapon.[14] Derived from the collective subjectivities of the institutions that contribute to strategic decision-making, and representing the world according to perceptions and world views embodied in the state, it enters into domestic and international political processes, influencing the perceptions of its citizens and of other states. It is the product of a collective subjectivity acting upon other individual and collective subjectivities. To gain the ideological impact, there must be real physical capability underlying the strategic decisions and, to some degree at least, the ideological terms must be shared. In war, when the terms are not shared, the result may be like that in France in 1940 with one side playing a different and superior game. Similarly, it has been argued that the North Vietnamese government in the 1960s never doubted the US government's resolve to commit thousands of men to the Vietnam war and bomb North Vietnam; what it did doubt was the USA's ability to combat guerrilla war and the domestic political feasibility of the USA fighting a protracted war. American strategy failed in Vietnam because its enemy did not share the same strategic premises and was thus not deterred from its own goals.[15]

The military has further ideological functions within society, often serving as a model for behaviour (discipline, obedience), organisation (hierarchy) and ideology (duty, loyalty, patriotism, respect for authority). Part of this effect derives from the value attached in western cultures to 'the military virtues', but possibly more important now is the idea of 'military efficiency', supposed to pervade all things military and be ideal for getting things done. A moderately close study of military history and modern military organisations may suggest this idea owes as much to myth as to reality, but it is nonetheless a remarkably influential model, now spread throughout the industrialised countries and many of the underdeveloped countries.

Strategic decisions thus reflect the response of a state to world events and problems, a response whose formation and final form is shaped by both international and domestic conditions. The process by which the decisions are taken and the often obscure debates surrounding them reflect the way in which the state sorts out a response to its challenges. We can summarise strategy as an instrument, but not a straightforward instrument, of the state for organising force, at two levels – management and ideology. Understanding strategic decisions can give us some insight into some of the most important aspects of the political functioning of a state.

Notes

1. From *Soldiers and Soldiering* (1953), cited in B. Brodie, *Strategy in the Missile Age* (Princeton University Press, Princeton, NJ, 1965), p. 12.

2. See, for example, J.C.T. Downey, *Management in the Armed Forces* (McGraw-Hill, London, 1977).

3. Introduction in E.M. Earle (ed.), *Makers of Modern Strategy* (Princeton University Press, Princeton, NJ, 1971), p. viii.

4. See, for example, Introduction in J. Baylis (ed.), *British Defence Policy in a Changing World* (Croom Helm, London, 1977), pp. 14-15.

5. *Jane's Weapon Systems 1978* (Macdonald & Jane's, London), pp. 314-15, 340-1.

6. B.H. Liddell Hart, *Strategy* (Faber & Faber, London, 1954).

7. Take, for example, this passage, quoted from a senior civil servant answering questions from a Parliamentary committee about the staying power of British air defences: 'The size of force that we have described in the memorandum . . . is the minimum that we need to have an effective deterrent posture in air defence . . . How long and in what circumstances that force could fight I think even my professional colleagues may find it very difficult to answer. *What, of course, none of us can answer is how long it might be required to fight*': T.C.G. James, Assistant Under-Secretary of State (Air Staff), in *Second Report from the Expenditure Committee Session 1975/6: Defence*, HC 155 (HMSO, London, 1976), Minutes, Q 527, p. 137 (emphasis added).

8. The 1979 Defence White Paper provides a list of 43 British companies which received £5 million or more in defence contracts in 1977/8, but the *Defence Equipment Catalogue* lists several hundred British companies which produce defence goods: *Statement on the Defence Estimates 1979*, Cmnd 7474 (HMSO, London, 1979), Annex J; *British Defence Equipment Catalogue 1978*, 10th edition (Combined Service, Farnborough, Hants, 1978), vol. III, pp. 138-240.

9. See M. Kaldor, *European Defence Industries – National and International Implications*, ISIO Monograph 8 (University of Sussex, Brighton, 1972); also Chapter 6 below.

10. B.H. Liddell Hart, *History of the Second World War* (Pan, London, 1973), p. 656.

11. P.G. Bennett and M.R. Dando, '"Fall Gelb" and Other Games: A Hypergame Perspective of the Fall of France, 1940', *Journal of the Conflict Research Society*, November 1977, vol. 1, no. 2.

12. Sun Tzu, *The Art of War*, trans. S.B. Griffith (OUP, London, 1971).

13. See the argument for this view in U. Albrecht, J. Galtung, P. Joenniemi, D. Senghaas and S. Verona, 'Is Europe to Demilitarize?', *Instant Research on Peace and Violence*, 1972, no. 4, p. 192.

14. The term 'ideology' is often used pejoratively to mean, more or less, views with which the writer disagrees; to avoid confusion, since the term will recur, I should state that I am not using it that way. Rather, I use the term, particularly in the context of institutional and collective ideology, to designate modes of perception and especially of identifying and responding to problems and challenges, on the basis of definite, though not fixed, practices, traditions, continuing historical development and circumstances.

15. See A.L. George and R. Smoke, *Deterrence in American Foreign Policy: Theory and Practice* (Columbia University Press, New York, 1974), p. 82.

3 NATO, NUCLEAR DETERRENCE AND SUPER POWER RIVALRY

More than 90 per cent of Britain's annual military budget is devoted to British commitments in NATO; there are now very few extra-NATO or extra-European activities for British armed forces. Discussing British defence policy means first looking at the context of the alliance in which British military preparations are almost wholly organised.

The North Atlantic Treaty was signed in Washington, DC, on 4 April 1949 and took effect on 24 August of that year, the date of the formation of NATO. In December 1950, General Eisenhower was appointed as Supreme Allied Commander in Europe (SACEUR); the command became operational on 2 April 1951. Initially, NATO had twelve member states (Belgium, Britain, Canada, Denmark, France, Iceland, Italy, Luxembourg, the Netherlands, Norway, Portugal and the USA); in 1952 Greece and Turkey acceded, and in 1955 the Federal Republic of Germany (FRG). Nine days after the FRG joined NATO, the Warsaw Treaty was signed on 14 May 1955, creating the Warsaw Pact (WP) consisting of the USSR together with Albania, Bulgaria, Czechoslovakia, the German Democratic Republic, Hungary, Poland and Romania. Albania withdrew from the WP in September 1968.

From the outset, NATO was more than an instrument of collective defence against a perceived threat from the USSR. Alongside the US Marshall Aid programme for West European economic development, NATO's formation played a crucial role in the political reconstruction and stabilisation of post-war Western Europe. This was largely an American project, and both the process of reconstruction and NATO itself were vehicles of American influence in the early years of a new political formation in Western Europe. This was the period of economic and political reorganisation of capitalism under the USA's international hegemony, backed both by military strength and a dominant economy, a period of recovery under American leadership from the debris of war and of the economic disasters of the 1920s and 1930s. Domination of some of the major institutions of the renewed system was an integral part of generalised American leadership.

Figure 3.1 outlines the civil and military structures of NATO. Formally, all activities are subject to the approval and authority of the NATO Council of representatives of the fifteen member states, with

Figure 3.1: NATO Civil and Military Structure

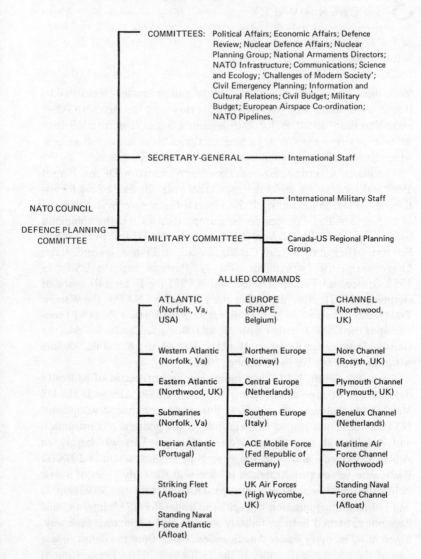

COMMITTEES: Political Affairs; Economic Affairs; Defence Review; Nuclear Defence Affairs; Nuclear Planning Group; National Armaments Directors; NATO Infrastructure; Communications; Science and Ecology; 'Challenges of Modern Society'; Civil Emergency Planning; Information and Cultural Relations; Civil Budget; Military Budget; European Airspace Co-ordination; NATO Pipelines.

SECRETARY-GENERAL ———— International Staff

NATO COUNCIL
DEFENCE PLANNING COMMITTEE

MILITARY COMMITTEE

International Military Staff

Canada-US Regional Planning Group

ALLIED COMMANDS

ATLANTIC (Norfolk, Va, USA)

Western Atlantic (Norfolk, Va)

Eastern Atlantic (Northwood, UK)

Submarines (Norfolk, Va)

Iberian Atlantic (Portugal)

Striking Fleet (Afloat)

Standing Naval Force Atlantic (Afloat)

EUROPE (SHAPE, Belgium)

Northern Europe (Norway)

Central Europe (Netherlands)

Southern Europe (Italy)

ACE Mobile Force (Fed Republic of Germany)

UK Air Forces (High Wycombe, UK)

CHANNEL (Northwood, UK)

Nore Channel (Rosyth, UK)

Plymouth Channel (Plymouth, UK)

Benelux Channel (Netherlands)

Maritime Air Force Channel (Northwood)

Standing Naval Force Channel (Afloat)

Source: *NATO Handbook* (NATO Information Service, Brussels, 1976).

military activities subject to the Defence Planning Committee of representatives of *thirteen* states — the odd ones out are France which withdrew its forces from NATO command in 1966 but is still a member of the alliance, and Greece which has held a similar position since the autumn of 1974.

The two main NATO command areas are Europe and the Atlantic, both of which are and always have been headed by American officers, reflecting the early unquestioned American leadership, while the lesser Channel command is headed by a British officer. British officers have also always filled the posts of Deputy Commander for Europe and the Atlantic, reflecting Britain's undoubted right to second place in the hierarchy in NATO's early years. The niceties of this process of apportioning commands are suggested by noting that the British-led Channel command has a mere Commander-in-Chief, whereas the two American-headed commands have Supreme Allied Commanders. Symbolic of changes since the system was constructed was the appointment in the mid-1960s of a West German general to head the new command for Central Europe, the most important sub-command area in NATO, and since 1978 there has been a second deputy to SACEUR, once again a West German general, underlining the FRG's growing military importance. The Commanders-in-Chief for Northern and Southern Europe are always a British general and an American admiral respectively.[1]

The USA's authority in NATO was reinforced by its monopoly within the alliance of nuclear weapons and its extension of nuclear deterrence to cover Western Europe — the American 'nuclear umbrella'. As a result, NATO strategy has been largely American strategy, with which in the end, notwithstanding prior consultation, other members have had to fit in as best they can. Some West European commentators have bemoaned a history of thirty years during which initiatives for change have almost all been American ones, to which West European states are asked to respond, and which may be replaced before the response is developed.[2]

NATO has always seen itself as a defensive alliance, fending off a hostile and potentially aggressive adversary in the WP. This has become a virtually unquestionable article of faith in western strategy and ideology. Nuclear deterrence has seemed the natural consequence of this basic premiss, which has meant reliance on American nuclear deterrence, reinforcing American leadership. By accepting nuclear deterrence as the basis of their defence, West European states have accepted that the first fact about their defence policies should be an American capability — yet American nuclear doctrine and the development of its nuclear arsenal is guided by American interests, not West European ones.

The Evolution of US Nuclear Strategy

With transitional periods between them, four major phases mark out the evolution of American nuclear strategy.[3] Following the atomic bombing of Hiroshima and Nagasaki in August 1945, the USA enjoyed a nuclear monopoly until 1953, though a monopoly whose forthcoming demise was signalled as early as 1949 by the first Soviet nuclear test. From 1954 until 1960, the strategic doctrine was known as 'massive retaliation', under which the USA threatened to respond to aggressive actions with massive force 'instantly, by means and at places of our choosing'.[4] A rather indeterminate period from 1961 to 1963 is followed by, from 1963 to 1968, a twin doctrine of 'assured destruction' and 'damage limitation'. Some time between 1969 and 1974 the American government adopted a new strategy, which still holds, known as the doctrine of 'limited strategic options'.

The problem with massive retaliation was its lack of precision about the level of provocation which would invoke the nuclear response. It is likely that this was not clear even to the American administration. In 1953, the USA hinted it would use nuclear weapons against China if the Korean truce negotiations broke down, and in 1955 again threatened a nuclear attack on China during the dispute about the islands of Quemoy and Matsu; but in 1954, President Eisenhower rejected a proposal to use air power, possibly including nuclear bombs, to aid the beleaguered French garrison at Dien Bien Phu in Vietnam.[5]

Nevertheless, the strategy was transferred to NATO in Europe, where numbers of American tactical nuclear weapons (TNW) were built up as an adjunct to conventional (non-nuclear) forces. The West European governments were delighted, for not only did it appear to relieve them of the unpopular chore of raising mass armies and preparing to fight a major conventional war, it also made it seem that the USA was committing not just its power but its very survival to the defence of Western Europe. Ever since, West European governments, with the exception of France, have resisted moves which seemed to 'decouple' the fate of the USA from nuclear deterrence in Western Europe. Indeed, the era of massive retaliation has a malign influence on NATO strategy to this day. The over-sized TNW arsenal in Western Europe (over 7,000 warheads), the refusal of most West European governments to contemplate reductions in the arsenal, and the centrality of TNW in NATO planning all date from that time.

By the end of the 1950s, the strategy's imprecision was increasingly criticised in the USA, as was, in some quarters, the very coupling of the

USA's fate to Western Europe's. The strategy neither offered an adequate way of relating to the USSR in rivalry, nor did it aid local military actions by the USA around the world. Henry Kissinger argued that massive retaliation together with insufficient attention to conventional forces added up to a concentration on total war, renouncing other options for the use of force, and thus abandoning the strategic initiative; if all-out war was not warranted, he argued, there was no capacity for a military response to threats to American interests.[6] Clearly, the suggestion that the USA was unable to use force was an exaggeration, as the US Marine's intervention in the Lebanon showed in 1958, but there is little doubt that these concerns were widely and genuinely shared in the American political establishment. The incoming administration of President Kennedy swiftly jettisoned massive retaliation.

Nuclear strategy during the Kennedy and Johnson administrations (1961-8) has been described as 'flexible response',[7] but this misses both the uncertainty of the first two years of nuclear planning and the extent to which, from 1963, nuclear strategy slipped into what was essentially a modification of massive retaliation. The new administration sought to develop flexibility in US forces, both by strengthening conventional forces and by developing a more flexible nuclear strategy. Robert McNamara, the Defense Secretary, outlined the government's nuclear thinking in June 1962, emphasising the need for control during the course of a nuclear war; instead of a single nuclear spasm and the all-enveloping holocaust, he envisaged what is known as intra-war deterrence. In the event of a Soviet first strike against American missile forces, the USA should be able to retaliate against remaining Soviet nuclear forces, avoiding damage to cities, even implicitly holding cities hostage to deter a further Soviet nuclear strike. The intention was twofold: to fight and win a nuclear war if need be, and to minimise destruction of American cities. The strategy was known by various names: 'damage limitation', 'no cities', 'controlled response'.[8]

To some, this has seemed to set the tone of American nuclear strategy in the 1960s but this is not so. The emphasis on limiting damage to the USA was gradually replaced by emphasis on inflicting unacceptable damage on the USSR and convincing it that under any circumstances, however powerful the Soviet first strike, the USA's retaliation would devastate the USSR. This was the strategy of assured destruction. Neat sums were calculated in the Office of Systems Analysis in the Pentagon to quantify the level of destruction.[9] By the mid-1960s, the US government accepted that the USSR could also assure the USA of destruction if it were to launch the first strike; the situation of mutual deterrence was described as 'mutual assured destruction', with the appropriate acronym of MAD. The basic threat within MAD was no different from massive retaliation, but now the declared position was that nuclear retaliation was reserved for nuclear attack. Thus US nuclear strategy through the Johnson administration was characterised by the twin poles of assured destruction – the deterrence threat – and damage limitation – if deterrence failed.

During this period, NATO strategy seems to have lagged behind American strategy, still tied to a doctrine essentially of massive relatiation with conventional forces seen as little more than a tripwire to nuclear escalation. The dominant feature during this period was the controversy surrounding the American proposal for a multilateral nuclear force in NATO, and the tensions within the alliance which led to the eventual abandonment of the proposal, and to French withdrawal from the military organisation. In 1967, NATO adopted the strategy of 'flexible response', in which the declared position is that any level of aggression would be met with an 'appropriate' response, including a nuclear response if deemed necessary, whether or not the WP had already used nuclear weapons.

The major problem with assured destruction, as seen by its critics and by the incoming Nixon administration in 1969, was the passivity inherent in it. It was essentially a doctrine of response, positively eschewing the initiative. Worse, it would respond only to nuclear attack on the USA. By this doctrine, the whole point of having nuclear weapons was not to use them. And although McNamara had aimed at flexibility for US forces as a whole,[10] one of the main ways in which criticism was voiced was to attack the narrow range of options it provided. Nixon raised these problems in 1970, asking if a president should have 'the single option of ordering the mass destruction of enemy civilians in the face of the certainty that it would be followed by the mass slaughter of Americans' and if assured destruction should be the only form of deterrence.[11] In January 1974, James Schlesinger, the Defense Secretary, announced that there had been 'a change in the strategies of the United States with regard to the hypothetical employment of central strategic forces'.[12]

Through Schlesinger's opaque language in the first announcement and others following, a number of strands were discernible: first use of strategic nuclear forces was now possible; targeting doctrine was changed to allow greater flexibility including precise, limited strikes; more emphasis was placed on counterforce strikes (that is, strikes against enemy forces) and therefore on warhead accuracy since counterforce targets are smaller than cities, with structures strengthened to withstand nuclear blast; it would be possible to fight 'sub-holocaust' engagements — limited nuclear war. Thus, the president had more options, deterrence could be applied to a wider variety of threats, both nuclear and non-nuclear, and nuclear weapons were more useful. The strategy became known by a variety of names: 'counterforce', 'the Schlesinger doctrine' and 'limited strategic options'.[13]

Strangely, the Carter administration seems to have claimed that it has changed US nuclear strategy — but changed it to a strategy of limited options. It was already the position that the ability to retaliate to nuclear attack should include the capacity for 'controlled counterattacks',[14] that is, for damage limitation; in late 1978 there were reports that the 'existing' strategy of 'relying upon large-scale retaliation' for deterrence was being questioned, with further reports in early 1979 that that strategy had been discarded in favour of one including counterforce targets and options for limited use of nuclear weapons.[15] One cannot escape the conclusion that this is either ineptitude by the press or mere deception; the doctrine announced by Schlesinger in January 1974 was at no time discarded, and has now simply been reaffirmed.[16]

Apart from this, the newness of the doctrine at the time of its 1974 announcement is itself controversial. It has been argued that the doctrine was American strategy throughout the 1960s, made public only to justify Pentagon requests for yet more accurate and more numerous nuclear warheads. The point is that assured destruction, relying upon the threat of destroying cities, would require a relatively small number of warheads, well protected in submarines, for example, and certainly far fewer than the 7,600 then in the American arsenal.[17] Milton Leitenberg has shown that the Single Integrated Operational Plan (SIOP) and General Strike Plan, the US nuclear targeting programmes, have included counterforce targets since the early 1950s when the USSR first had strategic bombers and missiles, and that scenarios for planning always included American first strikes.[18] Similarly, Robert Aldridge argues that counterforce was 'the Pentagon's clandestine military doctrine since at least the 1950s' and cites Schlesinger's 1974 report to Congress where he stated that a variety of targeting options 'have been part of US strategic doctrine for some time'; because the SIOP included counterforce targeting, Aldridge argues that the assertion by Schlesinger and others that the president had previously only the choice between surrender and annihilation was false.[19]

There is some force to this case, and American strategy in the 1960s with its element of damage limitation involving counterforce strategy was criticised on similar grounds as giving the appearance of a plan for nuclear first strike;[20] by ignoring damage limitation when presenting the new doctrine, Schlesinger did mislead. But in a crucial respect the strategy of limited options was a new departure. What Schlesinger announced was a change in targeting *doctrine*, not a new list of targets. Counter-force targets were always part of the damage limitation strategy, and the SIOP could contain precisely the same types of targets and yet embody a different doctrine. By concentrating on the targets, some critics have lost the crucial point, which is a change in *attitude* – genuinely, a change in doctrine.

The essence of the change lies in the emphasis on flexibility, select-ivity, precision, limited nuclear war and, therefore, on the utility of nuclear weapons. The shift was made possible by technological develop-ments, not least more accurate warheads and the Command Data Buffer (CDB), a computerised system which can retarget a *Minuteman 3* missile in 25 minutes, and the entire force of *Minuteman 3*s in ten hours, a task which used to take weeks.[21] The CDB programme began in 1971, around the time that the shift to a new doctrine was developing.[22] The CDB and greater accuracy are the technological basis for selectivity and precision in nuclear strikes, but, in addition, so Schlesinger argued, in-doctrination and pre-planning within the Strategic Air Command (SAC) were crucial. Although SAC had previously had a hypothetical ability for limited nuclear strikes, especially with manned bombers, it had not had the necessary training or attitudes.[23]

The problem which the new strategy attempted to solve is a long-standing one, taking us back at least as far as the period of massive retaliation: in essence, it is the problem of the utility of force, especially extreme force.

Russell Weigley has argued that the characteristic American way of war is a strategy of annihilation – active, aggressive use of force. Deter-rence through massive retaliation was 'a thoroughly negative kind of strategy', incompatible with 'positive goals' in US foreign policy.[24] It did not make force useful, and the Eisenhower administration's trimming of conventional forces hampered policy-makers further. The Kennedy administration tried to revive the utility of force for a 'positive' policy largely by expanding conventional forces, but this path led to protracted war in Vietnam, and massive public disillusion with the use of American soldiers, and sacrifice of their lives, in combat abroad. At the end of the 1960s, the response was the 'Nixon doctrine': other governments would receive American equipment, advice and training, but would have to do their own fighting. Yet here the Nixon administration teetered on the edge of renouncing direct use of conventional forces, while its nuclear forces were there only to deter nuclear war. The new strategy was an attempt to release the inhibitions on the use of nuclear weapons – and the nuclear alert of October 1973 (before the strategy was made public) over suspected Soviet troop movements to the Middle East suggested how nuclear forces might be directly useful if those inhibitions were released. Thus, the strategy of limited options was an attempt to supersede the passivity of previous nuclear strategies in order to compensate for the new passivity of conventional strategy, an attempt to surmount the main problems for American foreign policy in the early 1970s – problems, indeed, which remained throughout the decade.

Nuclear deterrence is always a risky and dangerous strategy, full of uncertainties. It is hard to know if the adversary is actually deterred from any desired action, and thus difficult to know if deterrence is successful. It is not clear whether or not the adversary believes the deterrent threat – and Soviet views on nuclear war suggest the USSR does not accept the deterrence equation as the USA lays it out. It is even hard to be sure that there is some specific threat or action to deter, or if the deterrent threat is aimed at the right target. The threat of nuclear devastation entrenches hostile attitudes and suspicions, possibly precluding other ways for two states to relate, other ways to pursue and settle differences. It runs the risk of accident, of war through misperception, miscalculation or mischance. It is, in the end, a sophisticated gamble with awesomely high stakes, and one from which the deterring state may gain little advantage.

But the shift from nuclear passivity to nuclear utility raises new risks. By raising the option of 'limited' nuclear war, it makes the use of nuclear weapons more thinkable, and therefore more likely, yet at no stage has it been, or could it be, guaranteed that the war would stay limited, and only reluctantly was it admitted how destructive even a limited nuclear war would be.[25] As we shall see, the USSR has not yet shown it accepts the terms of the game of limited strategic options: it believes, or claims to, that nuclear war must be total, making nonsense of the American emphasis on flexibility, selectivity, and precision. Horrible as a limited nuclear war would be, there is the yet more ugly prospect of an American government sailing gaily into a limited war, and ending up with the holocaust.

However, every policy-maker must realise the dangers of any strategy which risks any level of nuclear retaliation. As McGeorge Bundy has argued in a well known corrective to the excessive sophistication of some strategic debates, it is always possible to calculate a figure of 'acceptable' casualties in a nuclear war numbering many millions, but

> In the real world of real political leaders — whether here or in the Soviet Union — a decision that would bring even one hydrogen bomb on one city of one's own country would be recognised in advance as a catastrophic blunder; ten bombs on ten cities would be a disaster beyond history; and a hundred bombs on one hundred cities are unthinkable. Yet this unthinkable level of human incineration is the least that could be expected by either side in response to any first strike.[26]

Yet Bundy's well-founded assertion of the inhibitions against risking nuclear retaliation on the home country raises another prospect, which should be firmly set in any of Western European's thinking about American nuclear strategy: it is conceivable that the definition of what made a nuclear war 'limited' would in part be geographical — that is, the USA and the USSR themselves might not suffer nuclear attack, but their respective allies might.

The logic of Bundy's position would be to forswear any attempt to use nuclear weapons to serve 'positive' foreign policy goals — in other words, to return to the passivity of assured destruction. But then, unless the use of conventional forces in combat can be made politically feasible again, the result would be close to an effective renunciation of the use of force to support foreign policy, a return to the position diagnosed by Kissinger (with some exaggeration) in the 1950s. Yet if, despite the declared strategy, American policy-makers feared the Soviets did not accept the rules of the limited strategic options game, and therefore feared to use nuclear weapons for the very reasons Bundy argues, it is arguable that, like it or not, the USA has made that renunciation. As Weigley concludes, 'At no point in the spectrum of violence does the use of combat offer much promise for the United States today.'[27] And that precisely encapsulates one of the major dilemmas of US foreign policy in the late 1970s.

The inability of the Carter administration, or any possible administration, to resolve this dilemma probably lies at the heart of the impatience of parts of the American establishment and political élites in Western Europe at apparent American inactivity in the international arena. The widespread scorn with which Carter and the US Congress are viewed is symptomatic of the USA's generalised relative decline in the 1970s, both politically and economically, against both rivals and allies. Carter gets rather a rough ride, for although two Washington columnists accurately identify 'a kind of diplomatic masochism that lies just under the administration's surface attitude of occasional hard-headed diplomacy',[28] the administration has also shown it can pull off spectacular diplomatic coups. American foreign policy is handicapped by more than the occasional blunder: unresolved dilemmas extending back over two decades must dominate any perspective at present. The essential problem is the constraints, both domestic and international, on the USA using its awesome military power – and perhaps the essential danger is that one day an impatient administration may not perceive those constraints.

The continuing dilemmas, finally, have left the USA with a contradictory strategy. It subscribes both to a passive nuclear strategy – for assured destruction, partnered by damage limitation, has never been abandoned – and to a positive one – limited strategic options. And while conventional force is so far unusable, the strategy of limited options asserts that nuclear force can be used: the higher and more destructive level of force is said to be more acceptable as an instrument of policy than the lower level. This obstinate contradiction provides the focus for understanding the main dilemmas of American nuclear strategy in the 1980s.

Military Power in Soviet Foreign Policy

Since the mid-1960s, while the USA has faced these problems, we have seen the emergence of the USSR as a genuine global super power. Of course, since the late 1940s, the USSR has been seen as the main and sometimes the sole adversary of the USA and its allies, the source of most of their problems, both international and domestic. And the assumption of the boundless ambition and evil intent of the USSR has consistently hindered serious discussion of Soviet policy. In particular, study of the subject is hampered by what might be called a monolithic obsession – the USSR is seen as a monolithic system lacking contradictions, and thus the problems within Soviet foreign policy, based on fundamental weaknesses in the domestic system, are obscured. Indeed, these problems are disguised more by western preconceptions than by the deliberate policy of the Soviet leadership. Assessments of Soviet policies and, in the broadest sense, capabilities are marred by overeagerness to either condemn or glorify, often in similar terms, for while one camp sees Soviet socialism as proof of the evil of Soviet foreign policy, another camp takes Soviet socialism as proof of its virtues.[29] Despite the genuine power available to the Soviet state, there are sound reasons for viewing the USSR as 'a sheep in wolf's clothing'.[30]

Precise dating of the emergence of the USSR as a super power is impossible: it is the result of a process under way since at least the end of World War II, which may have passed a decisive turning point some time in the mid-to-late 1960s. Militarily, this has been marked by expansion of the strategic nuclear arsenal, wider naval deployments, and all-round development of the armed forces.

It is, however, important to retain a sense of perspective on these military improvements. In the next chapter, I shall show that the improvements are less dramatic than many assessments would have us believe, and have been, at the least, matched by changes in NATO's forces. It is, moreover, instructive to recall for how long we have heard about Soviet build-ups: in a recently declassified secret report of January 1951, Stuart Symington, then Chairman of the US National Security Resources Board and later a US Senator, asserted that, 'As things are going now, by 1953 if not 1952, the Soviet aggressors will assume complete command of the world situation.'[31] Impending Soviet domination is a recurrent obsession in NATO countries. Nevertheless, since 1968 the USSR has more than trebled its inventory of strategic nuclear warheads (bringing it to around half the American figure).[32] More capable combat aircraft have been introduced, especially in the European theatre, providing a more even balance between air defence and air attack forces to replace the former tilt towards air defence, and air transport has been expanded and improved; despite this, Soviet air capacity for offensives and transport is probably still below NATO's.[33] Perhaps the most impressive development relates to the navy, and this can be regarded as the most accurate indicator for dating and defining Soviet emergence as a super power.[34]

The Soviet navy, however, has not grown in numbers; it has fewer ships than in 1958, is replacing them at a rate below one-to-one, and has slower naval construction rates than NATO states.[35] What has happened is not naval growth, but an expansion in the areas of naval deployment together with improved capabilities for newer ships. Despite this last point, the Soviet navy is on average older than in 1958: Barry Blechman notes that in 1958, 40 per cent of submarines and 75 per cent of major surface warships were less than eight years old; by 1977, the figures had changed to 20 per cent and 15 per cent respectively.[36] The changed pattern of deployments is instructive: until 1957 Soviet naval activity outside the Black and Baltic Seas was rare; there was no continuous naval presence in the Mediterranean until 1964, and no significant growth in it until 1967; surface warships ventured to the Pacific only in 1963-4, and to the Caribbean in 1969; regular deployment to the Indian Ocean began in 1968, increased sharply, and then appeared to level off in the early 1970s.[37]

These wider deployments have been part of a more outgoing world policy by the USSR, showing greater eagerness to intervene actively in international politics. Naval presence has both expressed Soviet power in a general way, and, apparently, underwritten increased intervention in African politics, while improved air transport has made that intervention physically possible. When expressed intelligibly, concern among NATO policy-makers has been directed at the loss of 'overwhelming authority' on the world's seas and the freedom of action which went with it;[38] as Michael Klare has argued,

> It is not western *shipping* that is threatened by Soviet naval deployments, but Washington's strategy for continued Western hegemony in remote Third World areas.[39]

The history of American command of the seas and, before that, of the crucial role of naval strength in British global power has made western perceptions particularly sensitive to the effects of these expanded deployments, and probably encouraged the Soviet leadership to use the instrument of naval power ever more strongly.[40]

The past fifteen years or so can be taken as the second major phase in the growth of Soviet international power, the first being immediately after World War II when friendly governments were established in Eastern Europe, thus securing a defence buffer zone against invasion from the west (which Russia had experienced three times this century). It is often assumed that in that period the USSR was acting from a position of strength, its conquests then being a prelude to snatching yet greater prizes. Certainly, by comparison with the countries of Eastern Europe the USSR was in a position of great strength. But the war had devastated the Soviet economy, killed one-tenth of the population, and ravaged agriculture; Soviet industry equipped its armed forces only thanks to British and, far more important, American aid. To be sure, in May 1945 the USSR had 11 million men under arms – but the USA had 12 million, with an incomparably stronger industrial and agricultural base.[41]

The USSR imposed its leadership on Eastern Europe from a position of relative weakness, and it was only possible because the USSR had the prior agreement of its wartime allies. Eastern Europe was one of the fruits of victory, and can be seen as parallel to the fruits of victory gained in Western Europe by Britain and, especially, the USA. If Eastern European states were established as Soviet allies and as a buffer zone, the Federal Republic of Germany was set up as a front-line anti-socialist state, its entry into NATO immediately raised, and its economy assured through Marshall Aid. Stalin kept to the letter of the agreement dividing Europe, to the extent of ordering the strong French and Italian Communist Parties to co-operate with the reconstruction of capitalism, and ordering the Greek party to lay down its arms.[42] What is different about Soviet leadership in Eastern Europe lies not in the principle that states victorious in war generally try to profit from victory, but in the ways in which the USA and USSR separately went about enjoying the fruits of victory, and the contradictions on each side since then.

Weakness within strength continues to characterise Soviet policy even as it has developed from being a regional great power to a global super power. The Soviet economy continues to grow at an impressive rate, albeit more slowly than in the late 1960s, but in many respects it is inflexible and, as the weak performance of 1974 and 1975 showed, stemming as it did from miserable harvests in both years, is vulnerable to its agricultural weakness.[43] Central to its problems is the difficulty which has been found in pushing through industrial innovation except by imitating and importing western technology. But this carries with it the problem of debt to the West, now standing at $40 billion,[44] with a weak performance in the export of technology. United Nations data for 1976 show that Soviet technology exports, including those to Eastern Europe, amounted to $6,257 billion — only marginally above one-eighth of American technology exports (at $49,509 billion) and, perhaps more strikingly, little more than a third of the British figure ($18,175 billion).[45] There could hardly be a more eloquent testimony to Soviet industrial and economic problems, even though we may envy the general stability of the economy in an age of wild inflation and fluctuations in exchange rates in the capitalist world economy.

The problem is that there is no mechanism to drive innovation apart from political directives. Arthur Alexander points out that Soviet military industry 'is considerably more innovative than the civilian sector, partly because the former faces international competition of a particularly forceful nature'.[46] Lacking competition, the Soviet economy equally lacks any other mechanism able to perform a similar function. The systematic exclusion of the vast majority of citizens from participation in decision-making means that there is no democratic socialist alternative to the market to mediate between producers and consumers. Rudolf Bahro argues, in his monumental study from within the Eastern European system, that social need is mediated not by the market, but by the economic plan, which rests on 'the dictated balancing of interests from above'; success in fulfilling the plan wins, for the economic managers, only 'avoidance of anger', and the outcome is that 'every level of economic management is characterised by a predominance of inertial forces'.[47] This in turn consolidates the role of authoritarian directives in both the economic and political systems, and in both generates the conservatism and increasingly impoverished ideology which is so characteristic of the Soviet leadership in many of its actions.

For foreign policy, the consequence is an amalgam of caution and limited adventurism. The historical experience of the Soviet state – including counter-revolutionary foreign intervention during the civil war, enforced isolation, the failure of socialist revolution in Western Europe and the Stalinist thesis of the possibility of 'socialism in one country', and post-1945 American anti-Sovietism – conditions a response to the USA and NATO which is perforce competitive. American policies are seen to challenge, and do challenge, the Soviet state and its interests: Soviet policy does not flinch from the competition. But there is no evidence that the USSR is any more sanguine about the prospect of nuclear war than the USA is (although attempts have been made to show otherwise – see below), and the Soviet requirement for western technology necessitates relatively cordial relations. The USSR has an identifiable interest in the maintenance of peace, in avoiding tensions which might lead to war or, at least, overly hostile military confrontation, and no identifiable interest in incinerating Western Europe. Indeed, in the European context the USSR is firmly committed to the *status quo*, as was shown by its determined pursuit of international recognition of existing borders in Europe, for which it was even prepared to concede potentially embarrassing clauses on the protection of human rights in the Final Act of the Conference on Security and Co-operation in Europe in 1975.

Military confrontation in Europe remains important to both NATO and the WP as a political expression of continued competition, important for its effects on their own populations' perceptions as well as for its wider international impact. It may yet be more directly instrumental in European politics again, in, for example, deciding the fate of Yugoslavia or of any NATO or WP state seeking to break from the system in one way or another. It has its own dangers. But to some extent the locus of continued competition has been shifted from the European arena, and if there the USSR favours the *status quo*, elsewhere, and especially in Africa, it has a more thrusting policy designed to secure political change in its favour.

Yet here the USSR faces a decisive disadvantage: its low level of technology exports, only one-eighth of the USA's, indicates its lack of a weapon which is perhaps the most powerful, and most insidious, available to capitalist states and their interests. Control of technology has, both directly and in more diffuse ways, become an instrument for dominance and influence in poorer countries, providing the chance to shape policies and entire social systems. The very attractiveness of capitalist technology is a trap for poorer states.[48] Soviet technology is simply not so attractive. What is left for the USSR is to step in where western capital and states pull out, and to provide military support to liberation movements (with whose aspirations there is a degree of genuine political alignment) and certain states (often those it has aided in their former liberation wars). Important here, of course, has been the use of Cuban forces in Angola and Ethiopia; although final judgements on the events there and the nature and motivation of Cuban involvement must still hang fire, it does appear that this represents a modified Soviet version of the Nixon doctrine – crucially, its own troops have not yet been involved in combat. Equally important are the improvements in air transport and expanded naval deployments noted earlier. But the very visibility of military power is the result of the USSR not having a great deal else to offer.

In its own way, with both armed force and economic exploitation, the West has been far more thrustful, violent and effective in maintaining its influence than the USSR can ever be. In many respects, the USSR is essentially attempting to catch up – and it is not equipped to do it very well. Proper analysis of these developments has been hampered by what I earlier referred to as the monolithic obsession: contradiction and failure on the Soviet part are just not seen. Equally obfuscating has been the temptation to analyse events in a single geographical region as if they had a single political cause – the USSR – and without reference to a wider context: the *New York Times* commented acidly on *The Economist*'s identification of 'a crumbling triangle' from Addis Ababa to Kabul, and on Zbigniew Brzezinski's picture of 'an arc of crisis' around the Indian Ocean, suggesting that the USSR might see 'a crescent of collusion' between Japan, China and the USA, or 'a diameter of defection' from Egypt to Romania.[49] Close analysis of events in Afghanistan, Iran, South Yemen and Ethiopia reveals the intellectual poverty and gross distortion of fact entailed in the Brzezinski approach.[50]

Soviet nuclear strategy has been part of the competitive response to American power since 1945. The USSR was behind in developing nuclear weapons, and has lagged in every single phase of the qualitative arms race ever since. The broad outlines of the evolution of Soviet nuclear strategy seem less complex than in the American case, partly because we know less of the debates surrounding its formation and development. That such debates have taken place, and with great intensity, is clear. One such period of debate preceded the 1956 Congress of the Communist Party of the Soviet Union (where Khrushchev denounced Stalin), and resulted in discarding the old view that war between capitalism and socialism is inevitable, while asserting that were a major war to occur it would certainly be nuclear.[51] This led to a strategy sometimes known as 'minimum deterrence' and to a reduced emphasis on conventional forces. Like the American doctrine of massive retaliation it raised problems of the inutility of force, and can in some ways be seen as a natural counterfoil to that doctrine.

By the early 1960s, further debates had modified this perspective, returning a major role in future warfare to conventional forces, while still insisting on the near certainty of nuclear escalation. During the 1960s, the Soviet armed forces developed doctrines and capabilities for using nuclear weapons on the battlefield to punch holes in NATO positions which could then be rapidly exploited by armoured forces equipped to fight in a radioactive environment.

This, however, retained a perspective on force focussed largely upon a future major war with NATO. Following the downfall of Khrushchev, there was a gradual introduction of an approach known as 'flexibility with caution' better suited to the needs of an emergent super power. Four main premises underlie this approach which remains, with some modifications, the heart of current doctrine on the use of armed forces. First, nuclear war must be avoided and, secondly, reliance on strategic nuclear strength is the best way of doing this; thirdly, strong conventional forces are required to sustain Soviet interests in Europe and against China while, fourthly, more versatile conventional forces are needed to support Soviet global interests. Expanded naval deployment and improved air transport are natural partners for this shift of emphasis towards a worldwide military role.

A characteristic feature of Soviet nuclear strategy is that nuclear forces are not qualitatively divorced from conventional forces to the extent that they were in American doctrine before limited strategic options. This does not mean that one type of weapon is not distinguished from another: rather, that all kinds of force are seen within an integrated totality. A consequence of this is emphasis on battlefield use of nuclear weapons alongside conventional forces, and on the undesirability of delay or artificial limitations in employing nuclear weapons.[52] A further consequence, of which much has been made in NATO states, is that nuclear war is seen as displaying no fundamental difference from other types of war, and, accordingly, would produce victory for one side.[53] On the basis of this, Richard Pipes, a pace-setter among those who like to produce less confident assessments of Soviet policy than the US government, has asserted that the USSR 'thinks it could fight and win a nuclear war'.[54]

Such bold conclusions, however, must be taken carefully. The burden of Pipes' (and others') case is that, believing it could fight and win a nuclear war, the USSR would be prepared to launch one under certain circumstances. But Fred Kaplan has shown that many Soviet military authors start from the assumption that it is only aggressive American imperialism that would launch a major war. Further, the similarity between nuclear and other war is that nuclear war would still, at root, be an extension of policy by other means; the peaceful policies of the USSR would therefore not lead to war, but the aggressive policies of the USA might do. Thus, these authors conclude, the USSR must be prepared to respond, with all means at its disposal, to the threat of American aggression.[55] What Pipes sees as preparations for Soviet aggression, looks from the other side like a peaceful response to preparations for American aggression. Kaplan also quotes from one Soviet source to argue that the view that nuclear war is winnable is based on the expectation of the American masses responding to the war by rising up to overthrow imperialism and so assure the victory of socialism.[56] This, however, is a less convincing response to Pipes' argument, for should the USSR retaliate to an American nuclear first strike, the first victims would be precisely those American masses who should be rising up to overthrow imperialism, which suggests that the USSR should not retaliate to a nuclear attack upon it — but there is no evidence that this logic really is followed through. Moreover, it is unlikely that the American masses would respond like that, and even more unlikely that the Soviet leadership would be prepared to rely on them. If the logic were followed through, the USA could get away with utterly devastating the USSR without suffering retaliation, and it is hardly conceivable that the USSR would even hint at a policy giving the USA the unfettered right to annihilate it. More likely is that the argument Kaplan quotes is rather shallow propaganda.

There is, however, a contradiction within Soviet nuclear strategy, between its emphases on nuclear escalation and on winning the war, which, again, is missed by the monolithic obsession. If war between NATO and the WP must lead to full-scale strategic nuclear war, the result can only be the devastation of all combatant and many non-combatant countries. If there are any victors at the end, they will be in a poor state to enjoy the fruits of victory which, in any case, they will be hard put to find. As a general principle, nuclear war can be thought of as 'winnable' only if it is extremely limited compared to the destructiveness embodied in the super powers' arsenals. Nevertheless, the USSR has been reluctant to concede the case that nuclear war could be limited: its reaction to Schlesinger's announcement of the strategy of limited options in January 1974 was uniformly hostile, and well in keeping with its own nuclear doctrine.[57]

This obviously raises severe problems for the American strategy; the Soviet rejection of the rules of the limited nuclear war game undermines any benefits the USA would hope to get by asserting the utility of nuclear weapons for limited engagements. One reaction to this was simply to argue that the USSR would accept the rules of the game once it started, since it too would have an interest in keeping the war limited. But it has also been argued that the USSR may be a great deal more flexible than it makes out. Benjamin Lambeth argues that, despite the definite discrepancy between the American view of limited war and the Soviet view of escalation, Soviet views have displayed increasing flexibility since about 1967. He speculates, without clear evidence, that this may lead on to a Soviet concept of limited strategic options.[58] The increasing accuracy of the Soviet missile arsenal, though still inferior to the USA's, lends some weight to this speculation, since accuracy is the decisive capability required for precise, selective strikes.[59]

There is, then, a slim possibility, and it can be put no higher than that, of the USSR developing a doctrine for nuclear warfare similar to the USA's. This would require a major break with much of previous doctrine, but would be compatible with its strategic evolution in the sense that more versatile nuclear forces could be presented as the complement to more versatile conventional forces. It would, moreover, represent the USSR attempting to catch up in this field, as it has in African policy, and in its expansion of naval deployments to fit the pattern of past great powers' naval policies. American strategic thinkers and policy-makers might well welcome this attempt by the USSR to play the American game — and we may even see a perverse wishful thinking in Lambeth's analysis — but for the rest of the world the prospect would be unambiguously bleak. The possibility of both super powers having nuclear strategies which made limited nuclear war conceivable as an instrument of policy, with part of the definition of 'limited' being geographical in both cases so that the super powers only bombard each other's allies — this possibility is perhaps the grimmest of all.

Rivalry Through Detente

The prospect of such a dangerous pairing of American and Soviet nuclear strategies is something for the future. For the present, we can rather more sanguinely note the relatively improved international atmosphere, compared to the 1950s, which is summarised in the term 'detente'. Ending an era of particularly profound and dangerous tensions, there were hopes that detente could remove the main bones of contention between NATO and the WP and lead to a new era of lower levels of armament and reduced risk of war. These hopes cannot now be dismissed as mere illusion, for great gains have been registered, not least in Europe, but it is clear that they require some modification. Despite an improved atmosphere and more open communications, detente has not led to reduced arms levels or lower military spending: it has found little military corollary.

Dating the beginning of detente is difficult − it is a process which slowly gathered, and more recently somewhat lost, momentum. But most people would probably place its beginning some time after the Cuba missile crisis of 1962 when the world was on the verge of nuclear war, although in the late 1950s the term was already used to describe an apparent improvement in US-Soviet relations. It will be noted that the period of the emergence of detente during the 1960s coincides with the emergence of the USSR as a super power, and there can be no evading the fact that the USSR sees detente as made possible partly by its own increased strength.

However, detente is not the result of a single policy by any single state, nor is it embodied in any single international agreement. It is the sum of a variety of policies of both NATO and WP states, some of which are similar with clearly similar ends in mind, some of which are different but complementary. It is therefore a complex process, describing a whole range of economic and political relations, which is certainly not susceptible to the kind of crude substitute for analysis offered by, for example, the right wings of the British Conservative or American Republican parties. Perhaps the apotheosis of these non-analytical analyses comes from Alexander Solzhenitsyn who, because of his own ill-treatment and eventual expulsion by the Soviet authorities, gained a particular credibility as a crusader against the USSR and detente. For him, detente was simply Soviet deception, made successful by western gullibility and decadence. But on the basis of his understandably profound anti-Sovietism he produced a series of crass misjudgements about the extent of Soviet influence in Portugal, India, the Middle East and virtually everywhere else that he turned his attention. In essence, Solzhenitsyn called for a renewed cold war, isolating the USSR, and building up NATO's military power.[60]

Whatever else may be said, this recipe for a new arms race held nothing for the Soviet people. As Roy Medvedev argued, such a policy would further legitimate the Soviet leadership's repression of intellectual dissidents and oppositional groups; it would sweep away the slim prospects of a more democratic socialist society.[61] Equally, seeing the apocalypse just around the corner, Solzhenitsyn essentially called on the people of NATO countries to join in galloping towards it.

The foremost achievement of detente has been to reduce the danger of nuclear war — and no call to reject detente can, with honesty, evade the consequence of increasing that danger. Central to understanding the process are concepts of crisis management and crisis avoidance.[62] Into the former category falls a series of US-Soviet agreements, starting with the 'hot line' agreement of 1963 (updated in 1971, and paralleled by a British-Soviet hot line agreement in 1967), and continuing with agreements on reducing the risk of war (1971), preventing incidents on the high seas (1971 and 1972) and preventing nuclear war (1973).[63] In the second category are certain other arms control agreements and negotiations, the 'confidence building measures' (such as prior warning of military manoeuvres) and confirmation of existing European borders agreed at the Conference on Security and Co-operation in Europe in 1975. The basic effect of such agreements is to create a safer relationship in which, although the levels of armaments remain as high as ever and continue to increase, and although competition is not eliminated, nuclear war seems less likely. It is the shared interest in avoiding the nuclear catastrophe that forms the context and basis of such measures. It is a process which both sides find preferable to the previous pattern of armoured confrontations in Berlin.

Perhaps as important for laying the basis for the process as a whole has been the USSR's desire for access to certain aspects of western technology, and the eagerness of NATO states to sell to the USSR and WP states in a situation of international economic crisis, surplus industrial capacity, and tight markets. As long as these complementary interests exist, the complete discarding of detente by either side is unlikely, even if developments on both sides are capable of eroding it and putting its achievements at risk.

By itself, detente is not a process which can supersede the limitations of the present world political system: it is itself a product of the system and of relations within it. Thus, Carter was basically right to stress the dual nature of the US-Soviet relationship — co-operation and competition, in uneven balance — in a speech which showed a far clearer grasp of the complexities of the process, its opportunities and shortcomings, than is possessed by most of his hawkish critics.[64] But what these critics point to is the continuation of the USSR's emergence as a super power; this is seen as threatening American state interests, and so indeed it is, but two further points should be made: first, that it is extremely unlikely any American policy could have prevented this emergence, and, second, that the development of detente has depended on a relationship of approximate equality (assessed, for example, as the mutual ability to destroy each other several times over). The USA is at least as much at fault as the USSR for not having sought a genuine detente in the period of its clearest superiority. The tensions and dangers of the cold war could give way to a new, still competitive, but safer relationship only because the USSR was becoming a super power.

Yet this is enough to indicate the fragility of the process of detente, its gains and its prospects. This fragility is perhaps most clearly evident in the relationship between detente and nuclear deterrence, for the former attempts to construct what the nature of the latter undermines. The threat embodied in nuclear deterrence to massacre the enemy's population is appallingly inhumane (usually, less emotive terms than 'massacre' are preferred in strategic writings, but that is the nature of the threat); such inhumanity can only be justified if the enemy can be depicted as itself inhumane and aggressively minded — then, instead of being inhumane, the threat seems only realistic. Thus, for public acceptance (and in one sense political leaders are also part of the public, susceptible to the perceptions they also broadcast) nuclear deterrence depends upon hostility and suspicion towards the other side, while detente depends at least in part on breaking down those barriers of hostility and suspicion. It is, moreover, impossible for the deterrent threat not to carry connotations of blackmail — which again is hardly the basis for relaxing tensions. In this sense, we may ultimately find that detente and nuclear deterrence are incompatible.

The ideology embodied in nuclear deterrence may explain why it has been so easy for both sides to retrench somewhat after the first flush of detente. That there has been a retrenchment is undeniable and cause for serious concern; recent actions of both sides are all too reminiscent of the kind of petty irritations indulged in during the 1950s. We have seen, for example, mutual expulsions of US and Soviet diplomats on an apparent tit-for-tat basis;[65] in February 1978, the USSR put pressure on West Berlin for the first time in many years,[66] and in July the USA restricted exports to the USSR and temporarily banned visits there by senior US government officials.[67] And while the 1978 Soviet trials of dissidents seemed to many western commentators like an infringement of the 1975 Final Act of the Conference on Security and Co-operation in Europe, Carter's statements in July 1978 that he shared West German aspirations for German reunification must have seemed to eastern observers like a flagrant violation of those parts of the Final Act which guarantee the existing national boundaries in Europe.[68]

In part, the retrenchment can be traced to domestic political considerations on both sides. At a time of political and economic crisis in capitalism, it is hardly surprising to find anti-Sovietism re-emerging as a kind of ideological social glue. The welding together of British Conservatives in 1975, by Thatcher's powerful anti-Soviet rhetoric, at a time when they were stunningly disunited, is one example of the process. The use of fear of the USSR to legitimate the repressive *Berufsverbot* regulations in the Federal Republic of Germany is another. And the USSR and its allies have their own need for ideological social glue. Their inability to tolerate even relatively disorganised dissent is perhaps suggestive of their assessment of the risks of a genuine cultural and political openness, of a kind it has been thought would be encouraged by the relaxation of international tension.

At least as important, and possibly more so, has been the discovery by NATO states of another way of pursuing rivalry with the USSR – through use of the so-called 'China card', developing a pseudo-alliance with China on the basis of its desire for western technology and for isolating the USSR. The Chinese invasion of Vietnam, an ally (but far from a 'satellite') of the USSR, is striking evidence of what should have been clear throughout: as a trump card for NATO states, China has a will of its own and its own game to play. If China and NATO cosy up together and agree that they have a common enemy, it is not surprising if the USSR is suspicious and hostile. The further development of NATO-Chinese relations cannot be discussed here, but one thing is clear: attempting to view those relations as a ploy in NATO-WP relations will be misleading, and attempting to conduct them as such a ploy will be short-sighted and potentially dangerous in its effects on detente.

Retrenchment and this flirtation with the 'China card', however, do not mean that detente is at an end. The erosion of it has been irresponsible in the extreme, but it is neither complete nor irreversible. The problem for NATO states and for their citizens is how to generate a reasonably mature response to the basic facts of Soviet power: the hysteria which emanates from some quarters, and which is all too sadly fed by Chinese pronouncements, does not constitute anything like the desired response. Claims that the USSR is having things all its own way, that NATO is conceding and losing right down the line, are factually incorrect. The USSR is powerful but not omnipotent; its military power is great, but so is NATO's, and this very strength disguises the USSR's genuine economic and political weaknesses and handicaps. There is every reason to believe that its foreign policy will continue to be characterised by that mixture of caution and limited adventurism we now see. Given continuity in basic NATO policies and strategy, this suggests a continued relationship of competition. Yet there is also every reason to believe that detente can and will continue; it represents a realistic way, and perhaps the only realistic way, of preventing the competition from becoming too dangerous. It is, of course, limited by that very competition — but it may also ultimately provide a point of departure for qualitatively different international relations. If American eyes remain firmly fixed on gaining political benefits through such instruments as the strategy of limited options, and even worse if the USSR follows suit, the path which is chosen could lead towards nuclear destruction — but it is quite possible to choose differently.

Notes

1. *The Military Balance 1978-1979* (IISS, London, 1978), pp. 16-18; for a similar outline of Warsaw Pact command structures, see p. 12.

2. For example, see U. Nerlich, 'Continuity and Change: The Political Context of Western Europe's Defence', in *idem* and J.J. Holst (eds), *Beyond Nuclear Deterrence: New Aims, New Arms* (Macdonald & Jane's, London, 1977).

3. This periodisation, and much of the account which follows, is based on, but at points deviates from, the narratives in: J.H. Kahan, *Security in the Nuclear Age* (Brookings Institution, Washington, DC, 1975); *World Armaments and Disarmament: SIPRI Yearbook 1974* (MIT Press, London, 1974), Chapter 5.

4. Secretary of State, John Foster Dulles, in *US Department of State Bulletin*, 25 January 1954.

5. Kahan, *Security in the Nuclear Age*, pp. 18-20.

6. H.A. Kissinger, *Nuclear Weapons and Foreign Policy* (Harper & Row, New York, 1957); *idem*, 'Force and Diplomacy in the Nuclear Age', *Foreign Affairs*, April 1956, vol. 34, no. 2.

7. *SIPRI Yearbook 1974*, pp. 76-80.

8. Secretary of Defense, Robert McNamara, in *US Department of State Bulletin*, 9 July 1962; definite parallels can be traced between McNamara's speech and, for example: H. Kahn, *On Thermonuclear War* (Princeton University Press, Princeton, NJ, 1960); *idem*, *Thinking About the Unthinkable* (Avon, New York, 1962); A. Wohlstetter, 'The Delicate Balance of Terror', in H.A. Kissinger (ed.), *Problems of National Strategy* (Praeger, New York, 1965).

9. A.C. Enthoven and K.W. Smith, *How Much is Enough? Shaping the Defense*

Program 1961-1969 (Harper & Row, New York, 1971), p. 170 *et seq.*

10. See R.S. McNamara, 'The Spectrum of Defense', in Kissinger (ed.) *Problems of National Strategy*.

11. R.M. Nixon, *US Foreign Policy for the 1970s: A new strategy for peace*, Report to Congress, 18 February 1970.

12. 'Flexible Strategic Options and Deterrence', Excerpts from press conference of US Secretary of Defense James Schlesinger, 10 January 1974, reprinted in *Survival*, March/April 1974.

13. For discussions of the strategy see especially *World Armaments and Disarmament: SIPRI Yearbook 1975* (MIT Press, London, 1975), Chapter 3; and L.E. Davis, *Limited Nuclear Options: Deterrence and the New American Doctrine*, Adelphi Paper 121 (IISS, London, 1975).

14. *Department of Defense Annual Report Fiscal Year 1979* (US DoD, 1978), p. 55.

15. *International Herald Tribune*, 1 December 1978 and 6-7 January 1979; *The Guardian*, 26 January 1979.

16. *Department of Defense Annual Report Fiscal Year 1980* (US DoD, 1979), pp. 74-81.

17. My estimate based on various sources: see Table 4.7 below, Chapter 4.

18. M. Leitenberg, 'The Race to Oblivion', *Bulletin of the Atomic Scientists*, September 1974, vol. XXX, no. 7.

19. R.C. Aldridge, *The Counterforce Syndrome* (TNI, Washington, DC, 1978), pp. 3-6.

20. Kahan, *Security in the Nuclear Age*, pp. 91-2.

21. General G.S. Brown, *United States Military Posture for FY 1979* (US DoD, 1978), p. 23.

22. 'Command Data Buffer', *Market Intelligence Report* (Defense Market Survey, Greenwich, Ct, 1975).

23. *Hearings before the Subcommittee on Arms Control, International Law, and Organization*, Committee on Foreign Relations, US Senate, 4 March 1974.

24. R.F. Weigley, *The American Way of War* (Macmillan, New York, 1973), p. xxii and p. 398.

25. See S.D. Drell and F. von Hippel, 'Limited Nuclear War', *Scientific American*, November 1976, vol. 235, no. 5, and text to n5 in Chapter 1, above.

26. M. Bundy, 'To Cap the Volcano', *Foreign Affairs*, October 1969.

27. Weigley, *The American Way of War*, p. 477.

28. R. Evans and R. Novak, *International Herald Tribune*, 5 March 1979.

29. See the outline of four different but equally inadequate approaches to study of Soviet policy in E. Jahn, 'Four Approaches to the Analysis of Soviet Foreign Policy', in *idem* (ed.) *Soviet Foreign Policy: Its Social and Economic Conditions* (Allison & Busby, London, 1978); for a notable exception to the dreary rule, see R. Edmonds, *Soviet Foreign Policy 1962-1973* (OUP, London, 1975); what I refer to as 'the monolithic obsession' is called 'the Riga axioms' and penetratingly analysed by D. Yergin, *Shattered Peace* (Houghton Mifflin, Boston, 1978).

30. M. Frankland, *The Observer*, 11 February 1979.

31. *International Herald Tribune*, 9 October 1978.

32. See Table 4.7 below, Chapter 4.

33. R.P. Berman, *Soviet Air Power in Transition* (Brookings Institution, Washington, DC, 1978), see pp. 54-5 and 63-5.

34. On the importance of naval strength in Soviet writings on political power, see: G.E. Hudson, 'Soviet Naval Doctrine and Soviet Politics, 1953-1975', *World Politics*, vol. XXIX, no. 1; T.W. Wolfe, *Soviet Naval Interaction with the United States and its Influence on Soviet Naval Development* (Rand, Santa Monica, Calif, 1972), P-4913.

35. See Admiral J.L. Holloway, *Fiscal Year 1979 Military Posture and Fiscal Year 1979 Budget of the United States Navy* (US DoD, 1978), p. 69; see also Table 4.3 below, Chapter 4.

36. B.M. Blechman, *The Changing Soviet Navy* (Brookings Institution, Washington, DC, 1973), p. 10; 1977 figures are based on *Jane's Fighting Ships 1977/8* (Macdonald & Jane's, London, 1977).

37. Blechman, *The Changing Soviet Navy*, pp. 12-15.

38. Admiral J.L. Holloway, *FY 1977 Military Posture of the United States Navy* (US DoD, 1976), p. 9.

39. M.T. Klare, 'Superpower Rivalry At Sea', *Foreign Policy*, Winter 1975/6.

40. See K. Booth, *Navies and Foreign Policy* (Croom Helm, London, 1977), pp. 57-71.

41. See Yergin, *Shattered Peace*, pp. 64-5; A.B. Ulam, *The Rivals* (Penguin, New York, 1976), Chapter 1; I. Deutscher, 'Myths of the Cold War' in D. Horowitz (ed.), *Containment and Revolution* (Anthony Blond, London, 1967).

42. For an account of this period, see F. Claudin, *The Communist Movement: From Comintern to Cominform* (Penguin, Harmondsworth, 1975), Chapters 5 and 6.

43. *Allocation of Resources in the Soviet Union and China – 1976: Hearings before the Subcommittee on Priorities and Economy in Government*, Joint Economic Committee of the US Congress, 24 May and 15 June 1976.

44. *International Herald Tribune*, 10 October 1978.

45. Figures are for Standard International Trade Category 7, comprising all electrical and non-electrical machinery and transport equipment, in *Bulletin on World Trade in Engineering Products 1976* (United Nations, New York, 1978).

46. A.J. Alexander, *Decision-making in Soviet Weapons Procurement*, Adelphi Paper 147/8 (IISS, London, 1978), p. 25.

47. R. Bahro, *The Alternative in Eastern Europe* (NLB, London, 1978), pp. 159, 219-21.

48. See D. Ernst (ed.), *The New International Division of Labour, Technology and Underdevelopment – Consequences for the Third World* (Campus Verlag, Frankfurt aM, and Praeger, New York, forthcoming).

49. *International Herald Tribune*, 13-14 January 1979.

50. F. Halliday, 'The Arc of Revolution', *Race and Class*, Spring 1979, vol. 20, no. 4; see also E. Shaw, *Cold Peace* (The Labour Party, London, 1978).

51. This account is again based on *SIPRI Yearbook 1974*, Chapter 5.

52. See A.A. Sidorenko, *The Offensive*, trans US Air Force (US Government Printing Office, Washington, DC, 1970), pp. 109, 115, 132-4.

53. V.D. Sokolovskiy, *Soviet Military Strategy* (1968 edn) (Crane & Russak, New York, 1972), p. 15.

54. R. Pipes, 'Why the Soviet Union Thinks It Could Fight and Win a Nuclear War', *Commentary*, July 1977.

55. F.M. Kaplan, *Dubious Specter: A Second Look at the 'Soviet Threat'* (TNI, Washington, DC, 1977), pp. 6-14.

56. Ibid., p. 9.

57. See D. Holloway, 'Soviet Strategists Attack Schlesinger', *New Scientist*, 5 November 1974.

58. B.S. Lambeth, 'Selective Nuclear Operations and Soviet Strategy', in Holst and Nerlich, (eds), *Beyond Nuclear Deterrence*, pp. 95-101.

59. *Department of Defense Annual Report Fiscal Year 1979*, p. 62.

60. A. Solzhenitsyn, *Detente: Prospects for Democracy and Dictatorship* (Transaction, New Brunswick, NJ, 1977).

61. R.A. Medvedev, *Political Essays* (Spokesman, Nottingham, 1976), especially Chapters 1, 2, 4, 8 and 10.

62. A useful outline of these concepts is in P. Williams, 'Crisis Management', in J. Baylis, K. Booth, J. Garnett and P. Williams, *Contemporary Strategy: Theories and Policies* (Croom Helm, London, 1975).

63. J. Goldblat, *Arms Control: A Survey and Appraisal of Multilateral Agreements* (Taylor & Francis, London, 1978), pp. 229-34, 237-8.

64. President Carter, *US-Soviet Relations — Cooperative and Competitive Aspects*, Official Text of address to US Naval Academy, Annapolis, 7 June 1978, International Communication Agency.

65. *The Guardian*, 20 January 1978.

66. *The Sunday Times*, 5 February 1978.

67. *The Guardian*, 20 July 1978 and 26 July 1978.

68. *The Guardian*, 15 July 1978; *The Sunday Times*, 16 July 1978; *International Herald Tribune*, 19 July 1978.

4 OF NUMBERS AND NUKES

The presumption of the aggressive intentions of the USSR has always been matched by fears at the size of its conventional armed forces and their build-up. These have helped form the basis of general attitudes in NATO countries to the USSR, and lie at the core of NATO strategy and policy planning. Lately, these fears have also been transferred to the USSR's strategic nuclear forces, and the 1970s have seen a proliferation of alarmed and alarming analyses of every aspect of Soviet power. Our response to these analyses should be tempered by remembering their predecessors in the 1950s and 1960s — there has never been a period when assessment of Soviet power was marked by a generally shared confidence, although, on the other hand, there have usually also been authoritative sources for more confident and relaxed assessments. But during the 1970s, these assessments seem to have been more muted and rare. Therefore, the discussion of rivalry, of each side's strategies and the problems and dilemmas within them, must be supplemented by a discussion of the realities of military power deployed by NATO and the WP.

In undertaking this task, a series of problems must be confronted, and awareness of them must qualify not only the analysis in this chapter, but also every analysis of the comparative military power of the two alliances. It is actually extremely difficult to compare military power, if by that we understand the ability of adversaries to accomplish hypothetical military missions. Most assessments of the NATO-WP military balance seem unaware of such problems. They tend to equate quantity, of personnel and equipment, with capability; finding that the WP possesses numerical superiority, they conclude that NATO states must spend more money to procure more equipment and recruit more personnel to counter the threat. Sometimes, more ambitious projects are justified by such assessments, as in the argument of one Conservative MP that while West European unity cannot be gained by conquest, and with the route to unity through economic integration getting bogged down, 'fear of a common enemy' might do instead, although he worries that we may not yet be 'sufficiently afraid'.[1]

The apparently uncluttered logic in many such assessments simply does not stand up in the face of what we know about warfare. Even if military power is assessed not just on the basis of numbers, but also by considering the quality of personnel and equipment, the result is still inadequate. In recent years, the successes of Israeli armed forces and American failure in Vietnam have been large and public demonstrations that morale, tactics and strategy are at least as important in defining military effectiveness as the numbers and quality of forces, the sheer weight of firepower each side has available. Indeed, this is a lesson recurring throughout military history. What counts is not only the capacity to apply force, but how it is applied and for what ends — and these are aspects which are non-quantifiable, and often not identifiable in advance.

Even bearing such reservations in mind as we approach the military numbers game with due caution, we still have to face major problems concerning the status of the data on which assessment must be based. The basic source, especially for data on the WP, is the American intelligence establishment, with its access to the results of airborne and satellite photography, electronic spying and other means of gathering information. Data from this source, released in reports to US Congress and on other occasions, forms the basis for virtually all comparisons of forces in NATO countries. Further references are the series of *Jane's* annuals providing technical and other details, various compilations of varying degrees of reliability, the yearbooks and other publications of the Stockholm International Peace Research Institute (SIPRI) collating data from a wide range of public sources, and finally — and probably foremost as a reference on numbers of personnel and equipment — there is *The Military Balance*, published annually by the International Institute of Strategic Studies (IISS) in London.

Without IISS, discussion of the subject would be sorely limited, but this should not prevent us from weighing the data it presents. Apart from some public sources, including various newspapers and figures released from the US intelligence agencies, IISS relies heavily on a network of contacts with western governments and on information supplied by military attaches at London embassies.[2] Gaps and unreliable data are compensated for by estimation. IISS, therefore, does not receive raw data — they have already been processed by the time they reach it, and this creates its own problems. It has been demonstrated that IISS' figures for South Africa are inaccurate,[3] and it would be surprising if this were the only case. A recent reference book on American arms exports also shows major discrepancies with IISS' data, although some of these can be explained fairly easily, and the book's own sources may not be wholly reliable.[4]

But the basic problem does not lie in the possible contamination of data: even with raw data, we are dealing not with facts but with estimates. There is no place in the innards of the Pentagon or US intelligence agencies where facts exist in 'unvarnished' form. Projections of future events involve speculation, but so do reports on the current situation; for an intelligence analyst, 'the outside world' is not ultimately 'knowable'.[5] Even the most honest and rigorous analyst cannot totally exclude the effects of normative assumptions and ideological preferences from any stage of the process.

A revealing illustration of the problem came in the annual reports in 1978 of the US Department of Defense (DoD) and the Joint Chiefs of Staff (JCS). The former reported 31 Soviet army divisions stationed in Eastern Europe, while the latter found only 27; the DoD put total NATO military personnel at 4,800,000 while the JCS' figure showed 100,000 more; the DoD reported WP military personnel at 5,200,000, but the JCS reported 5,600,000.[6] Given the totals we are dealing with, the discrepancies are not very large, but they do show that even in the basic sources there is no consensus about the facts — nor can there be, for there are no 'facts' as such, only estimates and approximations.

Caution about the status of the data must be accompanied by care about which data are used. In assessing the European military balance, for example, there is a controversy as to whether French forces should be counted, which arises because France is a member of NATO but its forces are not under NATO command. A common compromise, and one adopted against previous practice for the British 1978 defence White Paper, is to include only French troops stationed in the Federal Republic of Germany.[7] Yet this appears to suggest that France is expected to commit some of its forces if there is war with the WP, but by and large to stand back from the fight — combatant and neutral simultaneously. On the other hand, to conclude that all French forces (or, alternatively, none) should be included on the NATO side means first undertaking a political assessment of the French relationship to NATO and how a war might affect it. Similarly, since 1974 Greece and Turkey have looked more likely to go to war with each other than with the WP, though both are NATO members; including one, both, or neither on the NATO side makes a great deal of difference to the military balance in Southern Europe. Meanwhile, the conflict between Romania and its WP allies, long-standing but especially strong in late 1978, raises the issue of whether or not its forces should be counted on the WP side. It is now a commonplace, and the position of US intelligence in Europe, to suggest that the other East European states would be reliable components of the WP only in the event of a NATO offensive;[8] if NATO does not contemplate aggression against the WP, as it claims, this would suggest it should exclude all non-Soviet WP forces from the balance.

All of these issues show that we can only constitute the 'facts' on which our assessments are based *after* political debate, not before. Accordingly, all judgements on the military balance must be somewhat tentative and made within a range of possible scenarios and broad margins of error, otherwise they will be susceptible to slight changes either way in the assessment of data from one year to another, and these changes are as likely to result from changes in the estimating process, changed perceptions, as from genuine changes in force levels by either side. Equally, the variety of ways of looking at the military balance must be acknowledged. One study has shown that there is only limited agreement on the basic statistics, and demonstrated the internally consistent logic of both 'optimistic' and 'pessimistic' assessments of the balance based on fundamentally different assumptions, including whether NATO forces should be judged by their ability to deter war or their ability to fight it.[9]

Yet one more note of caution must be sounded. A discussion of the military balance of conventional forces is clearly necessary, because all presentations of defence policy are made against the background of the balance, if for no other reason. Yet such discussions tend to imply that action by conventional forces would be decisive in a future war between NATO and the WP, and that must be open to question. Indeed, it can be argued that both sides' conventional forces are no more than targets for the other's nuclear forces. Entering into a discussion of the balance should not, therefore, be taken to signify a view of how war would proceed. It is, however, reasonable to suspend disbelief during the discussion in order to arrive at a conclusion about the relative weight of armed force on each side. The concern in NATO states now does not seem to be a fear of invasion, but rather of military blackmail, an indirect use of Soviet force to influence West European states' policies.[10] It is still uncertain that there is a genuine issue here, since military blackmail would presumably have to be underwritten by a threat of military action, such as invasion, which is not so feared. Nevertheless, perceptions of relative military power do seem important among NATO states and it may be that in possible future crises their actions would be influenced by their perceptions of the balance. And it has been argued that although the USSR may not believe it has military superiority against NATO,[11] it must have noted apprehensions in the West and so might be tempted to exploit NATO's perceptions to its advantage.[12] Although armed force is a complex instrument for policy, it is an instrument, and therefore a relative assessment of the two sides' strength is in order, despite the difficulties and necessary reservations.

The Numbers Game

Some commentators believe the military balance is so bad for NATO that any talk of caution and margins of error is superfluous. Numerous techniques can be used to make this case, including a careful selection of the most alarming data in a way that is either dishonest or inept, and often both. A less disreputable technique is to construct a scenario of how a future war might go, in which an indecisive NATO response to WP aggression compounds the alleged inadequacies of NATO forces.

One example, which caused quite a stir at the time since it misleadingly claimed to be based on a NATO study, was an article by Lord Chalfont, grimly entitled, 'The West must act to defend itself while it still has the chance'.[13] On the basis of the USSR's assumed aim of conquering Western Europe, it outlined a scenario for a WP offensive and victory, proceeding via a pessimistic assessment of the European military balance, an erroneous assertion that a large scale attack could be launched without warning,[14] a calculation that Soviet forces would move faster against ground and air opposition than Dutch troops could in the face only of air harrassment, a justifiable suggestion that NATO would be reluctant to use nuclear weapons on West German soil, and a strange insistence on the advantages of the WP attacking when it was night in Washington, DC, and the president would have to be dragged from his bed. It must be said that analysing the worst possible case can be worthwhile: even if judgements are made within wide margins of error, NATO may want to know what might happen if the true situation is at the wrong end of the margin. But the worst possible case, like the best possible, is by definition the least probable; analysis of it may have a role in policy formulation, pointing to problems which may have been previously unsuspected, but it is misleading to try and set it in the centre of policy discussion. If the worst possible is set in the centre, there is no reason why the best possible should not join it there — each is equally unlikely, and each belongs at the edge of discussion. The desire to base NATO strategy on analysis of the worst possible case reflects only the desire to affirm presumptions as conclusions and ultimately lacks analytic integrity.

The official view of the military balance from Washington has not generally been so despondent. A major Pentagon analysis in the early 1960s concluded that, far from facing a disadvantage, NATO had superior conventional forces in Europe; with the USA trying to get its NATO allies to increase their military spending, the report was thought 'sensitive' and was referred to publicly only three times, all in 1963, with no precise figures given.[15] Enthoven and Smith, senior Pentagon officials during the period, confirm that this remained the official view through the 1960s.[16] Similar conclusions emerged in a Pentagon study reported in June 1973.[17] In 1975, NATO ministers reportedly agreed that NATO did not face conventional inferiority and had more combat-ready soldiers in Europe than the WP, while doubt was cast on methods of counting WP tanks, by noting a previous habit of counting up the tank sheds and estimating on the basis of that but regrettably overlooking the fact that many of the sheds were empty.[18] In his 1978 report, the Chairman of the Joint Chiefs of Staff, after page upon page apparently bewailing American disadvantages, noted that 'Science and technology have been among the principal factors in *continued overall US military superiority*'[19] (probably referring to nuclear as well as conventional forces). Thus, although it may sometimes be kept quiet, the official American view has been, for almost twenty years, far less alarmed about the military balance than most of the mass media and most commentators would wish us to be.

There is, however, another string to the bow — the Soviet build-up, which is claimed to erode the NATO advantages recorded by previous studies. That there has been a build-up is undeniable; it has been part of the USSR's emergence as a super power. But it is not of the dimensions often claimed for it. In an admirable analysis, Les Aspin quotes some of the more alarming assessments made in the USA, to the effect that the Soviet build-up even outpaces that of Nazi Germany in the 1930s, a comparison which has also been heard in Britain. He tabulates the rate of increase for Soviet forces for 1972-6, and compares it to Germany for 1935-9, Egypt and Syria combined for 1968-72 and Israel for the same period, China for 1966-71 and North Korea for 1971-5. In the case of increases in military spending, in the share of Gross National Product (or equivalent measure) devoted to the military, in numbers of men, aircraft, tanks and active divisions — by all of these measures the Soviet rate of increase is the lowest of all, and Aspin also shows that Soviet production of new equipment is only marginally more than what is needed for replacement.[20]

The problem of the Soviet build-up can be gauged in another way, by taking a set of comparable figures recording WP and NATO forces over a period of years. Table 4.1 compares selected forces in Europe for three years, 1969, 1973 and 1978, divided according to NATO command sectors, lumping the Northern and Central commands together. It omits several important types of forces — artillery, helicopters, anti-tank

Table 4.1: Comparison of Selected NATO and WP Forces in Europe
1969, 1973, 1978

	NORTHERN AND CENTRAL[a]					
	1969		1973		1978	
	NATO	WP	NATO	WP	NATO	WP
Manpower[b] (000s)	600	925	600	900	626	943
Tanks[c] (000s)	5.25	12.5	6.5	17	7	21.1
Tactical aircraft:[d]	2,050	3,795	1,890	4,300	2,375	4,055
Light bombers	50	260	140	250	160	130
Fighter/ground attack	1,150	1,285	1,100	1,400	1,400	1,350
Interceptors	450	2,000	350	2,100	435	2,025
Reconnaissance	400	250	300	550	380	550

	SOUTHERN[a]					
	1969		1973		1978	
	NATO	WP	NATO	WP	NATO	WP
Manpower (000s)	525	375	530	320	550	388
Tanks (000s)	1.8	4.6	2.15	6.2	4.3	6.8
Tactical aircraft:	975	1,185	856	1,195	938	1,645
Light bombers	—	60	6	30	—	50
Fighter/ground attack	550	215	450	125	628	375
Interceptors	300	860	275	950	220	1,000
Reconnaissance	125	50	125	90	90	220

	TOTAL[a]					
	1969		1973		1978	
	NATO	WP	NATO	WP	NATO	WP
Manpower (000s)	1,125	1,300	1,130	1,220	1,176	1,331
Tanks (000s)	7.05	17.1	8.65	23.2	11.3	27.9
Tactical aircraft:	3,025	4,980	2,746	5,495	3,313	5,700
Light bombers	50	320	146	280	160	180
Fighter/ground attack	1,700	1,500	1,550	1,525	2,028	1,725
Interceptors	750	2,860	625	3,050	655	3,025
Reconnaissance	525	300	425	640	470	770

a. For NATO, the 'Total' area is the area of SACEUR's command. All French
forces, and British ground forces in Britain, are excluded. WP figures for
'Northern and Central' include the forces of Czechoslovakia, the German
Democratic Republic and Poland, Soviet forces stationed in those countries,
and most forces in western USSR. WP figures for 'Southern' include the forces
of Bulgaria, Hungary and Romania, Soviet forces stationed in Hungary and in
south-western USSR.
b. In 1969 and 1973, the IISS called this category 'Combat and direct support
troops available'; in 1978, 'Combat manpower in all types of formations'.
There may be a difference between the two.
c. Defined in 1969 as 'Medium/Heavy tanks available to commanders in peacetime';

in 1973 as 'Main Battle Tanks in operational service — in peacetime'; and in 1978 as 'Main Battle Tanks in operational service'. In 1973 and 1978, but not in 1969, it was noted that reserve tanks were excluded.
d. The area taken for aircraft is wider than that for ground forces. The figures include British and American aircraft in Britain, American aircraft in Spain, and Soviet aircraft in Western USSR. American aircraft in the USA with prepared bases in Europe are excluded, as are carrier-borne aircraft of the US Navy, and Soviet medium bombers.

Sources: *The Military Balance* (annual): *1969-1970*, pp. 62-3; *1973-1974*, pp. 88-91; *1978-1979*, pp. 109-12 (IISS, London, 1969, 1973, 1978).

weapons, surface-to-air missiles; like any such table it gives no idea of the age and quality of the equipment or how it is deployed: therefore, it cannot be taken to represent the military balance in Europe in any of the three years (though some might like to use it that way since it shows numerical advantages for the WP in most categories). The changes over time are shown in percentage terms in Table 4.2.

We can record the reservations before deriving the conclusions. First, some of the changes may be due to changed estimating techniques or use of different categories; second, the forces covered do not combine to show a comprehensively representative picture; third, these IISS figures show a different picture from the all-round assessments under-pinning the Pentagon's more relaxed judgements in the 1960s and 1970s; fourth, taking percentage increases obscures the absolute size of the increases, especially in the case of the WP's tanks where increases start from a much higher base-line.

Nevertheless, although the picture in air power in Southern Europe and in tanks in Northern and Central Europe is less cosy for NATO, the rates of increase in forces in Northern and Central Europe and in Europe as a whole show no major discrepancies over the ten years, 1969 to 1978. More revealingly, since 1973 NATO forces have been increased in all categories shown except three types of air power in Southern Europe, a more rounded increase in forces than the WP has sustained. In general terms, IISS' figures for the period indicate that the Soviet build-up has been roughly matched by the NATO build-up. The alarms of the second half of the 1970s correspond to a picture which, by these data, is now out of date, reflecting the position in the earlier years of the decade. Moreover, if we return to the 1973 Pentagon study which concluded that NATO forces then were adequate to their tasks and superior to WP forces in certain important respects,[21] we could conclude that NATO has about matched the Soviet build-up from a position thought to be already satisfactory by one important agency.

Table 4.2: Percentage Changes Over Time of Force Levels Shown
in Table 4.1

| | NORTHERN AND CENTRAL | | | | | |
| | NATO | | | WP | | |
	1969-73	1973-78	1969-78	1969-73	1973-78	1969-78
Manpower	—	4	4	–3	5	2
Tanks	24	8	33	36	24	69
Tactical aircraft:	–8	26	16	13	–6	7
Light bombers	180	14	220	–4	–48	–50
Fighter/ground attack	–4	27	22	9	–4	5
Interceptors	–22	24	–3	5	–4	1
Reconnaissance	–25	27	–5	120	—	120

| | SOUTHERN | | | | | |
| | NATO | | | WP | | |
	1969-73	1973-78	1969-78	1969-73	1973-78	1969-78
Manpower	1	4	5	–15	21	3
Tanks	19	100	139	35	10	42
Tactical aircraft:	–8	10	–4	1	38	39
Light bombers	—	—	—	–50	67	17
Fighter/ground attack	–18	40	14	–42	200	74
Interceptors	–8	–20	–27	11	5	16
Reconnaissance	—	–28	–28	80	144	340

| | TOTAL | | | | | |
| | NATO | | | WP | | |
	1969-73	1973-78	1969-78	1969-73	1973-78	1969-78
Manpower	...	4	4	–6	9	2
Tanks	23	31	60	36	20	63
Tactical aircraft:	–9	21	10	10	4	14
Light bombers	192	10	220	–13	–36	–44
Fighter/ground attack	–9	31	19	2	13	15
Interceptors	–17	5	–13	7	–1	6
Reconnaissance	–19	11	–11	113	20	157

All sources and definitional notes as for Table 4.1.
Percentages have been rounded and are positive (indicating growth) unless
otherwise shown.

To this we can add Table 4.3, which shows naval construction rates
(excluding ballistic-missile-firing submarines) and reveals that NATO

Table 4.3: Naval General Purpose Forces Construction Rates 1967-1976

	1967-71		1972-76		1967-76	
	NATO	WP	NATO	WP	NATO	WP
Torpedo and Cruise Missile Submarines:						
Diesel-powered	22	20	27	4	49	24
Nuclear-powered	35	24	16	15	51	39
TOTAL	57	44	43	19	100	63
Aircraft Carriers:						
+60,000 tons	1	—	1	—	2	—
30–60,000 tons	1	—	—	1	1	1
TOTAL	2	—	1	1	3	1
Surface Combatants:						
+8,000 tons	2	2	2	5	4	7
5,500–8,000 tons	7	6	12	6	19	12
3,500–5,500 tons	37	22	27	26	64	48
1,000–3,500 tons	44	24	19	—	63	24
TOTAL	90	54	60	37	150	91
Amphibious Warfare Vessels:						
Assault ships +30,000 tons	2	—	1	—	3	—
Assault ships –30,000 tons	2	—	—	—	2	—
8–17,000 tons	29	—	7	—	36	—
4–8,000 tons	4	8	—	11	4	19
TOTAL	37	8	8	11	45	19

Source: *The Military Balance 1977-1978* (IISS, London, 1977), pp. 90-2.

states sustain substantially higher construction rates than the WP.[22] It should, however, be added that construction rates do not tell the whole story; also important is the time when ships are declared obsolete and paid off, which appears to be earlier among NATO navies than in the WP. This factor also affects comparative figures for tanks and aircraft, with the WP tending to hang on to equipment which in NATO would long since have been scrapped (or sold to a poorer state). In any case, as I pointed out in Chapter 3, if there is anything which might be called a Soviet naval build-up, it has been in terms of expanded areas of deployment rather than an increase in the size of the navy.

The basis for some of the more alarming assessments of a Soviet military build-up thus tends to vanish in a puff of smoke if the available data are examined at all closely. But this is no discouragement to those who enjoy their work. Fred Iklé, formerly head of the US Arms Control and Disarmament Agency, seems sure that the USA is already 'number two', and revealingly remarks, 'The most disturbing picture emerges when we look, not at the detailed comparisons of weapon categories, but at the total magnitudes.'[23] Of magnitudes, the most total is the military budget. NATO governments and most commentators do not accept that the official Soviet budget represents the true extent of its military spending, and there has therefore been a major controversy about the level of the budget in comparison with the US budget.

In 1976, the CIA produced a higher estimate of Soviet military spending than previously, with the result that whereas US and Soviet spending had been thought to be about even, it now appeared that the Soviet figure was some 40 per cent higher than American spending.[24] From this, it has been concluded that the USSR is militarily superior, or at least fast catching up – in other words, it is used to sustain the image of the Soviet build-up.[25] However, the change in the figures, and the CIA acknowledges a possible margin of error of 15 per cent,[26] did not reflect a sudden increase in Soviet military spending. Rather, it represented changed perceptions in response to sustained and severe criticism of its former estimating methods.[27] The CIA has now decided that the cost of producing a given military output in the USSR is higher than it had supposed.

Apart from trusting the official Soviet budget, which is anyway misleading as a basis for comparison because of problems with the exchange rate, Soviet military spending can be measured either by assessing what it would cost the USA to buy Soviet forces and weapons programmes in US dollars, or by building a detailed picture of the costs of the programmes in roubles. The first method provides a basis for comparison with American spending; the second helps assess the economic weight and effects of military spending within the USSR. But the dollar figure is a very bad basis for comparing military strengths: if Soviet forces are costed in dollars they seem more expensive than American forces, but if American forces are costed in roubles, they appear more expensive than Soviet forces.[28] The answer changes depending on how the question is posed. The reason is fairly straightforward: in different societies, different things have different relative prices. In particular, Soviet conscripts are cheaper than US volunteer service personnel, while advanced technology is relatively more costly in the USSR than in the USA. A similar discrepancy exists if US and Soviet expenditure on education, for example, are compared.[29]

This does not mean examining Soviet military spending is completely uninteresting. It can be a part of general analysis of the Soviet economy, and it may help indicate the level of commitment to maintaining powerful armed forces, which is evidently very strong. But it is pointless to use it to try and compare military strength with that of other states, not least because it implicitly assumes that spending a lot of money necessarily buys a lot of capability, and this is not the case in either NATO or the WP.

Gross figures are, in fact, particularly complex for comparing military power, hiding at least as much as they reveal. Table 4.4 shows IISS' estimate of total service personnel for NATO and the WP; it will be noted that it differs from the two different figures quoted from the Pentagon earlier, but, like them, it indicates rough parity at this level.

Table 4.4: Total NATO and WP Armed Forces, 1978

WP		NATO	
Bulgaria	150,000	Belgium	87,100
Czechoslovakia	186,000	Britain	313,300
German Democratic		Canada	80,000
Republic	157,000	Denmark	34,000
Hungary	114,000	Federal Republic	
Poland	306,500	of Germany	489,900
Romania	180,500	Greece	190,100
USSR	3,638,000[a]	Italy	362,000
		Luxembourg	700
		Netherlands	109,700
		Norway	39,000
		Portugal	63,500
		Turkey	485,000
		USA	2,068,800
		Sub-total	4,323,100
		France	502,800
TOTAL	4,732,000	TOTAL	4,825,900

a. Excludes what IISS calls 'some 750,000 uniformed civilians'.

Source: *The Military Balance 1978-1979* (IISS, London, 1978).

However, in 1976 the Pentagon was offering a figure of 4,800,000 for Soviet forces alone. Table 4.5 shows how Les Aspin, on the basis of data provided by the Defense Intelligence Agency, 'halved' the Soviet forces by removing all categories of personnel not thought to threaten the USA, and also pruned American forces, less dramatically, to match. NATO figures could also be manipulated down, up and sideways, and one could think of further adjustments for WP forces, but what Aspin's exercise forcefully demonstrates is that simply taking the gross figures tells very little.

Table 4.5: Adjusted Comparison of Soviet and US Military Personnel, 1976 (in 000s)

Soviet Total	4,800	American Total	2,127
minus Internal Security and Border Guards	(430)	minus Chaplains and Construction	(3)
Construction Troops	(250)	Far East Troops	(115)
Military working on farms and railways	(150)		
Political Officers	(70)		
Civil Defence	(20)		
Supply, Storage and R & D Troops[a]	(170)		
Coast Guard	(60)		
Sino-Soviet Border Troops	(500)		
Czech Garrison	(55)		
Other civilians in uniform	(300)		
Sub-total	2,795		
minus Extra Air Defence Troops[b]	(475)		
Extra Strategic Forces Troops[b]	(275)		
Adjusted Soviet Total	**2,045**	**Adjusted American Total**	**2,009**

a. R & D: Research and Development
b. In these two missions the USSR maintains more personnel than the USA; believing that the excess implies no extra threat to the USA, Aspin has adjusted them out of his comparison.

Sources: Defense Intelligence Agency and Rep. Les Aspin (Dem, Wis) reported in *New York Times*, 24 April 1976.

Straightforward comparisons of personnel do not reveal, for example, how well trained for their tasks the people are; they do not reveal their commitment; they do not show how many are desk-bound bureaucrats; they pit an experienced professional soldier against a new recruit. But more important is that they obscure important trends, more strongly felt in NATO than in the WP, towards what may be called 'technological substitution' — using technological advances to reduce the requirement for manpower. If the same capacity to kill and destroy can be wielded by one person where formerly it took three, then, evidently, personnel comparisons are less interesting than before, especially when one side has exploited such developments more than the other. Indeed, if one takes the approximate personnel parity suggested by Table 4.4, whether or not one adjusts it on the model of Table 4.5, one could conclude that adding NATO's technological superiority to the assessment would indicate a clear superiority for NATO at this global level, but this would have to be qualified by considering where, how and for what ends military power is deployed.

In the 1979 British defence White Paper it was stated that NATO forces in the eastern Atlantic are outnumbered by the WP, by 30 per cent in surface ships and 50 per cent in submarines.[30] WP forces in this area seem to be equated by the White Paper with the Soviet Northern Fleet, but much of that fleet is permanently deployed to the north of the gap between Greenland, Iceland and Britain and it is elsewhere reported that only a handful of Soviet submarines deploy in the eastern Atlantic area.[31] The British figures are therefore misleading, giving no clear picture of the Atlantic naval balance, but even if they did not mislead in this sense, they would in another, for they would be taken as just one more piece of evidence of Soviet naval build-up and superiority when in reality they are no such thing. Table 4.6 shows that the WP navies, which effectively boil down to the Soviet navy, do not have greater numbers; particularly interesting is that the submarine force, a central component of most images of the naval threat, is not much larger than NATO's – 242 submarines against NATO's 213. Thus, if the USSR had a remarkably larger naval presence than NATO in an area such as the eastern Atlantic, it would be because it had made that a priority area for deployment at the expense of others where it was presumably prepared to accept inferior numbers. But in 1978, when the British government produced a similar comparison, it turned strangely coy when faced with a parliamentary question asking about those other areas: assessing Soviet naval forces elsewhere 'could only be conjectural' and 'would therefore be misleading'.[32]

What is required is assessment of the ability of NATO navies to complete specific tasks in specific areas; on this basis the US Chief of Naval Operations reported in 1976 that the US had 'a slim margin of superiority with respect to the Soviet threat in those scenarios involving our most vital national interests', a judgement confirmed the next year by the Chairman of the Joint Chiefs of Staff.[33] And unless the USA's 'most vital' interests have been redefined to exclude securing passage across the Atlantic, this judgement should calm the fears of the British government about NATO's reported numerical inferiority in the eastern Atlantic. If we add the not insignificant navies of other NATO states to the position of slight superiority that the US Navy is said to have, we could conclude that the total naval assets of NATO are clearly superior to those of the WP.

Table 4.6: Naval General Purpose Forces Active Strengths, 1977

	USSR	Other WP	WP Total	USA	Other NATO	NATO Total
Aircraft carriers	–	–	–	13	3	16
ASW Cruisers +30,000 tons[ab]	1	–	1	–	–	–
ASW Cruisers –30,000 tons	..	–	–	–	2	2
Cruisers	35	–	35	25	7	32
Destroyers	112	1	113	91	92	183
Frigates	108	4	112	166	64	230
Corvettes	106	6	112	–	35	35
Attack Submarines Diesel[c]	156	6	162	10	129	139
Attack Submarines Nuclear[c]	80	–	80	65	9	74
Amphibious Warfare Vessels + 4,000 tons	14	–	14	65	29	94
Replenishment, Support and Transport Vessels[d]	85	–	85	40	98	138
Coastal and Ocean-going Mine-warfare Vessels	289	86	375	25	248	273

a. ASW: Anti-submarine Warfare
b. There would be some dispute as to whether Soviet ships now being launched in this category should properly be called ASW Cruisers or Aircraft Carriers.
c. Includes submarines armed with cruise missiles.
d. Excludes small tugs, tenders, etc., and all merchant shipping which might be requisitioned in war.

Source: Taken from *Jane's Fighting Ships 1977-1978* (Macdonald & Jane's, London, 1977).

Were the British government still worried about the eastern Atlantic naval balance, its most obvious course would be to urge a relocation of NATO naval forces from other areas it thought less important. But here we confront the problem, also noted in Chapter 3's discussion of US nuclear strategy, that the deployment of the US Navy, the main component of NATO's naval strength, is guided by American interests, not by the interests of the USA's NATO allies. Although, around the world, the USA has other allies with whose navies it can co-ordinate,[34] deploying its own navy in support of its international role could detract from the commitment of maritime power to support NATO. Indeed, in this world role, the USA may, through NATO institutions, seek greater material West European assistance, which could further detract from what we are told are NATO's basic tasks in and around Europe.[35]

West European states might welcome such an invitation to a world role, not least for the greater leverage it would afford within NATO against the USA, but the general tenor of their assessments of the military balance with the USSR suggests that such a role would be a luxury, undermining the ability to respond to the immediate danger of Soviet military power in Europe itself. Although the general political situation between Eastern and Western Europe is more stable than in the 1950s, and although the locus of competition has to some extent been shifted away from Europe, it remains true that it is there that the greatest and most visible aspect of military confrontation exists. It is moreover true that although there is a large US military presence in Central Europe,[36] US forces make less of a contribution to immediately available NATO forces in Europe than they do to the gross figures of military strength.

The data in Table 4.1 show, in Northern and Central Europe, a WP numerical advantage of about 1.5 to 1 in combat and direct support personnel and about 3 to 1 in tanks; the British 1979 defence White Paper shows smaller WP advantages (1.1 to 1 and 2.8 to 1 respectively) and adds a further WP advantage of 2.7 to 1 in artillery pieces.[37] Were all French forces included, the personnel advantage for the WP would be eliminated and the other numerical discrepancies narrowed.

Closer examination of the data suggests that NATO faces a tight but not alarming situation in Europe. The first point to note is the absence from those data of important categories, such as helicopters and anti-tank weapons. By late 1978 NATO was expected to have 193,000 extremely accurate anti-tank guided missiles, not counting short-range one-man types; this figure represented an increase of 45,000, or nearly one-third, over the total at the end of 1976, and at the start of 1979 there were over 17,000 ground-operated launchers for these missiles, with more launchers on helicopters and fixed-wing aircraft.[38] The development of new types of anti-tank weapons has vastly increased the anti-tank abilities of infantry; according to one assessment, a single infantry company can now have more anti-tank capacity than whole battalions did before 1970.[39] Thus, counting tanks against tanks provides only limited and misleading information about the potential effectiveness of WP tank forces.

Counting tanks against tanks is misleading in another sense. One reason why the WP tank inventory has swelled to such large dimensions is because the WP tends to hang on to older models. A closer look at IISS data reveals that of an estimated 24,825 WP tanks in central Europe in 1978, 14,325 are operated by the USSR's allies.[40] All are Soviet-made tanks, but not only are the USSR's allies not equipped with the 1970s' Soviet models (T-64 and T-72 tanks), they do not even have the T-62s of the 1960s. All bar a few hundred are T-54/55 tanks, which first entered service in 1949, and of which the most recent variant entered service in 1958; the remainder are the even older T-34s, operated by

Bulgaria, Poland and Romania. Of the 10,500 Soviet army tanks in the same region, most are T-62s, which entered service in 1962 and were basically an improved version of the T-54/55. In 1978, production rates of the newer T-64s and T-72s were estimated together at 2,000 a year, which, since they entered service in 1976, suggests a maximum of 4,000 in the region if they have all been deployed there (which is not very likely).[41] NATO tanks are generally reckoned superior to the T-62, and thus also to the T-54/55, let alone the T-34. NATO tanks are thought to have faster rates of fire, to carry more ammunition and be better armoured;[42] it is also thought they have more accurate guns and greater accuracy on the move than the T-62 which may, however, have better armour-piercing shells.[43] In addition, the T-62 breaks down and needs extensive repairs every 100-125 miles, whereas for most NATO tanks the corresponding figure ranges between 150 and 200 miles.[44]

From the shape of WP ground forces, and from Soviet military writings available to us, it appears that those forces are largely designed for a mechanised offensive, integrating different kinds of army unit, but based on the tank forces. From this it would not be legitimate to infer aggressive WP intentions, since those same writings emphasise the offensive as a swift response to NATO aggression. The strategy of taking the fight off WP territory into NATO territory is reasonable, and need not imply intended aggression, though it should be added that it would require a hair-trigger readiness which could all too easily lead to over-eagerness. But the immediate point here is twofold: first, if NATO itself is not planning a tank-led offensive, the comparatively lesser weight of tanks within its total force structure need be no cause for alarm; secondly, that close examination of the WP tank inventory makes it seem a little less awesome, and the centrality of tanks in WP strategy means that this must materially affect our assessment of the entire military balance in Europe.

Considering ground forces alone, of course, is inadequate. Aircraft can support ground forces and harass the enemy, attacking their combat units, supply lines, communications and reinforcements, and must attempt to neutralise enemy air power. Table 4.1 shows a 1.7 to 1 numerical advantage to the WP in tactical aircraft in Europe, and a similar advantage for Northern and Central Europe. This discrepancy is largely accounted for by the WP's far greater numbers of interceptors, aircraft used for defence against attack aircraft; this will make NATO's air attacks harder, but does not directly threaten NATO ground forces, although if NATO attacks on WP airfields were ineffective the result would be greater pressure from WP attack aircraft on NATO ground forces. Table 4.1 does, however, exclude aircraft on both sides which could be immediately involved, including reinforcements from the USA and US naval aircraft in the Mediterranean. Moreover, the figures for 1973 in the Table are very different from those in the Pentagon study of 1973, in which it was calculated that numbers in a European air battle would be about even, at between 5,000 and 6,000 each.[45] This suggests that the figures for 1978, provided by IISS on the same definitions as used for 1973, may similarly understate NATO's air power.

It is generally reckoned in NATO that its aircraft and aircrews are superior to their WP counterparts. Robert Fischer has argued that WP aircraft may be able to carry out more missions in a given period, and are less vulnerable when on the ground (although this advantage is diminishing), but that NATO aircraft are more capable in both air-to-air combat and strikes against airfields, have longer ranges and greater payloads, more accurate munitions and more highly trained crews.[46] If the IISS data in Table 4.1 are taken, this difference in quality probably means that air power is about even, perhaps with a marginal advantage to NATO; if the present position is assumed to be similar to the numerical parity reported by the Pentagon in 1973, NATO has a definite superiority. However, surface-to-air missiles, like anti-tank missiles, are now extremely accurate and can be expected to take a high toll of manned aircraft, and although NATO types are again believed to be qualitatively superior, there are no firm data on which to make an assessment including this factor in the air balance.

A footnote must be added to this discussion, which has largely swung on tempering the numerical balance by also considering quality. To put it mildly, the next war would be extremely lethal to both people and machines. Expensive and sophisticated equipment will not always be less vulnerable than cheaper equipment of less quality and greater age. Therefore, the WP habit of keeping the inventory large by not scrapping old equipment has a certain logic. At the end of the day, it is possible that anything that moves will command the battlefield. Of course, what kind of battlefield will be left to command, and whether or not the victor will be in any shape to profit from it, are different questions entirely.

This discussion of the military balance has not been comprehensive. Yet further factors should be included, such as logistics arrangements, where it is NATO's view that, despite improvements since the logistic débacle during the invasion of Czechoslovakia in 1968, WP arrangements would collapse after about five days.[47] Speed of mobilisation should also be considered: here Fischer concludes that the WP numerical advantage in personnel (which he calculates at 1.36 to 1) would be translated to a superiority at peak of between 1.5 and 2 to 1, which he argues could be enough for local breakthroughs.[48] The comparison of military power in Europe then comes down to something like this: assuming that the WP mobilises its forces first, if its armoured offensive can be held by NATO's air power and anti-tank strengths, the offensive will shortly lose its impetus through deficiencies in logistics, and NATO will soon after restore numerical parity and gain military superiority; if the WP offensive were decisive in the first two to five days of the war NATO might be unable to recover.

This brings into focus criticisms which have been made of NATO that it is structured to fight a long war, whereas what will matter is its ability to fight a short war.[49] Against this it has often been argued that traditional military wisdom and experience suggest the attacker requires a 3 to 1 numerical advantage in the major categories. And against that it is argued that the 3 to 1 rule holds only if the attacker relies on brute force — manoeuvre and surprise can give an attacker superiority in important localities which may be enough for breakthroughs even with inferior numbers overall.[50] Although this is so, it misses the point, for what the 3 to 1 rule suggests is that, assuming NATO is not going to launch an offensive and will keep to its stated strategy, it starts with inherent advantages, which would have to be thrown away by bad leadership or any other non-quantifiable inadequacies before the WP's offensive were successful.

This discussion can be concluded by saying that, on the basis of the available data, with all the original reservations and caution in mind, the military balance in Europe, as elsewhere, by no means merits the diet of alarmism on which we have been fed. The one sure thing is that any clash between these immense military forces would be hugely destructive, even if nuclear weapons were not used. If NATO might justifiably look at the military balance and find it somewhat tight, there is equally nothing there to tempt a sensible and cautious Soviet leadership into launching an attack. Western commentators who profess to find enough NATO weakness to tempt such an attack do nobody a service.

Strategic Nuclear Weapons

Discussing the conventional military balance requires us to suspend disbelief about the prospects of a major non-nuclear war between NATO and the WP, but when we take up the question of nuclear weapons we enter a realm where rational discussion calls for yet greater effort. Henry Kissinger is reported to have asked, 'What in the name of God is strategic

Table 4.7: Development of US and Soviet Strategic Nuclear Forces, 1968-1977

	1968	1969	1970	1971	1972	1973	1974	1975	1976	1977
USA:										
Bombers[a]	562	512	512	479	430	430	390	369	348	348
Bombs[b]	2,248	2,048	2,048	1,916	1,720	1,720	1,560	1,476	1,392	1,392
SSBN	41	41	41	41	41	41	41	41	41	41
SLBM	656	656	656	656	656	656	656	656	656	656
SLBM warheads[c]	1,552	1,552	1,824	2,496	3,056	3,952	4,240	4,672	5,104	5,328
ICBM	1,054	1,054	1,054	1,054	1,054	1,054	1,054	1,054	1,054	1,054
ICBM warheads	1,054	1,054	1,074	1,274	1,474	1,674	1,854	2,154	2,154	2,154
USSR:										
Bombers[d]	150	140	140	140	140	140	140	140	140	140
Bombs[e]	300	280	280	280	280	280	280	280	280	280
SSBN	11	17	22	29	35	42	50	53	55	60
SLBM	59	155	248	360	456	564	664	700	732	812
SLBM warheads[f]	59	155	248	360	456	564	664	764	934	1,142
ICBM	900	1,200	1,498	1,527	1,527	1,547	1,567	1,587	1,552	1,452
ICBM warheads	900	1,200	1,498	1,527	1,527	1,587	1,647	1,707	2,172	2,392
Total of bombers and missiles:										
USA	2,272	2,222	2,222	2,189	2,140	2,140	2,100	2,079	2,058	2,058
USSR	1,109	1,495	1,886	2,027	2,123	2,251	2,371	2,427	2,424	2,404
Total of bombs and warheads:[g]										
USA	4,850	4,650	4,950	5,690	6,250	7,350	7,650	8,300	8,650	8,870
USSR	1,260	1,640	2,030	2,170	2,260	2,430	2,590	2,750	3,380	3,810
Independent targets:[h]										
USA	2,270	2,220	2,390	3,420	4,290	5,640	6,170	6,780	7,190	7,480
USSR	1,109	1,495	1,886	2,027	2,123	2,251	2,371	2,427	2,920	3,220

a. On the basis of the criterion used, the US medium-range FB-111A was excluded.
b. This assumes that each B-52 bomber carries four gravity bombs, all nuclear; however, they could be conventional bombs, as, for example, during their use in Vietnam. In addition, US bombers by 1977 carried at least 1,150 Short Range Attack Missiles, mostly on B-52s, which are excluded here.
c. Assumes US *Poseidon* SLBM carry an average of ten MIRV warheads each.
d. Here the Soviet *Backfire* merdium-range bomber is excluded.
e. This assumes two gravity bombs, both nuclear, on each bomber.
f. Figures from 1975 would vary depending on estimates of how fast one SLBM, the SS-N-6 *Sawfly*, was modified to carry extra warheads.
g. All figures here are rounded to ten.
h. Bombers, missiles with single warheads, and MRV were all counted as able to hit one target each; MIRV are counted as able to hit as many targets as they

carry warheads. US figures are rounded to ten, as are Soviet figures for 1976
and 1977.

Glossary

SSBN	Nuclear-powered submarines carrying nuclear-armed missiles.
SLBM	Submarine Launched Ballistic Missiles.
ICBM	Inter-continental Ballistic Missiles (land-based).
MRV	Multiple Re-entry Vehicles (that is, multi-warheads).
MIRV	Multiple Independently targeted Re-entry Vehicles (that is, multi-warheads in which each warhead has its own target).

Sources: For bombers, submarines and missiles, *World Armaments and Disarmament: SIPRI Yearbook 1977* (MIT Press, London, 1977), pp. 24-8: certain figures were changed reflecting my judgement about what weapon systems should be included — the criterion used corresponds to that for the US-Soviet Strategic Arms Limitation Talks; for bombs, warheads and independent targets, my estimates were based on data in: *SIPRI Yearbook 1977* and *SIPRI Yearbook 1974* (MIT Press, London, 1974); *The Military Balance 1975-1976, 1976-1977, 1977-1978* (IISS, London, 1975, 1976, 1977); *Jane's Fighting Ships 1975-1976* and *1976-1977, Jane's All The World's Aircraft 1976-1977*, and *Jane's Weapon Systems 1976* and *1977* (Macdonald & Jane's, London, 1975, 1976, 1977).

superiority? What do you do with it?'[51] Since full-scale strategic nuclear war would leave no victors in any meaningful sense, we can sympathise with his confusion and may ourselves have wondered about the same thing. But there are people who claim to know what strategic superiority is, and who also claim that the USSR either has it or is getting it.

Table 4.7 shows the development of US and Soviet strategic nuclear forces from 1968 to 1977. Since the mid-1960s, the USA has not increased its numbers of bombers and missiles, preferring to increase its strategic nuclear capacity through the technology of multiple warheads. Its 1977 lead in the number of targets its forces could hit still stands, with about the same margin — 9,200 to 5,000 at 1 January 1979.[52] In 1976 the USSR had (and still has) more explosive power in its arsenal,[53] but destructiveness is a product of both explosive yield and accuracy, and US warheads are still more accurate than the USSR's, reflecting the American lead in warhead-guidance technology. Each side is probably able to use about 60 per cent of its warheads at any one time.

Some recent assessments of Soviet guidance technology suggest that the accuracy of the USSR's warheads is increasing so much that American inter-continental ballistic missiles (ICBM) in fixed siloes on land will shortly be vulnerable to Soviet attack and condemned to obsolescence. One detailed analysis of the issue concluded that these claims are exaggerated, overlooking 'fundamental factors which limit the accuracy of inertially guided intercontinental missiles', but this has not prevented an intense debate about mobile basing for MX, the next American ICBM.[54] Among the ideas suggested are basing MX in trucks, trenches, aircraft and even at the bottom of lakes; a flurry of press articles in late 1978 testified to a major debate within the Carter administration as to the costs and technical difficulties of all the proposals, but it now appears that the Pentagon has committed itself to supporting a system in which MX missiles would be covertly moved among a large number of siloes, keeping the USSR guessing as to where they are.[55] The debate seems not to have been based on the problems of a strategy including limited nuclear options, possible US first strikes and limited nuclear war, but on the problem of retaliating to a major Soviet attack. This makes it even more strange that the debate has largely been confined, quite arbitrarily, to the question of land-based ICBM, ignoring the submarine-launched missiles whose warheads make up such a large part of the US strategic nuclear force. A recent study concluded that, even without mobile basing for MX, a major Soviet attack would still leave the USA with about 4,900 warheads and, if forces were especially alerted before the attack, about 7,500. These warheads could destroy about 90 per cent of military targets in the USSR, about 80 per cent of industrial targets, all Soviet government centres, and kill about 90 million people. Even after this the USA would still have about 1,000 warheads left for prosecuting the war even further.[56] American strategic analysts have whipped themselves into a frenzy about remarkably little. Should MX have a mobile basing system, this will be very costly, will make verification of arms limitation agreements harder, and may be more vulnerable to technical failure than the present basing system, raising the prospect of major accidents with nuclear weapons.

While some analysts worry about developments which might prevent the ICBM from being launched, others have fretted that they would be shot down in flight, not by anti-missiles which are limited by treaty agreement and anyway not trusted, but by a new Soviet charged-particle beam weapon, the result of a major technological breakthrough, which would work by directing hydrogen ions at the missiles. This view is traceable to the findings of one part of the US intelligence community, US Air Force intelligence, and especially to its former head, Major-General Keegan; it was first publicly promoted with force in May 1977.[57] Elsewhere in the intelligence community, the view was treated with scepticism with the USSR thought to be nowhere close to having a beam weapon even though it might have a research programme,[58] but in 1978, after a quiescent period, the stories emerged again and in greater detail.[59] In late 1978, a study at the Massachusetts Institute of Technology once again questioned the technical feasibility of such a weapon with current technologies, and argued that counter-measures to it were in any case relatively simple.[60]

Since the USA also has a research programme into beam weapons, it is unlikely that this will be the final word in the controversy. At the very most, it now seems a possible weapon for well into the future, and the storm which surrounds it is perhaps indicative of the lengths to which alarmism is able to go. But even if it seems that through the 1980s at least there will be no effective way to shoot down nuclear missiles, yet a third group of analysts has argued that Soviet civil defence programmes will so protect the population and industry that the USSR could 'ride out' American retaliation to a first strike. This issue has increasingly entered calculations of the strategic nuclear balance.[61] Les Aspin and Fred Kaplan have both challenged the evidence of a massive civil defence programme in the USSR, each arguing that more exists on paper than in reality and that there is no evidence of any rehearsals of evacuations involving city populations;[62] the US National Security Council's view is reportedly close to those of Aspin and Kaplan.[63] Nevertheless, civil defence spending in the USA has been boosted, with the largest budget for fifteen years being approved in 1977, and an administration proposal in late 1978 to spend $2 billion on a six or seven year programme to develop a plan based on evacuation.[64]

To put civil defence in perspective, this American programme would be based on the calculation that, if adequate warning of a Soviet attack were received, massive evacuation could save the lives of nearly two-thirds of the population. Put differently, even if there are massive evacuations, 70 million or more Americans would still die. And to the survivors would be left the prospect of slow and agonising deaths from radiation, with all food sources contaminated. In Britain, two MPs have estimated that effective civil defence could reduce deaths in a nuclear war from about 35 million to just 20 million.[65]

By the time we are discussing death on such a scale, the mind is anaesthetised, and the ill effects of that quickly become clear. Oklahoma City is one of only eight American cities with evacuation plans at present:

> 'We don't want to lay down and die in Oklahoma City,' said Clyde Mitchell, director of the city's civil defense. 'Folks around here say, yes, eventually we are going to come to a nuclear exchange with the Soviet Union. It's kind of inevitable.'[66]

If Mr Mitchell is right that folks in Oklahoma City think nuclear war is inevitable, they would be far better advised to direct their efforts towards changing the conditions which make that so. They may think it a slender hope, but it is a far more robust one than relying on evacuation to protect them if war does come.

It has been argued that a Soviet nuclear first strike against the USA would destroy a major proportion of US nuclear forces, without using all Soviet forces; US retaliation against Soviet cities would thus provoke another Soviet strike, against American cities, and the USSR's civil defence would then permit it to recover faster than the USA. Awareness of this could weaken the US incentive to retaliate to the first strike, leaving the USSR as the victor either way. This analysis comes from Jones and Thompson, whose concern is directed at the 'recovery-time gap' between the USA and USSR.[67] So after the 'bomber gap' of the 1950s, the 'missile gap' of the early 1960s and the 'mineshaft gap' of the film *Dr Strangelove* (the USSR is thought to have more mineshafts in which to protect its elite and breed a new population after the holocaust), comes the 'recovery-time gap', estimated by Jones and Thompson at 2 to 1.

Even if the evidence of the USSR's civil defence is accepted, three problems emerge in this odd logic. First, Kaplan shows that the surviving US force would be quite capable of thoroughly devastating all the largest 200 Soviet cities several times over.[68] Secondly, the analysis assumes a period of tension during which the civil defence plan would be implemented; this would be easily visible from satellites and the USSR would have to expect a pre-emptive strike from the USA. It is worth remembering that during the 1962 Cuba missile crisis British civil defence was not mobilised for fear of worsening the crisis and provoking a Soviet pre-emptive strike. Thirdly, the analysis assumes that the Soviet leadership would risk a war in which victory depends on recovering in five years against the ten it is said the USA would need. Perhaps, one day, the USSR would take such a gamble; if it does so it will be because it has been taken in by the distorted logic and fantasies of Soviet equivalents of Jones and Thompson.

In Britain, civil defence for the population is now rooted not in evacuation, but its opposite, a policy of 'staying put'.[69] The policy appears to be a pragmatic response to the problem that in a small country like Britain there would be no safe place to send the evacuees. It is a remarkably simple policy, quite deft in its cynicism. It is accepted that most people will try to go somewhere, anywhere, but trains will not be functioning, motorways can be cut and main roads out of towns and cities will be jammed by panicking citizens so badly that the policy will be largely self-enforcing. But if little pretence is made of protecting the population, for the state things are different. British civil defence has always been directed towards maintaining the state apparatus, even at a low level of functioning, under any circumstances, including nuclear war and revolution on a more or less equal footing.[70]

In the end, however sophisticated or original the logic, there is no getting away from the awesome destructiveness of a major nuclear war. It would be in nobody's interests and would make a mockery of the idea of 'victory'. That is, perhaps, the only relevant conclusion to draw from a discussion of the strategic nuclear balance.

Tactical Nuclear Weapons

Between NATO's conventional and strategic forces lie tactical nuclear weapons (TNW). Willingness to use TNW is a central component of NATO's strategy of 'flexible response' which is declared to be designed to

> enable NATO to meet aggression at any level with an appropriate response, while making it impossible for the aggressor to calculate in advance the nature of the response his attack will provoke, or how the conflict may develop thereafter.[71]

The two main elements here are the 'appropriate response' and uncertainty in the aggressor's mind. Whether or not the WP used its own TNW first, NATO's response to a major attack could include TNW, used on the battlefield, against WP airfields, logistic 'choke points', reinforcements or other targets.

Nuclear weapons were first introduced into Europe in 1948 when American strategic bombers were stationed in Britain. In 1953 the US National Security Council authorised the Joint Chiefs of Staff to develop plans based on using TNW. By 1954 the US Navy was operating nuclear-armed aircraft from its Mediterranean fleet, and US land forces in Europe, which apparently received their first TNW as early as 1952, were by 1955 equipped with *Honest John* nuclear missiles and nuclear artillery. In 1957 it was agreed that the USA should supply TNW to its European allies as well as increasing its own inventory.[72] Thereafter, numbers grew quickly, reportedly doubling between 1961 and 1966,[73] and reaching a peak in 1967.[74]

The number of NATO TNW in Europe is not precisely known. The figure usually given is 7,000 warheads to be delivered in a variety of ways, but figures vary from source to source and cannot be thought reliable. The number of TNW held by the WP is an even greater mystery, with estimates ranging from 1,750 to 5,000 warheads, while SIPRI gives 'a hypothetical figure' of 3,500 derived from the number of known Soviet nuclear delivery vehicles in Europe.[75] In 1978 the Pentagon would only say that NATO's inventory of TNW was 'very large' while the Soviet inventory was 'probably far smaller'.[76]

Apart from the normal problems of estimating data, much of this uncertainty about numbers stems from the uncertain definition of what constitutes a tactical weapon; the term 'tactical' is now intermittently replaced by 'theatre', meaning weapons for use in or near the theatre of operations, which can itself be defined widely or narrowly. Thus the Pentagon:

> The capability we maintain exclusively for theater nuclear warfare consists of atomic demolition munitions,[77] shells, bombs, warheads and depth charges, along with a few specialized delivery systems such as *Pershing* and *Lance* missiles. Otherwise, we depend primarily on our conventional ground forces, a number of dual purpose weapon systems such as cannon and tactical aircraft, and elements of our strategic forces for the execution of such theater nuclear options as may be available.[78]

Thus, both conventional and strategic forces can use TNW. Neither the power of the warhead nor the range of the weapon is a guide to what is a tactical (or theatre) weapon and what is not. What really matters is the target against which the weapon is used. A necessarily imperfect guide is that weapons used against military forces may be thought of as tactical, unless the targets are the enemy's strategic nuclear forces, and weapons used against cities, industrial centres, strategic forces and high level decision-making centres may be thought of as strategic, unless those targets are within the theatre of operations. Clearly, the definition has elements of circularity, but the operational military definition of TNW is fluid, and so must ours be.

Britain's contribution to NATO's TNW includes nuclear-armed *Buccaneer* and *Vulcan* bombers (the latter were earlier designated strategic), and a force of 264 *Lance* missiles with 20 launchers purchased from the USA in 1974.[79] The air force also has anti-submarine *Nimrod* aircraft equipped with nuclear depth charges,[80] and the army operates US-made M-110 203mm and M-109 155mm howitzers, both of which are capable of firing nuclear shells.[81] Finally, although the British government always refers to the four *Polaris* missile-firing submarines as part of NATO's strategic forces, the Pentagon has included them with NATO's TNW.[82]

Except for these British weapons and French TNW which, like all
French forces, are outside NATO command, NATO's TNW are under
American control. Should the American president decide to permit the
West European forces to use TNW, they would be released by the two-
man US Army teams guarding them and the coded locks (known as
Permissive Action Locks) would be undone.[83] American control is
further reinforced by the operational plan for NATO's TNW being
part of the Single Integrated Operational Plan for US strategic nuclear
forces.[84]

NATO's early decisions to build up its TNW inventory seem to have
been based on its obsessions with the supposed Soviet superiority in
conventional forces. As TNW numbers increased, US Army doctrine
viewed TNW as the way to neutralise the USSR's numerical superiority.[85]
The preponderance of WP conventional forces remains the basic rationale
for deploying TNW now, even though, as we have seen, there is no clear
basis on which to conclude that preponderance exists. But even if it did
exist, it is far from clear that TNW can ever be an intelligent way to respond to it. Tactical nuclear warfare would be even more lethal than
conventional war; TNW cannot substitute for manpower, and this has
been known since war games in 1952.[86] Even so, in the mid-1950s the
US Army exposed soldiers to radiation far exceeding safe levels at
nuclear weapons tests, not because of sloppy procedures as was first sur-
mised when details of this became public, but as a matter of deliberate
policy to duplicate nuclear battlefield conditions and see how long
contaminated soldiers could continue fighting.[87]

Despite the lengths to which planning for the nuclear battlefield has
gone, West European governments did not really see TNW as battlefield
weapons. For them, the point of TNW was to extend strategic deterrence
from the USA to Western Europe and to gain as concrete a commitment
as possible from the USA to link its own fate to that of the West European states. TNW were seen as Western Europe's strategic deterrent.[88]
It is from this that NATO's European members draw their insistence on
keeping open the option to use TNW whether or not the WP uses them
first; it is because of this that, time and again, NATO has turned down
WP proposals for an agreement outlawing first use of nuclear weapons,
virtually without discussion. And one of the effects is that if the deterrent relationship breaks down, the following war will almost certainly
be nuclear.

There is a view that conventional and nuclear weapons are qualitatively different, however powerful the former, however small the latter;
it believes there is a 'firebreak' between conventional and nuclear war —

crossing it by using TNW on any scale would initiate nuclear war, with no further firebreaks before the holocaust. But there is another view, that TNW are controllable and, not threatening the Soviet homeland, carry perceptibly less risk of escalation than strategic weapons. US doctrine asserts that first use of TNW should be limited and 'defensive in nature', yet sufficiently decisive 'to forcibly change the perceptions of (WP) leaders and create a situation conducive to negotiations.'[89] In other words, in the midst of the most destructive battles the world will have seen, NATO field commanders are expected to find a point where use of TNW is heavy enough decisively to alter the battlefield situation, yet light enough not to provoke retaliation and escalation. In all probability that point does not exist, and if it does there can be no sure way of identifying it.

If we accept NATO assumptions, and suppose that the WP has taken the risk of an offensive, it is far more likely that NATO's use of TNW will simply lead to the WP responding in kind, and possibly more heavily. Once a tactical nuclear war starts, all thoughts of control can be thrown out the window. Control depends upon fixing limits, which in turn depends partly upon both sides agreeing to them, and partly upon knowledge of the situation. On a nuclear battlefield, key parts of the situation will be extremely hard to ascertain, such as the explosive power of the TNW the WP is using, how many it is using and how many it has immediately ready, what effects they are having on NATO forces, and so on. One form in which energy is released in a nuclear explosion is the Electromagnetic Pulse (EMP), which can cause damage to electronic systems tens of kilometres from the point of a surface nuclear explosion.[90] Increased reliance on sophisticated electronic systems for communications and surveillance increases the damage the EMP can do to a military force. Even apart from the physical destruction TNW would cause, sections of the battlefield untouched by TNW may nevertheless suffer a communications black-out, against which counter-measures are possible but not guaranteed to succeed.[91] It would not even require a WP retaliatory strike for NATO communications to be affected by the EMP: if NATO uses nuclear artillery, with ranges now around 20 kilometres, it will be affected by its own nuclear bombardment.

Despite the apparent confidence of US doctrine, NATO's strategy for TNW lacks clarity. In 1975, a mere eighteen years after NATO agreed to a major TNW stockpile, the British government reported that, 'Studies are continuing on the political and military implications of possible defensive use of nuclear weapons by NATO.'[92] One senior NATO diplomat reportedly commented that the ideal target for TNW would be a

Soviet fleet invading Denmark[93] — a thought which owes more to wishful thinking than anything else, and is more than a little alarming if it is the best that can be offered. Early in the Carter administration, it was apparently the US government's view, based on the assumption of conventional inferiority, that war in Europe would quickly face NATO with the choice between nuclear weapons and defeat, but within a year a report described as 'A high-level US Administration analysis' concluded that if the WP retaliated with nuclear weapons to NATO's use of TNW, the consequences were not clear, but a NATO military advantage was a doubtful outcome.[94]

Unofficial rationales for NATO TNW argue that, as well as deterring first use of TNW by the WP, they contribute to deterrence of conventional war, and hedge against the possible failure of other parts of NATO's forces. A further use suggested for TNW has been to show resolve in the event of a WP attack, or even a crisis, by striking at a single WP city, outside the USSR, or at another major target; Alain Enthoven has commented that in eight years of studying the problem in the Pentagon, he never saw a scenario in which such use would make sense, but concludes that the capability is not expensive, so NATO might as well keep it.[95] However cheap it is to destroy a city, it would take a remarkably stiff Soviet upper lip not to respond in kind.

In fact, the strongest reason why NATO is not only maintaining but modernising its TNW force is that it already has several thousand. They are seen as concrete evidence of the USA's extension of nuclear deterrence to Western Europe, of its commitment to stand alongside West European states even in the face of Soviet aggression. They provide, so it is argued, the link between the fate of Western Europe and the fate of the USA so that, in a crisis, there could be no 'decoupling' of the two. Thus the removal of a portion of the TNW force, let alone the whole inventory, would raise the spectre of nuclear decoupling, suggesting that the West European states might have to stand alone. For some West European politicians, merely emphasising a requirement to improve conventional forces is tantamount to de-emphasising American nuclear forces and thus implies decoupling.[96] But West European fears about the USA ratting on its nuclear commitments cannot get round the fact that all the US president would have to do is refrain from releasing TNW to West European NATO forces. With large American forces, conventional as well as nuclear, in Europe it is not at all clear that there is a genuine issue of decoupling here, but if there is one it cannot stand up as an argument for keeping the large TNW inventory because the West European states simply have no way to prevent decoupling.

What is hard to understand is why West European governments should find the prospect of being incinerated by a WP response to NATO's opening nuclear bombardment so attractive. If TNW are used, the consequences will be appalling for NATO states themselves: it is therefore hard to see how a threat to use TNW can be thought of as a reliable deterrent. The standard response to this, a familiar argument, is that the important thing about TNW is that they cause uncertainty in Soviet minds. But while this uncertainty may complicate WP planning, which may possibly help deter aggression, it is equally likely that in an acute crisis it would only serve to make the Soviet leadership worry about NATO's TNW and accordingly launch a pre-emptive tactical nuclear strike.[97] The emphasis upon uncertainty, more than anything else, reflects the uncertainty in NATO's own planning and the fact that the consequences of using TNW cannot be calculated in any way which results in a conclusion that using them would make sense.

The Neutron Bomb

The USA's continuing programme of TNW modernisation will gradually change the shape of the NATO arsenal. The programme is extensive, including explosives and delivery systems as well as extra protection for TNW bases so they can better withstand nuclear attack.[98] One part of the programme has been particularly important, the development of miniaturised warheads for TNW (affectionately known as mininukes) in order to make their use and effects more precise. Along with this has gone the best known part of the overall programme – the neutron bomb. Although neutron warheads developed for the *Lance* tactical missile and eight-inch (203mm) artillery have not yet been deployed, they became the most controversial part of the modernisation programme from June 1977 when Walter Pincus, a *Washington Post* reporter, discovered a few lines tucked away in the Energy Research and Development Agency's budget and filed a story.[99]

The neutron bomb is a fission-fusion weapon.[100] A typical fission weapon releases about 50 per cent of its energy as blast, about 35 per cent as heat, about 10 per cent as residual radiation, about 1 per cent as the Electromagnetic Pulse and about 4 per cent as prompt or initial radiation.[101] The design of the neutron bomb so changes this pattern that about 80 per cent of its energy is released as initial radiation, mostly in the form of high-energy neutrons.[102] This also reduces the percentage of energy released as blast – thus the official term for the neutron bomb, the Enhanced Radiation/Reduced Blast warhead, and thus also the jibe that it is the perfect capitalist weapon since it kills people with radiation without damaging property with blast. In fact, all small nuclear weapons could be thought of as neutron weapons,

> In the sense that at ranges corresponding to the lethal radius of the weapon, even if it were completely a fission one, the energy released in the form of prompt radiation would be greater than the fraction that goes into blast and thermal radiation, and prompt radiation in the form of neutrons would dominate prompt radiation in the form of gamma rays.[103]

The point of the neutron bomb's design is to maximise this effect.

The effects of the neutron bomb would depend on a number of factors — the total energy yield, the height of the detonation, available protection, terrain and weather. Table 4.8 summarises the effects for three altitudes at which it could be detonated, using US Army nuclear casualty criteria, and comparing the anti-personnel effects on those in the open and on those with the benefit of armour protection (people below ground level in cities would have roughly the same protection as those behind heavy armour; those in vehicles without armour or with lighter armour than tanks have can be regarded as unprotected). The attraction of the neutron bomb for NATO is as an anti-personnel weapon against tank crews; it will be seen that if the bomb were detonated at 3,000 feet, at which altitude it would cause no property damage, its effect against tank-crew behind their armour would be delayed. For greatest effect against tank crews, some property damage is unavoidable if there are buildings close by, so that the jibe that the neutron bomb is a perfect capitalist weapon is just a jibe. The burst of neutron radiation is extremely brief (less than one millionth of a second) and dissipates quickly.

The neutron bomb is not as new as most people seem to think: the idea was first discussed in general terms in 1944 during the wartime Manhattan Project which produced the first nuclear bombs, according to one of the participants.[104] The possibility of nuclear weapons maximising initial radiation was recognised in the scientific community in the late 1940s and there was work on it throughout the 1950s at the Lawrence Livermore nuclear laboratory in the USA.[105] Discussions of the idea in 1957 led on to a study headed by Sam Cohen, a physicist at the US Air Force 'think tank', the Rand Corporation, which defined the basic concept of enhanced radiation weapons.[106] The first test of the neutron bomb was in 1963 — according to the Soviet Novosti press agency it was a technical failure although Cohen states it was success-

Table 4.8: Effects of a One-kiloton Neutron Bomb (radii in metres)

	Anti-personnel dosage			Tank destruction	Urban damage		
	8,000 rads[a]	3,000 rads[b]	650 rads[c]	blast	Severe	Moderate	Light
Detonated at 500 feet:							
Unprotected	750	900	1,200	165	420	540	750
Armoured	675	810	1,080				
Detonated at 1,500 feet:							
Unprotected	750	900	1,200	0	0	240	450
Armoured	675	810	1,080				
Detonated at 3,000 feet:							
Unprotected	300	600	1,050	0	0	0	0
Armoured	0	420	840				

a. A dose of 8,000 rads affects the central nervous system, causing incapacitation within five minutes of exposure; the victim would remain incapacitated for physically demanding tasks until death in 1-2 days.
b. A dose of 3,000 rads also affects the central nervous system, causing incapacitation within five minutes which lasts for about 30-45 minutes after which there is a slight recovery; the victim would remain 'functionally impaired' until death in 4-6 days.
c. A dose of 650 rads primarily affects the gastro-intestinal system, causing functional impairment within two hours; the victim may respond to treatment and survive, but the majority of cases will terminate in death in several weeks having suffered functional impairment throughout the intervening period.

Source: S.T. Cohen, *The Neutron Bomb: Political, Technological and Military Issues* (Institute for Foreign Policy Analysis, Cambridge, Mass, 1978), pp. 67-9.

ful.[107] The concept of an anti-personnel neutron weapon had by then been publicly discussed, though perhaps with less intensity than in the more recent controversy.[108]

After 1963 the idea of neutron warheads for TNW seems to have receded, perhaps because of technical problems, perhaps because McNamara, then US Defense Secretary, did not favour a further development of NATO's TNW arsenal. Neutron technology, however, re-emerged for the warhead of the *Sprint* anti-ballistic missile (ABM — an anti-missile missile) and was tested in 1965.[109] But from the mid-1960s the American ABM programme was subjected to intense criticism on various grounds — either that ABM would not work, or that if they did they would de-stabilise the US-Soviet strategic balance by providing a defence against nuclear missiles and thus undermining mutual deterrence. As the steam went out of ABM, so interest revived in neutron warheads for TNW.

Soon after Nixon's presidential inauguration in 1969 work on neutron warheads for TNW was authorised at the same time as there were reports that the administration intended to rely more heavily on TNW in Europe.[110] Discussion of tactical neutron warheads began in the specialist literature in 1971, while in 1972 the administration announced its interest in 'smaller, cleaner' TNW for deployment in Europe, but a 1973 request by the US Army for funding for new low-yield nuclear shells for eight-inch and 155mm artillery was turned down by Congress.[111] As US Defense Secretary, Schlesinger seemed a more committed advocate of neutron warheads than his predecessors, and discussed them with his counterparts in NATO at a June 1974 meeting of the Nuclear Planning Group (NPG). Full details were made available to the NPG in January 1976, and an article in a specialist journal in May 1976 shows that the US Army was already changing its criteria for nuclear casualties because the deployment of TNW with low yields meant radiation was replacing blast as the main way of producing casualties.[112] In November 1976, President Ford signed the production order for eight-inch neutron shells and for the *Lance* missile neutron warheads, and in June 1977 the rumpus started.

The controversy was always confused. Critics and proponents used a variety of arguments, moral, political and strategic, with critics calling neutron warheads 'dirty' as loudly as proponents insisted they were 'clean'. Military attractions of the warheads seem to hinge on two points. First, they could kill WP tank crews with initial radiation despite their armoured protection, and also kill infantry supporting the tanks. The threat of this would force WP tank formations to be more dispersed, limiting their concentrated striking power. Secondly, neutron bombs would cause less collateral damage (a term which refers to dead civilians, annihilated towns and other unintended or unwanted casualties of war) than existing NATO TNW. This opened a more attractive image of tactical nuclear warfare even if the nuclear battle took place on Federal German territory as NATO planning tends to suppose.[113] Precisely because it limited blast and relied on initial radiation, the neutron bomb looked like a precise controllable weapon.

The first problem with this lies in the idea of precision. The implication, possibly unintended, in many advocacies of neutron bombs is of a single weapon detonated against a single small target. But the frontage of a single company of WP tank forces is about one kilometre;[114] an armoured division can be expected to 'concentrate' in an area of at least 20 to 25 square miles. Moreover, US doctrine is for TNW, in order to have a decisive tactical effect, to be used in 'packages' possibly numbering up to 40 warheads, delivered by a variety of means.[115] Indeed, given the size of the area in question, it would be most odd if the doctrine were to use weapons in ones and twos. And if deployment of neutron weapons does force WP tank formations to be more dispersed, the relevant area will be even larger.

It is also believed that reducing collateral damage will reduce the risk of escalation to more destructive nuclear warfare.[116] But this is extremely questionable: if NATO believes reducing collateral damage makes nuclear weapons more useable, it will go ahead and use them, and if its calculations are correct it will do a lot of damage to WP armoured forces, to which the WP is almost certain to respond with its own TNW and there will indeed be escalation, which is likely to cause a great deal of collateral damage. A former Deputy Commander of the US Army in Europe, arguing against neutron bombs, drew on experience of NATO war games to show that even limited first use of TNW must expect a sudden and massive nuclear response.[117]

Fending off critics' moral arguments against the neutron bomb, proponents tended to argue that it is 'just another' nuclear weapon. Indeed it is – and all the risks of nuclear retaliation raised by using TNW are also raised by using the neutron bomb. There has never been an argument able to show that the WP will retaliate less devastatingly if its tank formations are broken up by neutron weapons than if it is done by other TNW. Even if only neutron weapons were used, and even if WP commanders realised that as their divisions ground to a chaotic halt, it is asking rather much to expect them to play the game and respond differently. Precision, controllability, reduced collateral damage, less escalation – it is a myth, the product of over-heated imaginations.

The neutron bomb caught the public's attention because the idea of a bomb designed to kill by radiation seemed so awful. Frankly, I find this morality somewhat arbitrary: the moral distinction between weapons which kill by blast with radiation and fall-out as a lethal side effect, and weapons which kill primarily by radiation, evades my undoubtedly unrefined moral sensibilities. It is, however, unacceptable that proponents of the bomb described it as 'clean', and perhaps sadly ironic that another project, to produce a bomb maximising blast and minimising radiation, is also described as 'clean' by US government spokespeople.[118]

The controversy also revealed the depths of illiteracy which pass for strategic debate. The heavy-handed propaganda campaign by the Soviet government was bad enough — absurd extremes were reached when it was raised in the UN Human Rights Commission and an effort was made to have a special disarmament agreement for the neutron bomb alone.[119] The effects of Soviet nuclear weapons would not be exactly humane, after all. But even worse was the way that campaign was used as an argument in favour of the neutron bomb. As one Conservative MP put it, 'The row being made by the Soviet Union should be a good indication that we are on to something which is in our best interests and not theirs.'[120] So we can forget the rest: if they don't like it, we must have it. But this substitute for thought is at least matched by the habit of defending the neutron bomb by showing it is far less destructive than the warhead on the new Soviet medium range missile, the SS-20. General Haig, NATO's commander in Europe, thought it was 'ludicrous' to hear so much about the neutron bomb and so little about the SS-20 given that the latter is 2,000 times more powerful 'warhead for warhead'.[121] Since the neutron bomb is so much more powerful, shell for shell, than Soviet tanks, perhaps General Haig thinks the same logic will let us stop bothering about Soviet tank divisions? Indeed, what neutron bomb proponents could never explain was why, if the basic concern is the WP tank force, NATO could not simply procure more conventional anti-tank weapons, which are highly effective and stay on the right side of the nuclear firebreak.

It may be that that kind of illogic really reflects bewilderment in NATO at the intensity of the controversy. The concept for the neutron bomb has been around a long time and detailed work on it has lasted at least two decades. Since 1969 or 1970 it has been a US weapons programme, and since mid-1974 it has been discussed by NATO's Nuclear Planning Group. Apparently, Carter was unaware that the neutron bomb was in the budget he inherited from Ford,[122] and this is probably not because it was consciously hidden from him, but because it was not thought important enough for his personal attention in the first months of his presidency. After the controversy began, the West European governments, previously all in favour of the project, backed off, while Carter evidently sought their active approval as an instrument against its US Congressional critics. At the December 1977 meeting of NATO defence ministers, Leber, the Federal German minister, proposed that production of the bomb be postponed to let the fuss die down. In the first quarter of 1978, there was intense pressure on Carter not to postpone, but he still did not receive the active public approval from other NATO governments that he wanted. The decision was taken in March 1978 and announced in early April (though it had leaked out a few days earlier). Carter put off the production decision, stating that whether or not the bomb was eventually produced would partly depend on whether the USSR would offer any concessions in its own arms programmes. Many observers concluded that the decision's actual meaning was cancellation.[123]

There was an immediate chorus of attacks on Carter, most of them seeming to misunderstand the decision and misrepresent the circumstances. He was accused of not understanding the decision-making process in either the USA or Western Europe. He was accused of seeming to surrender to Soviet pressure, which would not have been the case, of course, if some of the proponents had made more sensible arguments. He was criticised for making NATO's defences look weak, which was the fault of proponents for exaggerating their case. And he was accused of leaving the USA's allies dangling, even though they had more than six months to make up their minds.[124] The Federal German government reportedly believes the neutron bomb is essential for NATO,[125] which leaves us wondering why it was the Federal German defence minister who proposed postponement.

It is also not clear that the decision actually did amount to cancellation. The decision was to continue modernising the weapon systems (eight-inch artillery and *Lance*) so they could in future use neutron warheads, and to continue work on neutron technology, but to delay the decision about production and deployment. What Carter has done is to keep all options open. In October 1978 funds were released to produce eight-inch nuclear shells and W70-MOD 3 warheads for *Lance* in a way which continues to hold open the option of making them neutron weapons.[126] Should Carter, or his successor, finally decide to go ahead with the neutron bomb, production could follow the decision almost immediately.

Carter has stated that the decision will partly depend on whether or not the USSR comes up with any concessions. The first Soviet response was to reject the principle of bargaining over the neutron bomb,[127] but this was shortly followed by an offer that if the USA would renounce it, the USSR would do likewise, an offer which Carter unhesitatingly turned down.[128] This was hardly surprising: the offer to forego a weapon thunderously denounced in every available forum, and which the USSR had shown no sign of wanting to have for itself, did not amount to a great deal. More recently it has been reported that, according to Brezhnev, the USSR once tested a neutron warhead, but abandoned it.[129] It is hardly realistic to expect the USA to accept renunciation of a weapon the USSR has already decided it does not want as equal exchange. Of course, it can be argued that the final decision should not be based on what the USSR does, but one cannot argue that from a Soviet perspective now that it has accepted the principle of bargaining over the neutron bomb by making that offer.

It is therefore quite possible that the USA will finally produce, and NATO will deploy, the neutron bomb. If it does so, it will be because it thinks it has here a usable nuclear weapon, one which can help resolve the basic dilemma of the utility of force discussed in the previous chapter. Drawing on the weakness of the case that the neutron bomb would be useable in Europe against a WP offensive, two suggestions have been put forward for alternative explanations of NATO's desire for it. One, from Daniel Ellsberg, argues that it is really wanted as a weapon for armed interventions in the Third World; the other, from Eric Burhop, who argues that it is 'the weapon *par excellence* of the aggressor determined to take over intact cities and industries', suggests it is an instrument for a clandestine aggressive NATO strategy.[130] But, in the first case, the basic problem remains the political utility of force which cannot be solved simply by the weaponry available; in the second, it is not clear why NATO would want to conquer depopulated ghost towns in Eastern Europe. It may be that NATO or US government thinking has tended in either or both of these directions, in which case the implications are awful to contemplate.

However, in my view a more convincing explanation is that NATO governments, wrapped in a dimly lit world of distorted logic and hazy perceptions, are on the verge of making a gross mistake. The neutron bomb cannot solve the problem of making nuclear weapons usable. It cannot make use of nuclear weapons immune to retaliation. It solves nothing, but if NATO continues to dream it is a solution it may start thinking it can use nuclear weapons without having nuclear war, and that may be the most dangerous thought of all. It is likely we shall hear more of the neutron bomb, for its inventor, a tireless advocate, has now speculated that the USSR does actually have the weapon in its arsenal,[131] and, of course, as we know, if they have it, so must we.

How to Win World War III

During 1978 it seemed as if a new trend in strategic studies was beginning: two books appeared describing how World War III might begin and how it might proceed. The first, by General Hackett and others, appeared in the summer and put the war in 1985; it announced that General Hackett had been helped 'by experts of the highest calibre (some anonymously)'.[132] The other, written by a team (all of whom gave their names) led by Shelford Bidwell, came out a few months later, but made up for its tardiness by placing the war two years earlier, in 1983.[133] In the Hackett book, NATO wins the war, partly thanks to major increases in military spending by NATO countries for several years before the war. The Bidwell book ends with the war turning nuclear after NATO defences, weakened by inadequate spending during peace-time, have been overrun. So, two books, and two plots, with a single message: increase military spending.

By itself, this would not be very remarkable, but it is worth enquir-ing a little further into the two books for both contain two common assumptions: first, that in 1978 the military balance was pretty hopeless for NATO; second, that a greater military effort would permit NATO to win, or at least avoid losing, World War III. Since these theses are fairly widely accepted, both books may be fairly influential.

We can start by considering the quality of the works. Therefore, although nit-picking is not such a pleasant pastime, it is necessary to draw attention to a few flaws which, to be fair, are probably not very important. In the Bidwell book, if I took the table on page 41 seriously, I would probably conclude that neither East nor West European states imported any weapons between 1950 and 1974. I was also surprised to see from a map on page 61 that Sweden is a member of NATO, although this is offset by the news on page 137 that France is not a member – an understandable confusion, this, between withdrawing forces from NATO command and leaving the alliance. The reader may also be surprised to discover on page 136 that as war starts the US president must choose among options which apparently exclude using conventional forces. And it is embarrassingly necessary to point out that anybody who writes,

> The peoples of the Free World ... have a right to be enraged at the stupid and inaccurate way in which their journalists announced the so-called 'neutron bomb' in early 1978 (page 126)

should not be so stupid as to be inaccurate about when the neutron bomb appeared in the news – mid-1977, not early 1978.

Pointing these errors out is a little harsh, since why should facts get in the way of argument? But it does perhaps indicate that scrupulously providing accurate information for non-specialist readers was not the main concern of the Bidwell team. The Hackett team appears to score better on facts, but has a little inconsistency in describing how the war starts. While on page 49 we are told that the USSR had no master plan for conquering the world, but rather an opportunist foreign policy, thirteen pages later we are introduced to the fictional Ryabukhin Report which, to my eyes, looks remarkably like a master plan.

Part of the Hackett tale is based on major increases in military spending by NATO states, including Britain. As Britain emerges from the 1970s, political changes making this possible include shrugging off the 'massive burden of British trade unionism' and developing a new political approach, including the replacement of redistributive economic policy by 'more sensible attitudes'. Fortunately, devolution becomes less fashionable, Britain realises the world does not owe it a living, and support flags for 'what had previously been known as progressive education'. Crucially, the Scouts, Guides and St John's Ambulance all report rises in recruitment, as do the armed forces' volunteer reserves, while Officer Training Corps in universities become fashionable once more (pages 50-2). With all this, it is hardly surprising if military spending goes up.

In general, the Bidwell team manages to do without a similar assortment of unargued political prejudices, but does hinge part of the scenario on the indecisiveness of the British Labour government in 1983, 'the usual uneasy alliance of powerful left-wingers and timid moderates' (page 138). It is a little hard to understand how anybody can look at the history of post-1945 Labour governments, all dominated by the right and centre of the party with the left isolated and relatively weak, and come out with such a statement, but by that stage in the Bidwell book one is hardly concerned.

Military men are often accused of a syndrome known as 'fighting the last war' — that is, planning as if the next war will be like the last one — so it is refreshing to find that both books are quite unashamed about it. For Hackett, 'The situation at sea was uncannily reminiscent of the early months of the Second World War' (page 182), and while the Bidwell team are discussing the war in the Mediterranean we are told that 'Some might call it a futile struggle, but after all there was a precedent . . . established in these same waters 40 years before' (page 181). Even with a precedent the struggle might still be thought futile, so we are quickly reminded of Britain's long naval tradition (which is a little confusing since it is the US Navy which is doing the fighting).

It would be wrong to think of these two books as one. Notably, by Hackett's account the trans-Atlantic reinforcement convoy arrives successfully (losing just 12 out of 48 transports), an arrival suggestive of yet earlier wars since the convoy is code-named 'Cavalry', and is a crucial factor in eventual victory, whereas in the Bidwell book the convoy is a failure (losing 10 out of just 18 transports) and irrelevant as the nuclear holocaust begins. But the books do start from similar views and assumptions about the present, about the nature of military power and about the condition of British defence policy. In the end, both books are fantasies about the future based on fantasies about the present, even though the future-fantasies take different courses: the Bidwell book, predicated on continuation of what it sees as current NATO inadequacies, ends with nuclear catastrophe, while the Hackett book, with a more ambitious project, is predicated on improvements in NATO's military posture and political attitudes and ends with NATO victory – and in the process its logic runs out of control.

Readers of the Hackett book would presumably have various comments to make on the scenario of the war as it unfolds, on the extent to which it accurately reflects Soviet army tactics, Soviet strategic and political thinking, the developing technologies of warfare, and the degree to which its tale of the war's course convinces. But perhaps the basic point about the book is that the war occurs at all. That is, a presumably unintended moral of the story is that however much NATO states increase military spending (and even if Britain has a woman Prime Minister with a familiar artisan's name, Mrs Plumber), it is still not enough to deter the war.[134]

We can be thankful the fantasy collapses when it tries to go beyond showing the ill effects of what are thought to be bad policies and show the benefits of the 'right' policies. Otherwise, people might be tempted to take the fantasy more seriously. Both books set out to give advice on how to win World War III, and neither has any worth listening to, because the only important thing about World War III is that it must never happen, and the only important task is ensuring that it never does. Here, deterrence has a role to play – the very destructiveness of a future war must be something of a deterrent to it ever happening. But it cannot be relied on, for it is constructed around dangerous military strategies in both NATO and the WP, the former with its reliance on TNW, the latter with its emphasis on a swift offensive. Both depend on fast reaction and devastating firepower. There has to be a saner way of thinking about World War III: the challenge is to find it.

Notes

1. Julian Critchley MP, in *Official Report of the Eleventh Sitting of the Twenty-fourth Ordinary Session*, Assembly of the Western European Union, 22 November 1978, p. 4.

2. *The Sunday Times*, 18 June 1978.

3. S. Gervasi, 'Breakdown of the United States Arms Embargo', in Western Massachusetts Association of Concerned African Scholars (ed.), *US Military Involvement in Southern Africa* (South End Press, Boston, Mass, 1978).

4. T. Gervasi, *Arsenal of Democracy* (Grove Press, New York, 1977): sources are given as Congressional committees, the armed services, the Defense Security Agency, and major weapons manufacturers.

5. See L. Freedman, *US Intelligence and the Soviet Strategic Threat* (Macmillan, London, 1977), p. 9.

6. *Department of Defense Annual Report Fiscal Year 1979* (US DoD, 1978), pp. 75 and 80; General G.S. Brown, *United States Military Posture for FY 1979* (US DoD, 1978), pp. 69 and 109.

7. *Statement on the Defence Estimates 1978*, Cmnd 7099 (HMSO, London, 1978), p. 9.

8. Reported by R. Cook in *idem* and D. Smith, *What Future in NATO?*, Fabian Research Series 337 (Fabian Society, London, 1978), pp. 3-4.

9. *Assessing the NATO/Warsaw Pact Military Balance* (Congressional Budget Office, Washington, DC, 1977).

10. *Statement on the Defence Estimates 1976*, Cmnd 6432 (HMSO, London, 1976), p. 9; in more recent White Papers, the mode of expression of this fear has changed.

11. The Soviet view appears to be that the USA and USSR are 'about equal': *The Guardian*, 15 January 1977; since non-US NATO states mount far more military power than non-Soviet WP states, this would appear to concede the overall superiority to NATO.

12. B.M. Blechman *et al.*, *The Soviet Military Buildup and US Defense Spending* (Brookings Institution, Washington, DC, 1977), pp. 21-2.

13. *The Times*, 15 March 1976.

14. NATO is still apparently satisfied about warning time of a major WP offensive: *The Guardian*, 1 September 1977; *New York Times*, 15 September 1977.

15. M. Leitenberg, 'Background Information on Tactical Nuclear Weapons (primarily in the European context)', in SIPRI, *Tactical Nuclear Weapons: European Perspectives* (Taylor & Francis, London, 1978), pp. 22-3.

16. A.C. Enthoven and K.W. Smith, *How Much is Enough? Shaping the Defense Program 1961-1969* (Harper & Row, New York, 1971), especially Chapter 4.

17. 'Study Insists NATO Can Defend Itself', *Washington Post*, 7 June 1973.

18. *Christian Science Monitor*, 27 May 1975.

19. Brown, *United States Military Posture for FY 1979*, p. 105 (emphasis added).

20. L. Aspin, 'What are the Russians Up To?', *International Security*, Summer 1978, vol. 3, no. 1.

21. *Washington Post*, 7 June 1973.

22. See also M. McGwire, 'Western and Soviet Naval Building Programs 1965-1976', *Survival*, September/October 1976.

23. F.C. Iklé, 'What It Means To Be Number Two', *Fortune*, 20 November 1978.

24. *New York Times*, 23 February 1976, and 28 February 1976.

25. See, for example, Iklé 'What It Means To Be Number Two'; J.R. Schlesinger, 'A Testing Time For America', *Fortune*, February 1976.

26. *The Guardian*, 12 January 1977.

27. See, for example, W.T. Lee, *The Estimation of Soviet Defense Expenditures 1955-1975* (Praeger, New York, 1977), A.W. Marshall, 'Estimating Soviet Defence Spending', *Survival*, March/April 1976; for a review of the issues and methodologies, see P. Cockle, 'Analysing Soviet Defence Spending: the Debate in Perspective', *Survival*, September/October 1978.

28. L. Aspin, 'How to Look at the Soviet-American Balance', *Foreign Policy* 22, Spring 1976.

29. L. Aspin, *Are the Russians Really Coming?* (United Church Board for Homeland Ministries and Council on National Priorities and Resources, Washington, DC, 1976), p. 3.

30. *Statement on the Defence Estimates 1979*, Cmnd 7474 (HMSO, London, 1979), p. 8.

31. *The US Sea Control Mission: Forces, Capabilities and Requirements* (Congressional Budget Office, Washington, DC, 1977), pp. 36-40.

32. Cmnd 7099, p. 8; R. Cook, 'Mr Mulley's Balancing Act', *New Statesman*, 24 February 1978.

33. Admiral J.L. Holloway, *FY 1977 Military Posture of the United States Navy* (US DoD, 1976), p. 9; General G.S. Brown, *United States Military Posture for FY 1978* (US DoD, 1977), p. 77.

34. One comparison of the Soviet Navy with the total navies of NATO plus Australia, Japan, New Zealand, South Korea and Taiwan found that, excluding light patrol craft, the USA and its allies had a numerical superiority of 1,460 to 1,190: *New York Times*, 7 March 1977.

35. See Brown, *United States Military Posture for FY 1978*, p. 38.

36. This presence consists of about 190,000 army personnel, the 6th Fleet in the Mediterranean with two aircraft carriers, and 25 fighter/attack aircraft squadrons plus reconnaissance and transport aircraft in the region or within reach of it: *The Military Balance 1978-1979* (IISS, London, 1978), pp. 6-8.

37. Cmnd 7474, p. 9.

38. *Armed Forces Journal* January 1978; *Department of Defense Annual Report Fiscal Year 1980* (US DoD, 1979), p. 102.

39. S. Canby, *The Alliance and Europe Part IV: Military Doctrine and Technology*, Adelphi Paper 109 (IISS, London, 1974), p. 24.

40. *The Military Balance 1978-1979*, pp. 9 and 13-15; discrepancies between these figures and those in Table 4.1 taken from elsewhere in the same source need not alarm readers who should by now expect such things.

41. *Jane's Weapon Systems 1978* (Macdonald & Jane's, London, 1978), p. 332; here the T-64 and T-72 were regarded as one tank with two names, but they are thought to be two tanks: Brown, *United States Military Posture for FY 1979*, p. 70.

42. J. Record, *Sizing Up the Soviet Army* (Brookings Institution, Washington, DC, 1975). p. 25.

43. 'Tanks from the East and West', *Armies and Weapons*, September/October 1976.

44. R.D. Lawrence and J. Record, *US Force Structures in NATO: An Alternative* (Brookings Institution, Washington, DC, 1974), p. 12.

45. *Washington Post*, 7 June 1973.

46. R.L. Fischer, *Defending the Central Front: The Balance of Forces*, Adelphi Paper 127 (IISS, London, 1976), pp. 31-4.

47. *New York Times*, 15 September 1977.

48. Fischer, *Defending the Central Front*, pp. 15 and 25.

49. S.L. Canby, *NATO Military Policy: Obtaining Conventional Comparability with the Warsaw Pact*, R-1088-ARPA (Rand, Santa Monica, Calif, 1973); Lawrence and Record, *US Force Structures in NATO*.

50. Canby, *NATO Military Policy*, p. 13.

51. Quoted in *The Guardian*, 17 March 1977.

52. *Department of Defense Annual Report Fiscal Year 1980*, p. 71.

53. *The Military Balance 1976-1977* (IISS, London, 1976), pp. 106-8.

54. 'Could Russia Win an ICBM War?', *Flight International*, 2 September 1978; for examples of the mobile basing debate, see D.J. Ball and E. Coleman, 'The Land-mobile ICBM System: a Proposal', *Survival*, July/August 1977; C.S. Gray, *The Future of Land-based Missile Forces*, Adelphi Paper 140 (IISS, London, 1977).

55. *International Herald Tribune*, 15 November 1978, 16 November 1978, 22 November 1978 and 10 May 1979.

56. *Retaliatory Issues for the US Strategic Nuclear Forces* (Congressional Budget Office, Washington, DC, 1978), pp. 11-16.

57. C.A. Robinson, 'Soviets Push for Beam Weapons', *Aviation Week and Space Technology*, 2 May 1977.

58. *Allocation of Resources in the Soviet Union and China – 1977: Hearings before the Subcommittee on Priorities and Economy in Government*, Joint Economic Committee of the US Congress, 23 June 1977.

59. *Aviation Week and Space Technology*, 2 October 1978, 9 October 1978, 16 October 1978 and 30 October 1978.

60. G. Befeki, B. Feld, J. Parmentola and K. Tsipis, *Particle Beam Weapons* (MIT, 1978); see also Parmentola and Tsipis, 'Particle-Beam Weapons', *Scientific American*, vol. 240, no. 4, April 1979, and P. Laurie, 'Exploding the Beam Weapon Myth', *New Scientist*, 26 April 1979.

61. For example, H.F. Scott, 'Civil Defense in the USSR', *Air Force Magazine*, October 1975; E. Kozicharow, 'Nuclear Attack Survival Aspects Studied', *Aviation Week and Space Technology*, 14 November 1977.

62. L. Aspin, 'Soviet Civil Defense: Myth and Reality', *Arms Control Today*, September 1976, vol. 6, no. 9; F.M. Kaplan, *Dubious Specter* (TNI, Washington, DC, 1977), pp. 22-6; *idem*, 'Soviet Civil Defence: Some Myths in the Western Debate', *Survival*, May/June 1978.

63. *International Bulletin*, 3 December 1976.

64. *The Guardian*, 24 April 1977; *International Herald Tribune*, 14 November 1978.

65. R. Hodgson and R. Banks, *Britain's Home-defence Gamble* (Conservative Political Centre, London, 1978).

66. *International Herald Tribune*, 7 December 1978.

67. T.K. Jones and W.S. Thompson, 'Central War and Civil Defense', *Orbis*, Fall 1978, vol. 22, no. 3.

68. Kaplan, *Dubious Specter*, p. 25: this argument is based on data in an earlier article by T.K. Jones.

69. R. Cook, 'Challenge to Security', *New Statesman*, 8 April 1977.

70. 'Civil Defence or Internal Defence?', *State Research Bulletin* 8, November 1978.

71. *NATO Handbook* (NATO Information Service, Bruxelles, 1976), p. 17.

72. Dates taken from Leitenberg, 'Background Information on Tactical Nuclear Weapons', pp. 12-14.

73. *The Military Balance 1966-1967* (IISS, London, 1966), p. 14.

74. Leitenberg, 'Background Information on Tactical Nuclear Weapons', p. 8.

75. Ibid., p. 78; J.K. Miettinen, 'Enhanced Radiation Warfare', *Bulletin of the Atomic Scientists*, September 1977; *World Armaments and Disarmament: SIPRI Yearbook 1978* (Taylor & Francis, London, 1978), pp. 426-9.

76. *Department of Defense Annual Report Fiscal Year 1979*, p. 67.

77. Atomic Demolition Munitions (ADM) are nuclear explosives which could be buried and later detonated by timer or command, to create obstructions that could block or hinder WP advances, counter-attacks or withdrawals: *Employment of Atomic Demolition Munitions (ADM)*, FM 5-26 (HQ, Dept of US Army) August 1971.

78. *Department of Defense Annual Report Fiscal Year 1979*, p. 67.

79. 'United Kingdom Force Structure', *Market Intelligence Report* (DMS, Greenwich, Ct, 1976).

80. *The Sunday Times*, 2 May 1976.

81. Gervasi, *Arsenal of Democracy*, p. 209; *Jane's Weapon Systems 1978*, p. 407;

'Nuclear Weapons Systems', Memorandum submitted by the Minister of Defence in *Sixth Report from the Expenditure Committee Session 1978-1979: The Future of the United Kingdom's Nuclear Weapons Policy*, 348 (HMSO, London, 1979), p. 3.

82. *Annual Defense Department Report FY 1978* (US DoD, 1977), p. 148.

83. J.R. Schlesinger, *The Theater Nuclear Force Posture in Europe*, A report to the United States Congress (US DoD, 1975), p. 7.

84. *Planning US General Purpose Forces: The Theater Nuclear Forces* (Congressional Budget Office, Washington, DC, 1977), p. 6.

85. R. Rosecrance, *Strategic Deterrence Reconsidered*, Adelphi Paper 116 (IISS, London, 1975), p. 22.

86. Enthoven and Smith, *How much Is Enough?*, p. 125, n12.

87. *International Herald Tribune*, 25 January 1978 and 30 January 1978.

88. See B Brodie, 'What Price Conventional Capabilities in Europe?', in H.A. Kissinger (ed.), *Problems of National Strategy* (Praeger, New York, 1965).

89. Schlesinger, *The Theater Nuclear Force Posture in Europe*, p. 15; see also *Nuclear Weapons Employment Doctrine and Procedures*, FM 101-31-1 and FM FM 11-4 (Depts of the US Army and US Navy) March 1977.

90. E.J. Gaul, 'Electromagnetic Pulse', *Military Review*, March 1975.

91. See *Nuclear Blackout of Tactical Communications*, Nuclear Notes no. 4 (US Army Nuclear Agency, Fort Bliss, Tex, August 1976).

92. *Statement on the Defence Estimates 1975*, Cmnd 5976 (HMSO, London, 1975), p. 29.

93. R. Cook, '7,000 Warheads in Search of a Kill', *New Statesman*, 19 November 1976.

94. *New York Times*, 21 February 1977 and *The Guardian*, 7 January 1978.

95. A.C. Enthoven, 'US Forces in Europe: How Many? Doing What?', *Foreign Affairs*, April 1975.

96. R. Burt, *New Weapons Technologies: Debate and Directions*, Adelphi Paper 126 (IISS, London, 1976), p. 23.

97. J. Record, *US Nuclear Weapons in Europe: Issues and Alternatives* (Brookings Institution, Washington, DC, 1974), p. 18.

98. The modernisation process keeps on producing new facets and is not a watertight programme as such; for recent proposals, see *International Herald Tribune*, 13 June 1979.

99. *The Washington Post*, 6 June 1977.

100. In nuclear fission, energy is released through the splitting of atoms; in nuclear fusion, energy is released through the fusing of atoms, a process requiring intense energy which in currently deployed types is provided by a small fission device as the 'trigger'. Fission weapons are also known as atomic or nuclear weapons; fission-fusion weapons are also known as hydrogen or thermonuclear weapons. But in common usage and throughout this book, the term 'nuclear' embraces both types.

101. *A Primer on Nuclear Weapons Capabilities*, Nuclear Notes no. 6 (US Army Nuclear Agency, Fort Belvoir, Va, June 1977).

102. S.T. Cohen and W.R. van Cleave, 'West European Collateral Damage From Tactical Nuclear Weapons', in *RUSI & Brassey's Defence Yearbook 1976/7* (Brassey's, London, 1976).

103. F.M. Kaplan, 'Enhanced-radiation Weapons', *Scientific American*, vol. 238, no. 5, May 1978: 'kiloton' expresses the energy yield of a bomb – one kiloton is the equivalent to the energy released by 1,000 tons of TNT.

104. E. Burhop, *The Neutron Bomb* (CND, London, 1978), p. 11.

105. Kaplan, 'Enhanced-radiation Weapons'.

106. 'The Neutron Mess', *The Sunday Times*, 9 April 1978: in the narrative

which follows, details unsubstantiated by references are taken from this article; see also, S.T. Cohen, *The Neutron Bomb: Political, Technological and Military Issues* (Institute for Foreign Policy Analysis, Cambridge, Mass, 1978), pp. 5-8.

107. Colonel-Engineer M. Pavlov, 'Neutron Weaponry and Its Admirers', Novosti Press Release, 22 September 1978; Cohen, *The Neutron Bomb*, p. 27.

108. See S. King-Hall, *Power Politics in the Nuclear Age* (Victor Gollancz, London, 1962), p. 53; Cohen, *The Neutron Bomb*, pp. 13-30.

109. 'Why the West's New Bomb is in Limbo', *The Sunday Times*, 26 February 1978.

110. Leitenberg, 'Background Information on Tactical Nuclear Weapons', p. 53.

111. Ibid., pp. 54-5; it would appear that, although research on using neutron warheads on TNW was in progress, the 1973 Army funding request for eight-inch and 155mm nuclear shells did not refer to neutron explosives but to miniaturised conventional nuclear explosives, mininukes (see A. Frye, *Washington Post*, 17 July 1977 and G. Kistiakowsky, 'The ERW alias the Neutron Bomb', *Technology Review*, 1 June 1978), in which case they would have conformed to the wide definition of neutron weapons offered by Kaplan, 'Enhanced-radiation Weapons' (see text to n 103, above) even though they were not of the same design as the device which caused the controversy from June 1977.

112. A.S. Warshawsky, 'Radiation Battlefield Casualties – Credible', *Military Review*, May 1976.

113. S.T. Cohen, 'Enhanced Radiation Warheads: Setting the Record Straight', *Strategic Review*, Winter 1978.

114. Cohen and van Cleave, 'West European Collateral Damage'.

115. *Operations*, FM 100-5 (Dept of the US Army, July 1976).

116. *Collateral Damage*, Nuclear Notes no. 7 (US Army Nuclear and Chemical Agency, Fort Belvoir, Va, April 1978).

117. A. Collins, *Baltimore Sun*, 26 April 1978.

118. *International Herald Tribune*, 2 May 1978.

119. *The Guardian*, 9 March 1978 and 10 March 1978.

120. G. Pattie, MP, letter in *The Times*, 2 March 1978.

121. *Los Angeles Times*, 22 March 1978.

122. 'Furor over the Neutron Bomb', *Newsweek*, 17 April 1978.

123. For example, *The Sunday Times*, 9 April 1978; Lord Chalfont, *The Times*, 17 April 1978.

124. Editorial, *New York Times*, 6 April 1978; T. Sommer, *Newsweek*, 17 April 1978.

125. *The Sunday Times*, 9 April 1978.

126. Official Text of US Department of Energy Statement, and Excerpts from Press Briefing by T. Poston, US State Department, 19 October 1978, International Communication Agency.

127. *The Guardian*, 8 April 1978.

128. *New York Times*, 26 April 1978.

129. *International Herald Tribune*, 18-19 November 1978.

130. Ellsberg cited in *The Guardian*, 8 April 1978; E. Burhop, *The Neutron Bomb*, p. 12.

131. S.T. Cohen, *International Herald Tribune*, 10-11 March 1979.

132. J. Hackett *et al.*, *The Third World War August 1985* (Sidgwick & Jackson, London, 1978).

133. S. Bidwell (ed.), *World War 3* (Hamlyn, London, 1978): although, for the sake of brevity, I do not distinguish the individual essays in this book, it may be that not all the authors share all the views and assessments expressed in it.

134. This logic was also noted by a distinguished reviewer: M. Howard, *The Sunday Times*, 16 July 1978.

5 BRITISH DEFENCE POLICY IN THE 1970s

The 1970s opened with the election of a Conservative government which shortly increased military spending over the level it inherited from the 1964-70 Labour government and developed ambitious spending plans for the second half of the decade. But even before the Conservative government was defeated in the February 1974 general election some of its ambitions had had to be watered down. When Labour took office, under pressure from within the party to reduce military spending, it scrapped Conservative forward spending plans and set a target of a stable level of military spending through the rest of the decade, a target which was set aside in 1977 as part of a general NATO policy of increasing military spending from the late 1970s into the 1980s.[1] Until that policy took effect in Britain, with the 1979-80 budget, the last of the Labour government's military budgets in the 1970s, defence planners had had to accustom themselves to a squeeze on resources and a less ambitious military posture than they set out towards in the first years of the decade. As we shall see, the result was well short of satisfactory.

Yet by and large the Labour government achieved a stabilisation of military spending. As Table 5.1 shows, comparing annual spending in constant price terms, military spending under the 1974-9 Labour government never fell below the level it inherited from the Conservatives' 1974-5 budget. Fluctuations in the level of spending were relatively small and the increased budget for 1979-80 was still only six per cent higher than the level in 1974-5.

Table 5.1: Annual British Military Budget Since 1973 in Constant Prices

	1973-4	1974-5	1975-6	1976-7	1977-8	1978-9	1979-80	1980-1[a]
Defence budget in £ million at 1978 Survey prices	7,039	6,774	7,114	7,008	6,845	6,868	7,182	7,398
Change		−3.8%	+5%	−1.5%	−2.3%	+0.3%	+4.6%	+3%

a. Figures for 1981-2 and 1982-3 in Cmnd 7439 were notional, no expenditure decisions having been taken for those years, and are not shown here.

Source: *The Government's Expenditure Plans 1979/80 to 1982/3*, Cmnd 7439 (HMSO, London, 1979), Table 2.1.

This apparently successful administration disguises problems. Through the 1970s, the costs of military equipment continued to increase, far more quickly than inflation in the rest of the economy. Table 5.2 shows how the proportion of the budget spent on equipment has steadily increased, from 35 to 41 per cent, while that spent on manpower has equally steadily decreased, from 47 to 42 per cent. Yet the decline in personnel levels revealed in Tables 5.4 and 5.5 has been comparatively small. The result has been increasing strain on both the equipment and the manpower sections of the overall budget and a military posture which, impressive in outline, is tattered round the edges.

Table 5.2: Division of Military Expenditure By Main Categories, 1975-1979

	1975[a]	1976-7	1977-8	1978-9	1979-80	Average
Manpower	47%	45%	45%	43%	42%	44%
Equipment	35%	36%	37%	40%	41%	38%
(of which Production of new equipment		38%	42%	44%	44%	42%[b]
Production of spares		31%	27%	27%	26%	28%[b]
Research and Development		31%	31%	29%	30%	30%[b])
Other[c]	18%	19%	18%	17%	17%	18%

a. The 1975 *Statement*, Cmnd 5976, showed the shares of the total spent under these headings for 1974-5, *not* for 1975-6, and provided no breakdown of spending on equipment.
b. Averages here for 1976-7 to 1979-80 only.
c. Buildings, stores and miscellaneous services.

Sources: Successive issues of *Statement on the Defence Estimates*: 1975, Cmnd 5976; 1976, Cmnd 6432; 1977, Cmnd 6735; 1978, Cmnd 7099; 1979, Cmnd 7474 — (HMSO, London, annual).

Within this pattern of roughly stable budgets and an increasing proportion spent on equipment, the three services consume roughly equal shares of the whole (Table 5.3). This is the budgetary expression of the desire of the British state to maintain 'balanced forces', a desire which itself stems both from the view that a state with some pretensions to power should be able to mount forces able to carry out missions right across the military spectrum, or at least a respectable proportion of possible missions, and, in equal measure, from the roughly equivalent balance of power between the three services when it comes to politicking in Whitehall. As forces have been pulled back from imperial deployments around the world and squeezed by budgetary restraints, each service has successfully insisted that the other two must be equally

Table 5.3: Functional Analysis of British Military Expenditure

	Percentage of total expenditure[a]					
	1975-6[b]	1976-7	1977-8	1978-9[c]	1979-80	Average[d]
Nuclear Strategic Force	1.3	1.4	1.5	1.3	1.5	1.4
Naval General Purpose Forces	13.9	12.9	13.3	14.7	13.2	13.5
European Theatre Ground Forces	18.2	17.5	17.2	18.1	17.5	17.6
Other Army	1.9	1.1	1.1	1.1	0.9	1.1
Air Force General Purpose Forces	19.2	16.1	16.3	16	17.1	16.4
Reserve and Auxiliary	1.7	1.6	1.7	1.8	1.7	1.7
Research and Development	6.2[e]	12.4	13	12.6	13.4	12.9
Training	9.2	8.6	8.9	8.7	9.1	8.8
Production, Repair and Associated Facilities in Britain	7.5	7.3	7.1	6.5	6.9	7
War and Contingency Stocks	2.4	2.1	1.7	2.6	1.9	2.1
Other support	19.2	18.9	18	18.1	17.3	18.1

a. Totals may not add up to 100 due to rounding.
b. Figures for 1975-6 are not strictly comparable with other years since expenditure on Research and Development was split up among the other functional headings.
c. The figures for 1978-9 are more affected than those of any other year by receipts of offset payments from the Federal Republic of Germany.
d. Figures show average for 1976-7 to 1979-80 only.
e. This figure is the residue of spending on Research and Development not split up under the other functional headings.

Sources: Calculations based on sources for Table 5.2.

involved in trimming strengths and ambitions.

Civilian and service personnel directly employed by the military budget have decreased during the period of the 1974-9 Labour government, as Tables 5.4 and 5.5 show. Discrepancies between the two tables are probably due to Table 5.5 recording actual figures for the services' strengths, whereas Table 5.4 records the 'establishment' (that is, the intended) figure for each of the years. The total direct employment in 1979-80, including civil servants in the Department of Environment engaged on defence work and workers in the Royal Ordnance Factories, is about 643,000. To this figure should be added a further 400,000 or so jobs in industry meeting the military equipment programme, producing a total of about 1,040,000 jobs in Britain and abroad dependent on British military spending. The government estimates a further 140,000 or so jobs in industry derive from the production in Britain of military equipment for export.[2]

Table 5.4: Functional Analysis of Military and Civilian Personnel

Personnel in 000s[a]

	1975-6			1976-7			1977-8			1978-9			1979-80		
	Mil	Civ	Tot	Mil	Civ	Tot	Mil	Civ	Tot	Mil	Civ	Tot	Mil	Civ	Tot
Nuclear Strategic Force	2.6	3.8	6.4	2.8	4.1	6.9	2.8	4.2	7	2.8	4.1	6.9	2.5	4.4	6.9
Naval General Purpose Forces	34.3	10.9	45.2	32.7	9.9	42.6	32.7	9.3	42	32.4	8.4	40.8	32.2	8.2	40.4
European Theatre Ground Forces	100.7	30.3	131	103.1	30.1	133.2	102.6	29.2	131.8	101.8	28.2	130	98.4	27.7	126.1
Other Army	17.7	10	27.7	14.2	7.4	21.6	14.1	7.2	21.3	14.1	6.9	21	14.4	6.8	21.2
Air Force General Purpose Forces	61.4	14.5	75.9	56.6	12.7	69.3	54.7	12.1	66.8	53.7	11.6	65.3	53.8	11.4	65.2
Reserve and Auxiliary	2.5	3.6	6.1	2.6	3.6	6.2	2.6	3.6	6.2	2.5	3.6	6.1	2.5	3.5	6
Research and Development	1	33.1	34.1	1.4	36.7	38.1	1.3	35.2	36.5	1.3	33.7	35	1.3	33.2	34.5
Training	70.4	22.3	92.7	72.6	21.6	94.2	73.8	21.1	94.9	71.6	20.5	92.1	76.2	21	97.2
Production, Repair and Associated Facilities in Britain	10.4	98.4	108.8	9.5	97.5	107	9.6	93.5	103.1	9.9	88.3	98.2	9.7	87.2	96.9
Other Support	45.4	68.7	114.1	44.9	65.8	110.7	42.9	63.4	106.3	42.4	61.5	103.9	39	59.9	98.9
TOTAL[b]	346.4	295.6	642	340.4	289.4	629.8	337.1	278.8	615.9	332.5	266.8	599.3	330	263.3	593.3
Plus:															
Dept of Environment[c]		19			22			28			28			26	
ROFs[d]		23			22			23			23.5			23.5	
TOTAL			684			673.8			666.9			650.8			642.8

Sources: As for Table 5.2

a. The figures include foreign nationals employed locally by British forces.
b. The figure here is the total of those directly employed by the defence budget.
c. Department of Environment staff directly employed on defence work.
d. Employees in the Royal Ordnance Factories (ROFs) employed by the Ministry of Defence.

Table 5.5: British Service Personnel Strengths 1975-1979, in thousands

	1975	1976	1977	1978	1979[a]
NAVY and MARINES					
Officers	10.5	10.4	10.3	10	10
Servicemen and women	65.7	65.7	65.9	65.2	63.5
'Locally entered' personnel[b]	0.8	0.7	0.5	0.4	0.4
Total	77	76.8	76.7	75.6	73.9
ARMY					
Officers	18.7	18.5	18.2	17.7	17.1
Servicemen and women	148.4	151.3	149.1	143.2	141.1
'Locally entered' personnel	8.2	8	7.8	7.8	7.5
Total	175.3	177.8	175.1	168.6	165.7
AIR FORCE					
Officers	17.7	16.5	15.6	14.9	14.6
Servicemen and women	77.2	74.3	71.3	69.8	70.9
'Locally entered' personnel	0.4	0.4	0.3	0.2	0.1
Total	95.3	91.2	87.2	84.9	85.6
TOTAL[c]					
British personnel	338.2	336.7	330.4	320.7	317.2
'Locally entered' personnel	9.4	9.1	8.6	8.4	8
Total	347.6	345.8	339	329.1	325.2
RESERVES and AUXILIARY FORCES[d]					
Navy and Marines	37.1	36.5	36.6	35.1	35.3
Army[e]	170	170.7	179.7	187	191.8
Air Force	32	33.4	33.7	30.7	30.6
Total	239.1	240.6	250	252.8	257.7

a. Figures at 1 January 1979; for the other years, the figure given is for 1 April each year.
b. Men of all ranks recruited outside Great Britain.
c. Figures here and elsewhere in the table diverge slightly from those in Cmnd 7474, because totals in Cmnd 7474 do not always add up, due, one presumes, to rounding.
d. Includes both regular reserves and volunteer reserves and auxiliary forces.
e. Including the Ulster Defence Regiment.

Source: *Statement on the Defence Estimates 1979*, Cmnd 7474 (HMSO, London, 1979), pp. 81-4.

The 1970s saw a continuation of British withdrawal from its world-wide military role. Since the 1974 Labour government defence review, deployment has focussed on Europe, Britain and the eastern Atlantic, Channel and North Sea areas. Ground forces are deployed in Germany, in Britain for home defence, in Northern Ireland, with a small garrison left in Cyprus and another much smaller in Gibraltar. Naval forces concentrate on anti-submarine capabilities, with a lesser capability for operations against surface ships in the seas around Britain and out into the Atlantic, with a small force still in the Mediterranean. The air force is focussed on operations above the major land and sea deployments, for support of ground forces, maritime strike, reconnaissance and air defence, together with capability for long-range bombing. In addition the navy operates the fleet of four *Polaris* submarines equipped with ballistic nuclear missiles.[3] Deployments outside the NATO area are shown in Table 5.6, the most significant being in Belize in Central America and in Hong Kong.

Table 5.6: British Forces Deployed Outside NATO Area, 1979

	Army	Royal Navy	Royal Air Force
Antarctica		Ice Patrol Ship.	
Belize	$1\frac{2}{3}$ infantry battalions; artillery; air defence; engineers; helicopters; support.	Frigate.	*Harrier* aircraft; *Puma* helicopters; *Rapier* anti-air missiles.
Brunei	1 Gurkha infantry battalion.		
Diego Garcia		Naval Party.	
Falkland Islands		Royal Marines detachment.	
Hong Kong	3 Gurkha infantry battalions; 1 UK infantry battalion; Gurkha engineers; helicopters.	5 patrol craft.	1 Squadron *Wessex* helicopters.

Source: *Statement on the Defence Estimates 1979*, Cmnd 7474 (HMSO, London, 1979), paras 241-3 and Annex C.

But this brief outline of the basic statistics and deployments of British defence policy does not reveal the basic issues of policy, the underlying dilemmas and the major decisions which have to be faced. To understand these fully, it is necessary first to turn to the evolution of British defence policy since the 1950s.

Available Resources and Desired Capabilities

In 1957, the Conservative government's White Paper on defence announced its intention to 'make a fresh appreciation of the problem and to adopt a new approach to it'.[4] Since the Conservatives took office in 1951 there had been a series of reductions in defence spending, reducing the previous Labour government's rearmament programme to more manageable proportions. But now was the time to develop a new overall approach for defence to provide a stable basis for future planning; central to it were greater reliance on nuclear deterrence, with missiles to supplement and finally supplant bombers, reductions in British forces in Germany, a future elimination of fighter aircraft for air defence and the end of conscription. Commenting twelve years later on this White Paper, Lawrence Martin argued that its 'supposedly radical' approach was 'essentially traditional' – it was 'yet another attempt to continue the whole familiar gamut of British military roles within increasing economic constraints'.[5] One can make the same basic judgement about the attempts of successive British governments since 1957 to deal with the major problems of defence policy.

The evolution of policy from the 1950s is marked by withdrawal from Empire, narrowing the global scope of British military power, and by the increasing priority of the commitment to NATO. Yet this constant theme is punctuated by a series of chops and changes. Spending cuts from 1953 to 1959 were followed by five years of rising budgets and the abandonment of much of the policy of the 1957 White Paper. The major survivors from it were the end of conscription and the continuing search for a nuclear missile force. Conservative defence policy to 1964 showed no clear sense of direction or priorities – 'plotting the track of policy means logging a succession of tacks and jibes and course corrections, some of them very coarse corrections'.[6] The incoming Labour government in 1964 attempted to trim the military establishment with a defence review lasting to 1966. But the review was barely completed before further changes followed with the announcement of the intention to withdraw most forces from 'East of Suez' in 1967. The 1964-6 review had provided no stable basis for future policy because the need to resolve difficult questions of priorities was not confronted. Yet even the decision to withdraw from 'East of Suez' did not truly confront the tough questions: although it is retrospectively clear that it marked effective abrogation of most of the remaining British military world role, this was not the intention, for the idea was to do without permanent bases but to develop long-range air transport to fly forces quickly in to 'trouble spots'.[7]

The same White Paper affirmed there would be no change in the commitment to NATO in Europe, and by and large the Conservative government of 1970-4, although in opposition it had protested at the withdrawal from 'East of Suez', kept to the range of commitments left it by Labour. Defence spending was increased, but the increases were concentrated on NATO. By the time Labour returned to office, to institute a further defence review, there was no question of spreading imperial wings once again. With the exception of a few scattered bases around the world, the 1974 review completed the process of concentrating upon NATO in Europe, the eastern Atlantic and the seas around Britain, even withdrawing most forces from the Mediterranean. Within this framework the Labour government cut down its Conservative predecessor's ambitious forward spending programme, planning to stabilise defence spending for the rest of the decade. Reductions in planned spending were presented as defence cuts, and widely accepted as such in the press. But if the definition of a 'cut' is that less is spent after it, then the 1974 review resulted in no cuts. The reason for this shallow deception was an unsuccessful attempt to placate the left wing of the Labour Party which sought a reallocation of resources away from defence, and the Conservatives were naturally pleased to connive in the deception since it permitted them to attack the government for giving in to its left wing and cutting defence spending. Once again, the review was swiftly followed by further reductions in planned spending, largely achieved in the first phase by slippages in equipment programmes, abandoning some development work and penny-pinching in the availability of spare parts.[8]

Retrospectively, one can see that the optimism with which Martin concluded his 1969 study was unjustified:

> After years of disheartening retreat and upheaval, Britain is on the way to creating a compact and efficient military establishment designed for a fairly well-defined task . . . (T)he main lines of projected policy constitute a sound and sensible allocation of the resources being made available.[9]

Instead we have had increases in spending under the Conservatives until 1974, followed by a planned stabilisation of expenditure, followed by a series of marginal reductions, minor cancellations, delayed programmes and deferred spending, followed finally by a decision to meet NATO's target of a three per cent annual increase in spending for five years, taking effect from 1979.[10] In this, defence policy in the 1970s has followed the pattern set in the 1950s and 1960s: the chops and changes which punctuate British defence policy are themselves a constant theme of the policy over the past three decades.

Although this chopping and changing has been expressed in modifying strategic approaches or tactical doctrines, on each occasion its immediate roots are to be found in budgetary constraints. Successive governments have been unable to arrive at a stable match between the resources available for defence policy and the capabilities it is desired to have. The definition of available resources is, of course, subject to change depending on government decision. In general, the Conservatives like to make more resources available than Labour does, but the cuts in defence spending from 1953 to 1959 were carried out by a Conservative government pruning the plans left it by a Labour administration. Since 1957 the proportion of national wealth devoted to defence has declined from just over seven per cent of Gross Domestic Product to just under five per cent in the late 1970s, with increases in only two years, 1972 under the Conservatives and 1976 under Labour.[11] On present plans, with the three per cent annual increase in spending for five years, the GDP proportion will stabilise or increase slightly depending upon the economy's growth rate. Thus the failure to achieve a match between available resources and desired capabilities is not the sole responsibility of either one or the other of the two governing parties of the past 30 years.

It is not only government decisions which set the level of resources available; it is the outcome of economic performance as a whole and the way in which demands for shares of the national wealth are met as a result of the balance of power between social and political forces. No government is completely free to make resources available arbitrarily. But given the record of a slow but, over time, fairly steady decline in the share of GDP 'available', the enigma of British defence policy since the start of the 1950s is why it has been so difficult to match desired capabilities to resources. Undoubtedly, resource constraints in a context of increasing equipment costs place severe strains on the ingenuities of military planners, especially when tasked by the government with fitting a quart into a pint-pot, but why have governments so consistently demanded their quart? The fault cannot be laid wholly at the door of a succession of Cabinets and defence ministers: especially in the 1970s both the uniformed military and defence civil servants have constantly pressed for more resources, and undoubtedly tend to plan according to the resources they think ought to be made available rather than according to what is or is likely to be available.

To some degree the lasting failure to resolve the mismatch between resources and desired capabilities reflects a failure within the political and administrative elite genuinely to come to terms with Britain's decline. Perhaps one could say that for many years this was made harder by the fact that Britain's relative decline coincided with unprecedented economic growth rates: compared with other states Britain was worse off than ever before, yet compared with its past it was better off than ever.[12] In the 1950s the state attempted to sustain a position it held before 1939 which it could no longer afford; yet in the 1970s, when British decline is trumpeted in newspaper headlines and widely acknowledged, the effort is to keep Britain in a position it had in the 1950s, and which it can no longer afford.

Nostalgia and anachronistic pretensions do not constitute the whole explanation, however, for there is a second and quite different sense in which there is a mismatch between resources and policy. Britain has a major arms industry, among the largest if not the largest in Western Europe, which suffers perennial problems of surplus capacity. That is, given the demand for military goods provided by the defence budget, the industry requires a higher level of demand to absorb its potential output. This places continuous pressure on the state to increase military spending and continue major weapons programmes despite inexorable cost increases from one generation of weapons to the next, pressure which has not been eliminated by major reorganisation of the ship-building and aerospace industries culminating in nationalising them in 1977. Increasing arms exports is one way of utilising this excess capacity, but involves facing intense international competition from other states with their own problems of surplus industrial capacity, and faces its own particular risks. Management of British defence policy is a constant compromise between the availability of resources forever inadequate to provide desired capabilities, and the super-availability of military industrial resources able to produce what the budget cannot afford.

As the Ministry of Defence (MoD) contemplated spending plans from 1976 onwards it wistfully remarked, 'Forward planning of the defence programme is at present subject to an unusual degree of uncertainty.'[13] In fact, there is not much that is unusual in the 1970s about the need to chop and change — there has been no golden age of stability in defence planning since World War II. But it is the case that the problems intensify the longer the resources-capability mismatch remains unsolved.

Above the tangle of British defence policy since the mid-1950s stand two positive commitments — to NATO, and to the possession of a strategic nuclear force.[14] But the commitment to NATO has changed from one aspect of global military policy to the central rationale of defence policy. Since the 1950s the scope of defence policy has undergone a major reduction, but despite that the resolution of the resources-capability dilemma has evaded defence planners. At the end of the process Britain contributes significant air, ground and naval forces to NATO, including tactical and strategic nuclear forces. While the budget is lower than the French or Federal German budget, the force posture is more fully rounded and more widely extended than either, providing 'a balanced "mix" of capabilities' that is a substantial contribution from a state with Britain's economic debilities.[15] On the one hand, this rounded force posture can be seen as a mark of the success of British defence planning despite its economic constraints, although with shortages of spare parts and problems of morale the result is less impressive when examined closely; on the other hand, retention of this 'balanced "mix"' has been the particular form of the general failure to resolve the dilemma between resources and desired capabilities. For whatever else has happened, during the 1970s the forces' major equipment projects have tended to survive the reductions in planned spending. There has neither been a real effort to re-work the missions required of the forces committed to NATO in Europe, nor a government strategy enabling resistance to industrial pressure for the major projects to be continued, even though such a strategy is possible and has been spelled out.[16] And the result is a pattern familiar from the 1950s and 1960s: trying to do too much with too little and ending by doing most of it badly.

It has become fashionable to talk of military forces in terms of 'teeth' (combat forces) and 'tail' (the support infrastructure), a metaphor suggesting that spending on the 'tail' can be happily cut back without affecting the 'teeth'. A more appropriate metaphor than 'tail' would be 'gums' — when the gums are neglected, the beast becomes toothless. It is all very well keeping a rounded force posture with sophisticated weapon systems at its core, but not a great deal of it makes sense when RAF transport is cut right back, fuel and spare parts are in short supply, forces' living conditions inadequate, recruitment low and early departure from the forces high.

Moreover, the option which used to exist of reducing non-NATO non-European commitments was available only until withdrawal from Empire was completed; commitments outside Europe now have almost no budgetary significance. If there is to be another attempt to confront the resources-capability dilemma, either more resources must be made available or the core commitment to NATO must be pruned. The Labour government since 1974 was largely unable to make that choice; pressures from its left prevented increased resources being allocated to defence for most of its period of office, and pressures from its right and from the rest of NATO prevented it from planning for a lower level of resources. The strength of these latter pressures was tellingly revealed when Fred Mulley, Secretary of State for Defence, defended the government's record in Conservative terms, by listing the improvements in terms of army manpower and new weapons programmes he had seen through.[17] By 1978 if not before, the Labour government was politically incapable of generating its own concepts for defence policy; instead, it operated a pale imitation of what the Conservatives claimed they would do when back in office. Finally, a Labour government which once tried to win credit by deceptively claiming it had cut defence spending not merely accepted but welcomed the NATO decision to increase defence spending by three per cent annually for five years. But sadly for it and for the present government, three per cent is not enough to solve the basic problem: the budget increase could be swallowed up in making good minor deficiencies, and still leave hard choices over forthcoming expensive equipment projects.

Polaris

One such decision not only raises major issues of defence budgeting in the 1980s but should also force the British state to define the image it has of itself and its role in the world, the image it wishes other states and the British people to accept. This is the decision about whether or not to replace the *Polaris* nuclear force, and if so, how.

Under a 1962 agreement with the USA Britain was able to construct a force of five nuclear-powered submarines equipped with *Polaris* ballistic nuclear missiles. The force would be targeted according to NATO plans but could be used independently if Britain's 'supreme national interest' were jeopardised.[18] The 1964-6 Labour defence review cut the number of submarines to four, and the first was launched in 1966, the last in 1970. The submarines, which were built in Britain, each carry sixteen missiles of American manufacture, and each missile carries three British warheads with yields of 200 kilotons. Of the four submarines, never more than two and usually only one can be on patrol at any one time.

The MoD defines the force as 'an integral part of NATO's strategic nuclear force', although the US Pentagon has referred to it as part of NATO's forces for theatre nuclear warfare.[19] Given the relatively low accuracy of the missiles' multiple warheads, this suggests that *Polaris* is intended for use against major targets in Eastern Europe and perhaps the Western USSR, such as cities and major military bases. It is reasonable to speculate that its possible uses include the nuclear 'shot across the bows' — destruction of a non-Soviet WP city as a demonstration of resolve. Basic targeting information for the force comes from US satellites, and the force is probably included in the US Single Integrated Operational Plan for nuclear weapons.

This dependence on the USA effectively nullifies the effect of the clause in the 1962 agreement allowing independent British use and, even though *Polaris* can be seen as meeting 'a basic urge for independence, a say in the holocaust',[20] undermines that perspective. *Polaris* was the last step along a road which started with the decision of the 1945-51 Labour government to develop an independent nuclear force after the USA had excluded Britain from further nuclear weapons collaboration, which then led via the failed British *Blue Streak* ground-launched missile to a decision to purchase the US *Skybolt* air-launched missile, and finally, following *Skybolt*'s cancellation, to the 1962 agreement. The thinking of successive governments was always to do with an independent British force, and when the reality turned out rather differently the thinking in many quarters failed to catch up.

Although the Labour government refused to acknowledge it, a decision on *Polaris*' successor was almost certainly imminent in the late 1970s, and may, indeed, already have been taken. The estimated 'life' for the submarines is 20 to 25 years; since it takes a fleet of four boats to sustain a continuous patrol of one boat, the force will be effectively redundant as soon as the first boat goes out of service, an event likely around 1990, about 25 years after the first boat entered service. The submarines' operating life can be lengthened, most obviously by reducing the depth at which they patrol, but although this would lessen wear on the hull it is not clear that it would slow the build-up of background radiation from the submarines' nuclear reactors.[21] The decision to procure a new force would be required at least ten years before its planned entry into service, which means that the first years of the 1980s would be crucial.

Apart from these considerations, a deal of activity suggested the decision was imminent. From 1974 the Labour government ran a *Polaris* Improvement Programme also known as *Operation Antelope*, costing some £450 million at mid-1970s prices, apparently directed towards improving the ability of *Polaris* warheads to reach their targets by miniaturising them, enabling each missile to carry five or six warheads instead of three. It is hard to see why such a programme is necessary, since in the USSR there are almost no anti-missile defences through which *Polaris* warheads must penetrate, and in Eastern Europe there are absolutely no such defences. But as a way of keeping abreast of warhead technology, relevant not only to the existing force but also to a future one, and relevant not only to ballistic missiles but also to cruise missiles (see below), *Antelope* has some purpose. In Spring 1978 the MoD ordered a Cray-1 computer for the Aldermaston Atomic Weapons

Research Establishment, apparently this is a relatively unsophisticated 'number cruncher', ideal for solving certain problems of warhead design. In addition, several million pounds were committed to constructing an additional plant at the Chapelcross power station in Dumfries to provide an independent source of tritium, an essential ingredient of the British type of thermonuclear warhead.[22] The tritium plant could also be relevant if the army's new FH-70 howitzer, or its self-propelled version, the SP-70, were intended to fire nuclear shells.

Taken together these projects suggested that MoD had every intention of staying in the nuclear business and that, if the decision had not already been taken secretly by the time Labour left office in 1979, a powerful momentum had built up in favour of replacing *Polaris*. Intriguingly, Chapman Pincher 'revealed' that plans to keep a strategic nuclear force until the end of the century were 'far advanced', and that under Labour 'a technical decision' to replace *Polaris* with British-designed missiles had been taken.[23] In fact, by autumn 1979 the Conservative government, building on the groundwork laid by its Labour predecessor, was reportedly looking more favourably at the possibility of purchasing *Trident* missiles from the USA, to be armed with British warheads and fired from British-built boats, in a repeat of the 1962 Nassau agreement, though with less favourable financial terms. The new force would consist of five submarines, each firing 16 *Trident* missiles, with a much greater range than *Polaris*, and with perhaps as many as ten warheads per missile.[24]

The original decision in the 1940s to develop nuclear weapons was taken without the knowledge of the general public, Parliament, most of the Cabinet and much of the MoD. The crucial decision, after numerous small preliminary steps had virtually ensured development would be approved, was taken by an *ad hoc* Cabinet committee. Those who knew deliberately encouraged ignorance of the decision; not least, expenditure on nuclear weapons technology was hidden from public or Parliamentary scrutiny.[25] It appears that a similar pattern of events has occurred, again under a Labour government, even if the decision had not been taken by a Cabinet committee under Labour. Quietly, the way was opened for a Conservative government to take the actual decision. Only determined political pressure could have forced the decision, and the process which made the decision possible, to be at all open.

The issues weighed in the state's internal deliberations are unlikely to include the basic moral issues raised by the possession of nuclear weapons. The tendency to extend warfare to civilian populations, effectively invalidating the distinction between combatants and non-combatants, is taken to its fullest extent by nuclear weaponry. There is no moral argument which can justify such warfare, and it follows that to threaten such warfare is correspondingly immoral, even if the antagonist also threatens it. The possession of such power by the state not only raises questions of morality, but also tends to erode the principles of accountability of state actions, implicitly legitimising the extension and sophistication of the state's powers of control and secrecy.

We can be fairly confident that such issues will not figure in the state's own discussions or in the mainstream of debate on the issue. But if exponents of replacing *Polaris* seek instead a debate primarily on strategic grounds, it is not clear that their case can be a great deal stronger. As a contribution to the NATO-WP strategic nuclear balance, *Polaris* has little weight for either good or bad: its total of 192 warheads, of which a maximum of 96 can be fired at any one time, is of little significance beside American and Soviet totals of around 9,000 and 5,000 respectively, of which around 60 per cent can be used at any one time. The degree of overkill *Polaris* can add to the American overkill is of little if any meaning. So the argument for a replacement makes any sense only if it emphasises *Polaris* and its successor as an independent British force or as a down-payment for a future West European force independent of the USA. For those who wish to follow neither of these two routes, backwards to Imperial grandeur or onwards to a West European super-state, two other positions are available.

It is sometimes argued that if Britain had no strategic nuclear force, as, let us recall, the Pentagon has said was the case during the 1970s, then the only such force in Western Europe would belong to France. The unstated core of this argument is that Britain should arm not only in competition with presumed enemies but also with economic partners and political allies. The reason it has not been dismissed is because the view that possessing weapons of mass destruction gains status and prestige is too widely accepted, even though possession of *Polaris* has done nothing to halt Britain's economic and political decline.

On the other hand, it is often argued that the British force can technically be fired independently of the USA, and so could prevent the USA from reneging on its nuclear commitments to West European states by triggering a nuclear exchange. If the missiles can be fired independently, it is likely they would be extremely inaccurate, since the USA could simply withhold the latest targeting information from the satellite system which it alone possesses. This indiscriminacy might well not bother the British government. But it is not clear that firing *Polaris* would tempt the USA back into the fold; it is more likely to provide an object lesson in the costs of starting a nuclear war as Britain is incinerated by Soviet retaliation (and if we are worried about the USA ratting on Western Europe, we could be sure it would do its best to tell the USSR who it was who fired the first missile). It is, moreover, unlikely that British missiles will hold the USA more firmly to its NATO commitments than the presence of American troops and several thousand American nuclear warheads in Europe. We are back here with the arguments about the nuclear 'decoupling' of the USA and West European states encountered in relation to tactical nuclear weapons, and whatever the political significance of such arguments they are no more convincing in the context of Britain's nuclear force than they are in any other context.

This brings us to the arguments which regard *Polaris'* successor as a down-payment for a future unified West European nuclear force. These arguments depend on the assumption, first, that France would agree to pool its nuclear forces with Britain and, secondly, that other West European states would accept Franco-British nuclear leadership, as well as on a degree of wishful thinking about the prospects of solving the problems raised by rivalry within Western Europe. In fact, a unified West European defence system, though not under Franco-British leadership, is one possible outcome of current developments in West European politics. But it is not the most likely outcome and basing the decision on *Polaris'* replacement on a mirage of the future would be somewhat incongruous, though not much more so than basing it on a mirage of the past which is where arguments about an independent British strategic force take us.

These arguments are the unacknowledged core of most advocacies of replacing *Polaris*. They tend, however, to skate over the problematic and expensive fact that genuine independence in a future strategic force would also require investment in a sophisticated satellite system for surveillance and targeting. Even more marked by its absence from their case is a discussion of the uses of an independent force. Clearly, first use of nuclear weapons by Britain against the USSR must be expected to provoke overwhelming retaliation. It is therefore unlikely that a threat to use nuclear weapons would deter such prospects as a Soviet invasion of Britain or even a limited nuclear attack, leaving aside for the moment the likelihood of such events. A force of the size of the present one could cause horrendous destruction in the USSR, but the response would utterly devastate this small and crowded country, and this might occur both to the British Cabinet which might therefore be reluctant to make the threat and to the Soviet leadership which might therefore not take the threat seriously if it were ever made. The only circumstance in which Britain could use nuclear weapons against the USSR without needing to fear retaliation would be after Britain had been so annihilated by nuclear attack that there was nobody left in Britain to care.

An independent strategic nuclear force is both out of Britain's reach and anyway undesirable and useless. Yet this was the case in the early 1960s when the current force was procured. Paradoxically, if independence were a general aim for foreign and defence policy a strategic nuclear force would be the last thing for the British state to procure, for its practical effect has been to tie Britain more closely to the USA.

But there may be those who want a capability posthumously to incinerate Soviet citizens, or an irrelevant contribution to NATO strategic forces, or a prestige symbol against the French, or a down-payment on a possible unified West European defence policy. For them, the question of cost arises. No official estimates are to hand, but Ian Smart has produced convincing unofficial estimates of the cost of a force of five submarines, able to maintain a constant patrol of two submarines as a hedge against future improvements in anti-submarine warfare, each submarine carrying sixteen ballistic missiles equipped with three independently targeted, and therefore more accurate, warheads: in 1976 prices, he put the cost for development and production in a range between £2,245 million and £2,925 million.[26] This would absorb a large proportion of the equipment budget throughout the 1980s, making one wonder what other weapons projects the armed forces would be willing to sacrifice. It is therefore no surprise that advocates of staying in the strategic nuclear business have turned their attention to what seemed like a cheap alternative, cruise missiles, which are within Britain's technological reach and thought to be able to give Britain a new world role.[27]

There is a wide variety of cruise missiles, of varying ranges and capable of carrying nuclear or conventional warheads. Whereas ballistic missiles fly on a pre-set trajectory, cruise missiles fly under power, like aircraft but without a pilot. In the debate over *Polaris'* replacement the interest is in long-range cruise missiles (LRCM), which could be air-launched (ALCM), submarine-launched (SLCM) or even ground-launched (GLCM). During the 1950s the USA attempted to develop LRCM as strategic weapons; two shorter-range types, *Mace* and *Matador*, did enter service, but the long-range efforts were all unsuccessful. One, *Snark* developed by Northrop, had a sad habit of wandering off by itself after firing, and from firing ranges near Cape Canaveral in Florida several missiles cruised off to the Amazon jungle.[28] In the 1970s interest in LRCM for both tactical and strategic use was revived, based on the development of more efficient jet engines, of lighter conventional and nuclear explosives, and of micro-circuitry for the on-board computer.[29] The computer is the crucial technology in modern LRCM which can be thought of as computer-age versions of the German V-1 'doodlebug' flying-bomb used against Britain towards the end of World War II.

The belief was that with the aid of their computers LRCM would be extremely accurate as well as cheap. Small in size (fourteen to twenty feet long) and flying at altitudes as low as 250 feet they would be hard to detect on radar; they could be set meandering routes to deceive the enemy, and although flying at just about the speed of sound they could be shot down by surface-to-air missiles, they would be cheap enough to be procured in massive numbers, able to overwhelm enemy defences by saturation. To some, with their high accuracy, they seemed ideal for precise and limited nuclear strikes, even though this rather contradicted the idea of using them in large numbers. And although their technology is most advanced in the USA where development is being undertaken on the largest scale, it is within the reach of most countries with sophisticated aerospace and electronics industries, such as Britain, France, the Federal Republic of Germany, Italy and others.

But cheapness is a relative concept. Unit production costs for American ALCM have been calculated at $1 million for a run of 6,480 missiles, and for SLCM at $700,000 each for 1,160 missiles.[30] And when Smart costed a force of SLCM for Britain, assuming 17 submarines each carrying 24 LRCM, rejecting ALCM because airfields would be too vulnerable to surprise attack, he arrived at an estimate of between £2,740 million and £3,430 million, in 1976 prices, which is a higher range than he gives for a force of submarine-launched ballistic missiles.[31] A more recent study supports Smart's conclusions.[32]

Enthusiasm for strategic LRCM has waned on grounds other than cost. The testing programme in the USA has had numerous problems with engine failure and malfunctions of the guidance system.[33] There has been some consternation in the USA at reports, first denied but now confirmed, that Soviet fighters have successfully shot down missiles 'equivalent' to LRCM,[34] and at a report that the USSR is deploying a new surface-to-air missile, the SA-10, with high speed and great acceleration.[35] It is worth adding that some of this alarm seems to forget that the point of LRCM was to overwhelm defences by numbers, in which case losing even 1,000 to fighters and SA-10s would not matter. But it is clear that the manufacturers' original sales talk is beginning to sound a little hollow. The USAF, which has always argued that LRCM could only be an adjunct to manned bombers, not their replacement,[36] has now developed a doctrine for the bomber to fire LRCM shortly before entering enemy air space and then fly on to attack the main target — the so-called 'shoot and penetrate' concept.[37] And whereas it might once have been accused of blind allegiance to manned bombers, the USAF's view now has more support, and does tend to undermine the view that SLCM could be strategic weapons in their own right.

There is no cheap miracle waiting to provide *Polaris'* successor. At present, Britain, like France, has a fairly small development project for cruise missiles,[38] but this might relate to a shorter-range tactical missile. Cruise missiles are technologically available, but opting for them to replace *Polaris* will neither avoid the budgetary dilemmas nor restore faded glories.

In 1974 a Labour government was twice elected on manifestoes which included a pledge not to produce a new generation of strategic nuclear weapons. For the May 1979 election, the pledge was watered down to virtually nothing, and in between the groundwork was laid for, as it turned out, the Conservative government to proceed with replacing *Polaris*. At the time of writing, there has been no official statement confirming reports that the intention is to purchase *Trident* missiles, or to replace *Polaris* in any other way. It seems, however, that one will not be long delayed.

Replacing *Polaris* is little short of idiotic: for no gain, except a vain, shabby and transparent attempt at being a great power, MoD is apparently willing to sacrifice other equipment programmes. Purchasing *Trident*, rather than developing and producing missiles in Britain, will not reduce the costs of replacement by much. MoD should be asked to specify which other equipment programmes it is prepared to sacrifice. But it is more likely that the dilemma is being ignored in the hope it will go away. A decision to replace *Polaris* could be made on the cheap by upgrading nuclear-armed *Tornado* aircraft from tactical to strategic bombers, simply by changing the label; after all, when *Polaris* entered service, bombers previously designated strategic were downgraded to tactical. This would probably fool very few people, but it would be a cheap way of keeping the strategic nuclear status symbol, and is only a little more of a sham than most of the arguments favouring replacement of *Polaris*. On the other hand, replacing *Polaris* at full cost will simply be a further sign of the ineptitude of British defence planning.

The Multi-role Tornado

During the 1970s, debate about the future of the Royal Air Force (RAF) has largely meant debate about a single aircraft, the *Tornado*, formerly known as the Multi-role Combat Aircraft (MRCA), which will be the RAF's main front-line combat aircraft through the 1980s. It is a tri-national project between Britain, the Federal Republic of Germany (FRG) and Italy, produced by Panavia, a Munich-based consortium of companies from the three countries established especially for the project. It is Western Europe's major current military aerospace project, and in Britain alone is estimated to provide at peak, a total of about 36,000 jobs.[39] At present, Italy is expected to take 100 copies of *Tornado*, the FRG 322 and Britain 385 of which 165 will be a British-only air defence version, giving a total production run of 807 copies. In 1978, the government estimated the unit production cost at £7.9 million, and £9.4 million for the air defence version;[40] including the cost of research and development gives a bill for the British share of the project of about £4,000 million, and including the costs of operation and support gives a 'lifetime' cost for Britain of about £8,800 million.[41] Many commentators see *Tornado* as a model of West European collaboration, politically desirable as an example of unity in action, and practically necessary since none of the three states could have afforded the project independently.

For Britain, the history of *Tornado* goes back to the 1957 defence White Paper which announced the government's intention to reduce tactical air power in Europe, supplement manned bombers with missiles and eventually replace air defence aircraft by surface-to-air missiles.[42] Although these proposals did not come to much in the years that followed, they contributed to crisis in the aerospace industry and were part of a lively debate within the MoD about the future of air power. It was in the late 1950s that the concept for manned bomber operations of a fast and low-level penetration of enemy air space was developed;[43] in accordance with this concept, development work on the TSR-2 bomber and reconnaissance aircraft was started in 1959 by the newly formed British Aircraft Corporation, a merger of Vickers and English Electric. It is to this concept of bombing operations that *Tornado* in its strike role conforms.

Development of TSR-2 was ended in 1965 as part of the Labour government's 1964-6 defence review, apparently because of cost which the government estimated, for research, development and production, at £750 million for 150 aircraft.[44] But although TSR-2 was cancelled, the operational requirement it would have met was allowed to stand, and the intention was to meet it by purchasing American F-111 medium bombers, but problems in F-111 development led to cancellation of the order in 1966-7. Meanwhile, BAC joined with the French company of Dassault to develop a variable geometry (that is, swing-wing) multi-role aircraft, known simply as the Anglo-French Variable Geometry project

(AFVG). It was to be used for reconnaissance, air defence, and strike against land and sea targets. Neither Dassault nor the French government were enthusiastic about AFVG and withdrew from the project in 1967. For a year BAC worked on the UK Variable Geometry aircraft (UKVG) until new collaborators could be found; in 1968 UKVG was laid to rest as MRCA was born.

For the other participants *Tornado* also goes back a long way, to a 1958 NATO study which called for an aircraft capable of vertical take-off and landing for air combat and ground attack.[45] The FRG and the USA collaborated for a period on a project like this until the USA pulled out, leaving the FRG also looking for collaborators in a project to satisfy its air force requirements for the mid-1970s. In 1967 a working group was formed in which the Belgian, Canadian, Dutch and Italian governments joined with the FRG to discuss their requirements and see if they could be met by a single project. In 1968 the British government joined these five in initialling a Memorandum of Understanding declaring their common interest in developing a multi-role variable geometry aircraft of which a total of about 1,200 were expected to be produced. But within a year the six-country project became a three-country project: Belgium and Canada pulled out in late 1968 because of premonitions of excessive cost, and the Netherlands followed in mid-1969 shortly after the joint design for MRCA had been produced in a whirlwind, highly pressured few weeks from the end of January 1969 to the beginning of March; it was in those few weeks that the companies melded their different concepts and preferences into one.[46]

The project has generated a complex system of contracts, sub-contracts and sub-sub-contracts designed to provide each country with work in proportions which reflect the investment in the project made by each government (Britain and the FRG invested 42.5% each and Italy 15%).[47] BAC was responsible for development of the nose and rear fuselage, the German Messerschmidt-Boelkow-Blohm (MBB) for the centre-fuselage and Aeritalia for the wings. The prize airframe contract, for the centre-fuselage, thus went to a company, MBB, which lacked experience in variable geometry even though BAC's experience in this technology not only included AFVG and UKVG but pilot projects going back to 1945. This decision, unwise at first sight, was the outcome of the intense bargaining about the parcelling out of contracts which is a feature of all collaborative projects. Without the FRG and the large order it was expected to place, Britain and Italy could not have contemplated MRCA. Moreover, Rolls-Royce of Britain was bound to dominate development of the aeroengine, so the British had to concede design leadership in the airframe as a plum to guarantee the FRG's participation.

Development of MRCA has been plagued by delays, perhaps because of this unwieldy system of contracts, or because of the need to establish new multinational bureaucratic structures to run the project, or because of deficiencies in the original hastily produced design. In 1967, the FRG was hoping for an operational aircraft in the mid-1970s. In October 1973, Panavia expected the maiden flight in early 1974,[48] but this was delayed until August of that year because of engine problems.[49] In 1973 it was also thought that MRCA would enter service in 1977, yet by 1977 the British government did not expect entry into service until the early 1980s.[50]

This four year delay is the more remarkable since the maiden flight was delayed only six months. Some of the cause of it can be traced to the failure of Marconi-Elliott Avionics Systems (MEASL) to fulfil its development contract for the Stores Management System (SMS), that is, the main weapons computer. MEASL received the contract in 1972 and announced in 1974 it could not fulfil it; responsibility for this failure was attributed to the governments by a British defence minister, William Rodgers, who suggested that the contract's design specification had been over-ambitious and insufficiently detailed.[51] MEASL received the contract from the British government for a new SMS, but the FRG gave the new contract to an American company; the new SMS is less ambitious, which means that the aircraft will have less flexibility and capability than was thought necessary in 1972. There have also been difficulties in achieving a high enough airspeed — which came to light partly through the criticisms of an aviation scientist who worked on the project for a period, and partly through French and Swiss sources.[52] By May 1977, however, *Tornado* was apparently flying happily at about twice the speed of sound,[53] but further delays in deliveries resulted from changes shown to be necessary by the flight test programme.[54]

The important thing about *Tornado* is that it is a multi-role aircraft. Providing multiple capabilities, it is argued, permits production runs to be longer, thus lowering unit costs, and means that fewer types of aircraft are required, which both rationalises support and logistic arrangements and reduces total expenditure on research and development. It has even been suggested that having multi-role aircraft means that lower numbers of aircraft can be procured since each can perform more than one role, but this argument does not hold up since no aircraft can do more than one job or be in more than one place at any one time. Lower numbers of aircraft are procured now, but this is because, multi-role or not, they are more expensive than they used to be.

Table 5.7 shows the six different roles, plus training, demanded of MRCA by the participating governments as the project got under way. Together they look remarkably like the roles AFVG was being developed for in the mid-1960s, with air superiority and close support added on. This unprecedented range of roles led to it being dubbed in the FRG 'the egg-laying wool-producing milk-giving sow';[55] none of the three governments alone would have developed such an ambitious project, and there are several reasons for believing it has not made sense to try and get sows to lay eggs, especially when hens do it so much more comfortably.

Table 5.7: Roles of MRCA Tornado

Long-range strike and interdiction:[a]	for Britain, FRG
Land-based strike at maritime targets:	Britain, FRG
Close support of ground forces and battlefield interdiction:	Britain (secondary role), Italy
Air superiority:[b]	FRG (secondary role), Italy
Reconnaissance:	Britain
Air defence interception:[c]	Britain
Training:	All three

a. Interdiction missions aim to hinder enemy movement and activity by attacking airfields, concentrations of force, depots, railyards and railways, communication centres and so on.
b. The aim here is to gain command of a given area of air space, such as above the ground forces; also known as the air combat role.
c. This role will be met by a separate version of the *Tornado* developed individually by Britain.

Sources: *MRCA Fact Sheet* no. 1 (Panavia, Munich, October 1973); 'MRCA Programme Entering Production Investment Phase', *Interavia* no. 4, 1973; 'Operational Aspects of MRCA', *Flight International*, 28 March 1974; *Air Extra*, July 1977.

There is a general problem with multi-role aircraft, indeed, with any multi-purpose machine: they tend to do each task less efficiently than aircraft specialised for that task. The aircraft must have the performance characteristics needed to satisfy the most demanding role, and when less demanding roles are being carried out these sophisticated capabilities can be not just unnecessary but an actual hindrance, as the US Air Force discovered in South-east Asia.[56] The different roles place different and contradictory demands on the airframe and engine. Thus *Tornado*'s engine must be capable of a fast rate of climb and powerful acceleration, but have low fuel consumption for cruising on patrol; the airframe must be light enough for high manoeuvrability, but large enough for stable flight at low level at about the speed of sound. The wing-loading (the ratio between the aircraft's weight and the surface area of the wings) is ideally different for fighter aircraft and strike aircraft, and different again for the short take-off and landing demanded of it for close support of ground forces.

In fact, *Tornado*'s multiplicity of roles is rather less impressive when examined closely. Each additional capability increases the cost of the final product, but close support aircraft must operate in the face of dense opposition from surface-to-air missiles, anti-aircraft guns and enemy fighters; the preferable aircraft would be both cheaper and more rugged than *Tornado*. There may be an understandable reluctance to commit such an expensive product to this role. And the final design of *Tornado* appears to stress strike bombing to such an extent that it is hard to accept it could perform adequately as an air combat fighter. An analysis from a respected journal states that MRCA was recognised by the participating governments to be unsuited for close support and air combat as far back as 1970.[57]

If these two roles are cut out we are left with the requirements stated for the AFVG, and with the feeling that the Italian government has been sold a pup, though it could obviously still use *Tornado* in other roles. Of the remaining roles, Britain already has *Harrier* and *Jaguar* aircraft for battlefield interdiction, with a replacement even now under discussion, and numerous aircraft can carry out reconnaissance missions — there is no reason why a few extra *Jaguars* could not have been produced to extend their coverage of a role in which they already operate.[58] The MoD has argued that, as an aircraft, the *Tornado* air defence version will not be much better than the *Phantom* aircraft it will eventually replace, but that 'the weapon system is a complete step ahead',[59] which means that although the aircraft itself is not so hot, the missile, radar and main computer are major improvements on *Phantom*'s equipment.

And this brings us, finally, to the strike missions. What the RAF has got, what it has wanted and been fighting for ever since the 1957 defence White Paper threatened the future of manned bombers, is a modern, sophisticated, high-speed low-level bomber. It will be noted that the Federal German air force has got the same thing; for the FRG *Tornado* is a back-door entry to the long-range bombing mission, and Britain has helped it through that door so it too could stay in the bombing business.

One problem with a major collaborative project such as *Tornado* is that it is far harder to cancel. The agreement covering development and production is an inter-governmental agreement, with far more force than contracts between individual governments and corporations. Particularly once the project was well advanced, no single government could risk pulling out of it for fear of the retaliation it might face, in, for example, the various fora of the EEC. What is extraordinary is that there are some who believe that this difficulty in cancelling a project is a positive advantage.[60] Removing the ultimate form of control over a project, cancellation, necessarily decreases the ability of any individual government to control by sanctions the multinational consortia and bureaucracy it helped establish to run the project. Unforeseen delays, cost increases, mal-design, technical deficiencies, changes in the strategic environment, basic alteration of the original underlying rationale for the project — none of these need hinder a multinational project's steady progress to its consummation.

Yet all the signs are that the 'success' of *Tornado* and of collaboration has entered the official orthodoxy. The British government is eager to move on to a further collaborative project, so far identified only as Air Staff Target 403 (AST-403), to replace its current *Harrier* and *Jaguar* ground attack aircraft. Optimistically, it has been suggested that what is in hand is a 'cheap, simple fighter',[61] but there is already evidence of the temptation to produce another international cross between a hen, a cow, a sheep and a sow.

It has been reported that the British want the new aircraft to be capable of both supersonic speed and vertical/short take-off and landing;[62] already this is enough to eliminate both cheapness and simplicity. A slightly later report stated that vertical take-off and landing would not be required, but that both high manoeuvrability and a heavy weapons load would be,[63] and as time goes by AST-403 is being transformed from a cheap fighter into an aircraft for close support and battlefield interdiction which is also fully capable of air combat.[64] This evolution has occurred even before the attempt has been made to reconcile RAF requirements with those of other air forces that might collaborate. But the prospects for collaboration on the model of the *Tornado* project are not clear; an authoritative West German commentator has suggested that collaboration would be more complex the second time round because of conflicting requirements, with the FRG more interested in a specialised fighter aircraft, and MBB, the German participant in *Tornado*, has underlined this by undertaking studies on a future fighter together with McDonnell Douglas of the USA.[65]

Although this by no means rules out collaborative development of AST-403, it does seem probable that it will not materialise as an operational aircraft before the end of the 1980s. Both *Harrier* and *Jaguar* are undergoing improvements, with a 'Super *Jaguar*' already wheeled out, and *Harrier* has been modified both for operations from anti-submarine cruisers and in joint work with McDonnell Douglas who produce *Harrier* under licence in the USA for the US Marines.[66] Difficulties over collaboration may combine with pressure on the equipment budget to force upon MoD an incremental process of modifying existing types rather than producing a completely new aircraft. But there is little doubt that MoD's preference is both to go for a completely new type and to maintain the full range of missions by getting one aircraft to perform as many roles as possible. We have seen with *Tornado*, its multiplicity of roles shrinking under closer inspection, how illusory it can be to rely upon multi-role aircraft, but if it is thought impossible to do without certain roles then there is no other way. *Tornado* is a physical embodiment of the failure to resolve the dilemma between resources and desired capabilities.

The Royal Navy

Withdrawal from Empire has steadily reduced the scope of British naval deployment; with almost no forces left in the Mediterranean, and only small units outside the NATO area, of which the largest is a single frigate at Belize in Central America, the duties of the Royal Navy (RN) are concentrated on operating the *Polaris* force and on the eastern Atlantic, Channel and North Sea where it constitutes around 70 per cent of available NATO forces. Where once it was the global instrument and symbol of British power, the RN's main task now is anti-submarine warfare (ASW), with secondary capabilities for operations against surface ships, preparing for the task of seeing American reinforcements safely to Europe.[67]

The importance of trans-Atlantic reinforcements in a future war is a subject of unresolved and perhaps unresolvable debate. It is not clear that war in Europe would last long enough for reinforcements and their transports to be assembled in the USA, cross the Atlantic and arrive in time to have a role to play. Those who believe that the WP will reach the Rhine in two days and the Channel in a week implicitly hold that the war will be lost before the Americans arrive. On the other hand, both sides deploy such immense destructive power that they might have fought each other to a standstill, leaving only a nuclear graveyard by the time reinforcements appear. Moreover, reinforcements must not only cross the Atlantic, but disembark in Europe in ports the WP would almost certainly have attacked, and if they could disembark they would then have to travel to the battlefield along roads and railways which could also be destroyed.

The real problem is probably not whether reinforcements can cross the Atlantic. In normal peacetime conditions, only three or four Soviet submarines are deployed in the Atlantic, and to gain access to the Atlantic additional submarines must pass through the gap between Britain, Iceland and Greenland where strong ASW 'barrier' systems give NATO ASW forces an important advantage. Barrier systems are backed up by NATO submarines, ASW aircraft and surface ships escorting the reinforcement convoys, adding up to a formidable 'gauntlet' Soviet submarines must 'run'.[68] Although it would undoubtedly take time sharply to reduce Soviet submarine forces with this gauntlet system, the difficulties faced even by the first convoys in the Atlantic seem easier to overcome than those they would face once they reached Europe. Partly through awareness of this, and partly to bring some reinforcements in more quickly, emphasis has also been placed on pre-positioned warstocks in Western Europe, available for US troops flown in by civil airliners. The problems here are both expense, since each US division earmarked for airborne reinforcement must have a full equipment inventory in the USA for training as well as in Western Europe where the pre-positioned stocks must be maintained and guarded in peacetime, and its feasibility, because of the problem of keeping airfields with long enough runways open in the face of WP attacks.

If an assessment of the European military balance depends partly on seaborne reinforcements, then it could be argued that there is a clear need and role for adequate naval strength to assure their passage, and the RN's contribution to ASW in the eastern Atlantic is certainly not peripheral in this perspective, but problems attached to the arrival of the reinforcements suggest the RN may have some difficulty in carrying conviction in planning for its major task. Clearly defined though the task is, it could yet turn out to be marginal.

The decision to withdraw forces from 'East of Suez' was reflected not only in narrower naval deployment but also in the parallel decision to forego new aircraft carriers. This was based on the view that the use of carrier-borne aircraft to support ground forces could be more cheaply replaced in the areas of most concern to the British state by using landbased aircraft. The only reason to keep aircraft carriers would be for a maritime role unsupported by land-based aircraft, such as in the Indian Ocean, from which it was planned to withdraw; no rationale was left for procuring new aircraft carriers.[69] But it was not only carriers' strategic role that concerned the RN: aircraft carriers were the modern capital ship, the core of naval force structure and the flagship of the fleet, and although the navy could not reverse the decisions which eliminated its traditional world role, it could resist the impact they would have on its shape and self image.

The 1964-70 Labour government rejected naval proposals even for small aircraft carriers, but when the Conservatives took office in 1970 the idea was revived, and in 1971 a programme to construct Through-deck Cruisers was announced. During the 1974 Labour defence review these changed their name to ASW Cruisers and in May 1977, two years behind schedule, *Invincible*, the first of three, was launched.[70] By then it had been decided to procure a maritime version of the vertical take-off jet *Harrier*; each ASW Cruiser can carry five *Sea Harriers* and ten ASW helicopters, at a total unit production cost of £150 million in 1977 prices.[71]

In the 1960s the idea of the small aircraft carriers was simply to spread maritime air power by purchasing smaller and cheaper units. Although the basic idea has endured, albeit with some modifications, the rationale has changed. The ASW Cruisers will operate as the command ships of ASW task forces, as well as being ASW weapon systems in their own right. Expensive and attractive targets, they will be protected by frigates and destroyers from the very submarines they will go out to hunt, and by surface-to-air missiles from air attack. The decision to put *Sea Harrier* on the Cruisers turned them into 'genuine' aircraft carriers, even if small ones (the largest American carriers have about 90 aircraft on board). This is the only kind of aircraft carrier Britain could have afforded, and the only kind which could be rationalised in terms of current naval missions. Perhaps symbolising the 1970s' Labour government's acceptance of the reversal of the decision against aircraft carriers made by the 1960s' Labour government, the third ASW Cruiser will be named *Ark Royal*, the same as the RN's last 'proper' aircraft carrier which was paid off in 1978.[72]

In operations over land *Harrier* has appeared an extremely effective aircraft, but it has also proven extremely difficult to fly, requiring the best pilots and a conversion course longer than normal to become accustomed to it.[73] Changes for *Sea Harrier* have concentrated upon electronics,[74] and flying it from the Cruisers will probably be even harder than it is on land. And it is not clear that in return the RN will receive a particularly effective weapon system. An official from the MoD described it to a House of Commons committee as part of the ASW task force's air cover, but it is not primarily an air-to-air fighter, and the aircraft against which it is expected to use *Sea Harrier* are the relatively old *Badger* and *Bear* Soviet bombers which are also used for reconnaissance and mid-course guidance for missiles, in the hope that there will be no better replacement for them during the 1980s.[75] But it is not certain that *Sea Harrier* and its air-to-air missile could deal with either of these two except with very good radar warning and the advantage of surprise, and it is possible that it will also have to face the newer supersonic *Backfire* bomber.[76] It can probably chase all three types out of an area of air space, but it is not so sure it can shoot them down which one would have thought was the point of the exercise. Under pressure about *Sea Harrier*'s apparently limited capabilities, the same MoD official came up with a neat formulation: 'The Harrier will be versatile within the limits of its capabilities',[77] which sounds impressive but could equally well be said of bows and arrows and is no answer to the criticism that a lot of money is being spent for little purpose.

It is, in any case, not clear that the ASW task forces will need their own carrier-borne air cover since, at least in 1976, they were expected to operate under most circumstances within the range of land-based air cover.[78] This raises a possibility that underlying the RN's and MoD's insistence on having *Sea Harrier* and mini-carriers is the expectation or hope of having another task for which they would be more clearly suited. Speculation about this is given a little further force by doubts that ASW Cruisers are the best way of carrying out the ASW mission; in general, the most effective forms of ASW are submarines supplemented by land-based ASW aircraft such as the current *Nimrod*. Vice Admiral McGeogh has forcefully argued that the ASW Cruisers will be expensive, vulnerable and incapable of performing any one of their missions to adequate standards[79] – a familiar criticism of multi-role weapon systems. Where surface ships have a role in ASW it is hard to see an immediate justification for them being as large and expensive as the Cruisers, nor is it obvious that a command vessel must be larger than the ships under its command.

One is therefore entitled to speculate that the RN and MoD have had half an eye to possible future actions where what are essentially air-to-ground attack aircraft flying from ships could be handy assets. That is, ASW Cruisers and *Sea Harrier* keep open the option for a limited use of force in the future, overseas and outside the NATO area. The destroyers and frigates which are the other main components of the ASW task forces will have long enough cruising ranges to support the Cruisers in such actions. There can be no proof that is the intention behind the present shape of naval force structure; even close to home bases, long cruising ranges are justifiable as a way of extending the time spent on patrol, and *Sea Harrier* may simply be a buy of dubious merit with a possible undisclosed intention of also using it against Soviet surface ships. Whatever the conscious intention, it may be that the shape of the modern navy is conceived through assumptions which belong to a bygone era. But those assumptions derive from a time when overseas intervention was a high priority naval mission, and if the force is shaped in accordance with them it retains, even if anachronistically and incompletely, the capabilities for that mission.

In a sense, the ASW Cruisers are a compromise between what strategy suggests the navy should be doing and what the navy itself would like to be doing, between the reality of Britain's present international position and the history and traditions of the senior service. Despite the apparent precision with which ASW can be designated as the RN's main task, the navy's roles are ultimately not all that clearly defined. The 1979 defence White Paper merely asserts the importance of 'Freedom of the Atlantic', and previously there has been the assertion of the need for a naval strategy 'parallel' to the strategy in Europe which requires for the sake of deterrence that 'the balance of maritime power' should not swing too far against NATO.[80] What counts is 'naval presence', more as a boost to NATO's morale in times of crisis than to provide a tightly defined response to a threat. This leaves enough room for manoeuvre for the RN to be allowed, if it insists, to have its imitation aircraft carriers and to continue living partly in the past. And more worryingly, it could permit a government also living in the past to try and behave as if the sun really never did set on the Empire.

The Army in Northern Ireland and Europe

Since the formation of NATO the army has had two main roles: in the form of the British Army of the Rhine (BAOR) it has prepared for the defence of Western Europe, and it has been a colonial army. It is in the latter role that it has seen action, yet its equipment and force structure are almost wholly directed towards the BAOR role. Only since its active engagement in Northern Ireland began in 1969 has this situation changed, with the development of sophisticated techniques and equipment (both hardware and software) for counter-insurgency, and even then with little effect on force structure.[81] Specialised training was relatively quickly provided, drawing in part on the experience of the army in colonial engagements into the 1970s when British forces were still fighting in Oman, but there remains a contradiction between the BAOR role and the role in Northern Ireland: if in Western Europe Britain has had 'an imperial army in a European role',[82] in Northern Ireland it has had a European army in an imperial role. Although this is not the place to argue about the political definition of the army in Northern Ireland, an operational definition must find little basic difference between what it does there and what it has done in past urban colonial situations.

There is, however, a difference between action in Northern Ireland and action elsewhere in the past, and it is crucial and often under-estimated. At the time of writing, the army has sustained almost ten years of urban warfare, under constant pressure and stringent financial constraints, against an enemy and in a population unlike those of past colonial engagements. The enemy and population are white, speak the same language, live in much the same way the soldiers do back home, watch many of the same television programmes, have more or less familiar social structures and habits and share numerous cultural affini-ties. There are probably few in the army who think of it as a colonial action in the old sense. But if it is not quite a colonial action, nor is it quite a domestic role like breaking the firemen's strike in the winter of 1977-8. Soldiers may be told they are there to keep peace, maintain order or defeat the IRA, but this does not address the level at which they experience their environment and day-to-day duties. What makes this worse is that the army's role is not particularly popular in mainland Britain, even if there is little support for withdrawing the army. The truth is that not many mainlanders care about Northern Ireland and fewer understand. It is, almost literally, a thankless task, and the drab grimness of soldiers' life and work there[83] was dramatically emphasised in February 1979 when a trooper in the Royal Welch Regiment opened fire on men of his own unit, killing one and injuring another.[84]

The shamed glumness of most responses to the army's Northern Ireland morass is in sharp contrast to the optimism of August 1969 when the role was adopted (or, rather, re-adopted, if we have a proper sense of Irish history). This was typified in Richard Crossman's diary entry for 17 August 1969 where, although he worried that getting the army out once it was committed could be hard, he still thought that 'We have now got into something we can hardly mismanage.'[85] The pressure this commitment has put on the army has been compounded by general problems of low morale, relating not only to Northern Ireland but also to issues of pay, conditions and equipment, problems which extend also to the navy and RAF and will be discussed in the following section.

The BAOR has its own problems, in part through these general morale problems, and in part from the impact of the rigours of Northern Ireland on service discontent, but also problems of costs. Already BAOR has suffered through penny-pinching restricting the availability of spare parts and troop transport. Although the British state is obliged by NATO agreements to maintain BAOR at a level of at least 55,000 troops, the need to send soldiers to Northern Ireland has reduced actual numbers during the 1970s. In 1978 3,000 extra troops were committed to BAOR as a political gesture, but such gesturing is expensive; the 1979 White Paper estimates the cost of maintaining 58,000 troops in BAOR at £1,079 million – £18.6 million per 1,000 soldiers compared to £10.6 million per 1,000 in UK Home Forces.[86] And this cost is susceptible to changes in rates of exchange: during the sterling crisis in 1976 it was reported that halfway through the budgetary year the estimated 1976-7 cost of BAOR had risen from £400 million to £600 million solely because of the pound's decline.[87]

But a more important cost problem must confront the army as it plans BAOR for the years ahead. The core weapon system in BAOR is the tank; the development of precision-guided anti-tank weapons has not passed BAOR by, and it is now also being equipped with new heavy artillery in the form of the British-German-Italian FH-70 howitzer, but the tank remains the core. The present British tank is the *Chieftain* which entered service in 1967 and has perhaps the most accurate gun and strongest armour of its generation of tanks in either NATO or the WP; the strong armour has carried the penalty of weight, amid criticisms that its engine was under-powered.[88]

Chieftain's weight and consequent lack of speed is the result of British tank doctrine which has been prepared to sacrifice speed for protection and does not accept that high speed is essential. It is one of many doctrinal discrepancies in NATO that the FRG's *Leopard I* is faster and lighter even though it would operate in the same terrain against the same enemy; whereas *Chieftain* weighs 54 tons with a top road speed of 30mph, the corresponding figures for *Leopard I* are 39 tons and 44mph.[89] The lighter armour of *Leopard I* means it would be more vulnerable to enemy fire, which could result in less tactical mobility for German tank forces despite their greater speed; a particularly intense debate about these issues in the Israeli army in the 1960s was resolved in favour of having tanks which, like the British, sacrificed speed for survivability, and resulted in the spectacular tank victories of the 1967 Six Day War.[90]

The problem which arises now concerns *Chieftain's* replacement. Since the British and Federal German armies would fight alongside each other, a standard tank for the two seemed to make sense, but apart from the problems of reconciling two different tank doctrines, collaboration was blocked by the difference in replacement schedules; this difference seems more to do with British budgetary constraints compared to German eagerness than anything else, for *Leopard I* entered service only two years before *Chieftain* but will be replaced almost ten years earlier. The FRG and the USA attempted collaborative development and each produced prototypes of similar basic performance characteristics;[91] when the two tanks were tested against each other, the US army decided the American Chrysler XM-1, now named the *General Creighton Abrams*, was the better, whereupon the FRG complained the tests were unfair and withdrew into independent production of *Leopard II*.

Consequently, there are no potential collaborators with Britain for a new tank. In September 1978, the MoD announced plans for *Chieftain's* replacement, designated Main Battle Tank 80 (MBT 80). The most important thing about it is the estimated unit cost of £1 million for a production run of 1,000, which compares with about £300,000 for *Chieftain* in 1978,[92] an estimate, moreover, which pre-dates the two-year project definition programme (itself costing £60 million), the final choice of engine and any snags which might push the price up even higher. MBT 80, which is planned to equip BAOR from the late 1980s, includes two innovations; one, hardly innovatory by the time it enters service, is the nylon-titanium *Chobham* armour, a British development whose first recipient was the Shah of Iran and the specifications for which were given to France and the FRG back in 1972.[93] The second is a gun which, although it is rifled, is capable of firing shells stabilised in flight by fins, something only smooth-bore guns were previously capable of, thus permitting it to fire high explosive ammunition as well as the more modern fin-stabilised armour-piercing shells.

The difficulty for the army is not only the cost, but also the problem of how the British tank industry is to survive until production of MBT 80 begins. With no British requirement for a tank until the late 1980s, except for improved engines and other modifications, there seemed to be a clear strategy of keeping the tank industry busy by selling *Chieftain* on the world market, and the Iranian order for 1,200 seemed set to keep Britain in the tank business without cost to the defence budget. Even before the Shah was dethroned the deal was being reconsidered, and afterwards the cancellation of the contract surprised nobody, but the threat to jobs in Britain, though a major worry at a time of economic and political crisis during the winter of 1978-9, was less of a long-term problem than the threat to the survival of the tank industry.[94] World-wide there is rather a limited market for tanks — unless the British government had ambitions to sell *Chieftains* to China — and it is not clear how the gap between 1979 and MBT 80 could be bridged. And all of this brings home two rather uncomfortable questions.

After the Yom Kippur Arab-Israeli war of 1973, when Egyptian tank-hunting infantry teams took a heavy toll of Israeli tanks and the Israelis took a heavy toll of Syrian tanks, the demise of the tank as a major battlefield weapon system was widely predicted. That now seems to have been an over-reaction, but the battlefield authority of tanks has been sharply diminished by the advent of relatively cheap precision-guided anti-tank weapons. While tanks still have a place on the battlefield, especially as the core of offensives, it must be asked whether they have a place on the battlefield with a price tag of £1 million each in the armies of states facing severe budgetary constraints, states like Britain. Despite its *Chobham* armour, providing better protection than all previous tank armour, MBT 80 will be vulnerable to anti-tank weapons and its high cost may preclude procuring it in high enough numbers to constitute a significant force. It might make more budgetary sense to delete tanks from the army's force structure, and take the opportunity to develop a different kind of force prioritising the deployment of anti-tank weapons in small mobile units.

If the army does its best to suppress that question, or to answer it by sticking to its tanks, a second question arises. With the loss of the Iranian order and a tight international market for tanks, and with both the FRG and USA proceeding with independent production of tanks, it might seem more sensible to purchase the next British tank from abroad than go through the costly development process. But this question is almost as uncomfortable as the first, since it would require a change in the army's tank doctrine, and for the government raises the difficult prospect of abandoning Britain's prestigious tank industry. It is, of course, equally discomforting for the industry itself, although options are available for alternative production if it stops making tanks.[95]

The army thus has two main roles, in Northern Ireland and BAOR, with one of which there must be great unhappiness however stiff the public upper lip is kept, while the other is becoming increasingly expensive. As long as a BAOR of 55,000 soldiers or more is regarded as an irreducible commitment, and as long as it is structured around tanks, and especially if the next tank is MBT 80, the army appears to be heading for a particularly painful confrontation with the dilemma between available resources and desired capabilities that is the outstanding theme of British defence policy for three decades.

Men, Morale and Money

Perhaps the most painful confrontation with that dilemma is already occurring, evident in the problems of low morale affecting all three armed services, both the officers and other ranks. These problems can be seen as the outcome of three pressures on the forces: uncertainties about their roles or dissatisfaction with them, the effects of techno-logical change and the way in which the failure to resolve the resources-capabilities dilemma is reflected in terms of pay, conditions and some of the less visible aspects of military preparations. These pressures have resulted, in the words of one commentator, in putting the services 'on the brink of a serious crisis of confidence and morale' reflecting 'a growing frustration and resentment' in all ranks, 'a pervasive sense of cynicism and bitterness, with a potentially corrosive effect on discipline and morale'.[96] My own assessment differs in that I think the services are not 'on the brink', but already deep in the crisis, and my concern extends to the possible creation of a generation of servicepeople who may view the civil government as their main enemy, despite the effects of the services' own actions and priorities in building these problems.

The evidence of dissatisfaction is widespread and hard to ignore. Soldiers with four children earning £31 a week in December 1977 were naturally discontented with their lot, the more so since the fine for missing a hair cut or being late on parade could exceed their weekly pay;[97] working a ninety hour week during their four month tours of duty, ordinary soldiers in Northern Ireland averaged earnings of about 33p an hour. At the beginning of 1978 many servicemen were finding the married quarters provided by their services too expensive.[98] Pressures such as these on top of those of Northern Ireland and the ordinary ones of army life, including the senseless disciplinary system with such high financial penalties, can add up to an intolerable situation. The army itself and its way of operating makes life hard on the ordinary soldier, but the pernicious role of bad budgeting failing to provide enough for decent wages is not to be ignored.

In April 1978 the Armed Forces Pay Review Body concluded that service pay rates had fallen more than 30 per cent behind comparable civilian rates. As news of this report seeped into the press, leaks from the MoD to the Press Association showed that the number of army officers seeking early discharge had doubled since April 1977, while in the RAF and RN the number applying for early discharge had increased in the year by 77 per cent and 68 per cent respectively.[99] Of course, these leaks were designed to put pressure on the government to get pay increases — during 1978 the forces were not slow to use leaks to the press to make their case — but the dissatisfaction to which those figures attest is not to be denied. Based on the Pay Review Body's report, the Cabinet's response was to offer thirteen per cent from 1 April 1978, with further increases in each of the following two years to restore comparability with civilian rates. The outline of the decision was fuzzy enough to give any competent trade union negotiator cause for concern that loop-holes were being developed in advance, a concern which might have been intensified by the Prime Minister's refusal to meet the forces' Chiefs of Staff who on this but no other occasion might have acted rather like shop stewards.[100]

Hopes that the award might solve the problem were short-lived; barely a week after it was announced there were reports of resentment that the full 30 per cent had not been awarded immediately.[101] Confirmation of its inadequacy came towards the end of the year: despite some increase in recruitment early departures from the forces were still high, with the sharpest increases in the RN and Marines, and only the RAF was free of this generally rising trend, largely because it operates what is tactfully known as a 'controlled exit' system — it refuses to let people go when they want.[102]

Discontent extends beyond problems of low pay to resentment at deficiencies in equipment. Complaints about inadequate equipment are nothing new: most armed forces for most of the time either believe or pretend to believe that their equipment is not as good as it ought to be — it is one way of keeping up the pressure for more and better equipment. But more and more, armed forces must see themselves not just as bands of heroes, but as teams of technicians, and when as technicians they lack means for the task, frustration and resentment follow. Lists of complaints sent directly to *The Times* by army officers included delays in providing new radios, lower priority for necessary modifications to *Chieftains* than for tank exports, delays in the delivery schedule of a new reconnaissance vehicle and inadequate equipment for reserves.[103] The lack of mechanisation in the army is another standard complaint, especially since it compares badly with the FRG army operating alongside BAOR, leading to discomforting feelings of national inferiority.[104]

The upper echelons of the services cannot be exempted from responsibility for such developments. BAOR may lack items of equipment, but in April 1978 50 tanks were laid up for lack of *men*.[105] If, during the 1970s and before, equipment less visible than tanks had received proper priority in the planning in which senior servicemen participate, BAOR might now have fewer tanks but it might be able to run them properly. As one essentially sympathetic commentator pointed out, the services' basic instinct is to 'plead for a few more resources to complete the task they have been given instead of telling the politicians bluntly that the job cannot — and perhaps should not — be done.'[106] And it is not as if the forces are absent when decisions are taken about what jobs are to be done. Similarly with the navy: on successive days in 1979 a senior admiral warned that warships might soon have to be laid up for lack of skilled men and the government announced a firm order for a new £50 million Type-42 destroyer and its intention to order two more;[107] who will sail in them?

As the admiral's warning showed, the advance of technology by no means eliminates the human factor in military activity. According to an internal RAF report, flying safety was being jeopardised by low morale.[108] With recruitment low because of unattractive rates of pay and long-term commissions, and with applications for early departure from the RAF climbing, the proposed solution was to re-introduce short-term commissions of twelve years with an option to leave after eight, as well as the long-term commission lasting sixteen years or until the age of 38, whichever came first.[109] But here the problem of cost-effectiveness is encountered, for it now costs an estimated £1 million to train a pilot to the highest standard, at the end of which a short-term pilot could leave after only a further four or five years.[110] Whichever way it is looked at, it is in the end ludicrous that expensively trained technicians engage in 'moonlighting' — taking second jobs in order to make ends meet. This was widespread in the RAF as its own report acknowledged,[111] and it is no secret that it had reached epidemic proportions in the army. When the army was used to break the firemen's strike in the winter of 1977-8, resentment among soldiers that they were standing in for better paid firemen was widely noted; what was not publicly acknowledged was that a more serious frustration for soldiers, especially ones stationed in London, was that their round-the-clock substitute firemen's duties cost them their night-time jobs for security firms, nightclubs and others.

When the Conservative government was elected in May 1979, it immediately awarded the services a pay increase amounting to about 33 per cent. One presumes that this will go some way towards answering the problems of morale, but evidence quickly emerged that it will not be enough, for the Ministry of Defence announced in June 1979 that some of the older warships will be put on 'standby', a further 60 *Chieftain* tanks would be withdrawn from service, and most battalions in Germany would reduce one company each to skeleton manning levels.[112] And this, be it noted, after 1978 had been a record year for service recruiting following the April 1978 pay rise, and after the May 1979 pay rise was hoped to stop the flow of skilled and experienced men and women out of the services.

Although the forces' own complaints focus on identifiable issues such as pay, conditions and inadequate logistics, the true dimensions of the problem are not confined to them. Well before the pay grievances were so forcefully aired in 1978, British army recruitment and re-enlistment levels were falling steadily, apparently because of the commitment in Northern Ireland; throughout the 1970s NATO forces have faced upheaval and uncertainty, in the soldiers' movements in West European conscript armies and the US army before it became a volunteer force, and as was shown in a different way in the serious disciplinary problems of the US Marine Corps.[113] It has been a period in which the social and political environment, both within and without the services, has been uncertain and volatile. The social role of servicepeople is less now than ever before. That has exacerbated problems such as pay and conditions, which are serious enough on their own account and which can only be solved through a determined and sustained policy under which extra resources are devoted to the manpower section of the budget, at the expense of the equipment budget if need be, reversing the trend of the 1970s revealed in Table 5.2. The answer to these problems, in other words, is simply proper budgeting, yet to say that is to say a lot: in the 1970s British defence policy has provided a lesson in how not to budget, not because the Ministry of Defence does not understand arithmetic, but because it wants to do too much with too little.

Into the 1980s

The commitment to an annual three per cent increase in military spending for five years might appear to provide the solution to this dominant problem of British defence policy. There will undoubtedly be a temptation, especially with a new government, to see it as providing more resources permitting the deployment of greater capabilities, and so to re-open old files with shelved equipment programmes in them, to expand the horizons a bit, to seek new improvements and increases in forces. The temptation should be resisted – three per cent is no solution.

In 1975 a paper by David Greenwood outlined illustrative options for changes in military posture which could accommodate a reduction in annual military spending amounting to between 20 and 25 per cent. In a comment on that paper in 1977 Greenwood argued that the kind of changes he outlined – severe pruning of any combination of two of the three services – would be necessary in the early 1980s not to reduce the budget *but simply to hold it steady*.[114] Put the other way round, the argument is that to maintain the same kind of posture as the budget now supports, barely, budgetary increases of 20 to 25 per cent in real terms would be needed. The main validation of that judgement is to be found in the cost increases of major weapon systems, such as the MBT 80, costing over three times as much each as the *Chieftain*. If present doctrines, force structures and types of weapon system are kept to, and if the replacement of *Polaris* goes ahead, and if pay, spares and auxiliary equipment are to be at the desired levels, three per cent annual increases will not hold the line, and even six per cent increases will be barely adequate.

During the controversies over forces' pay in 1978, the Conservatives seized upon the issue as an argument for increasing the defence budget. Properly viewed it is no such thing; it is, rather, an argument for proper budgeting, in two senses: first, in terms of the allocation of resources within the budget, which should no longer concentrate on the prestigious weapon systems at the expense of other aspects of military preparations, and, second, in terms of planning on the basis of a level of resources which can reasonably be expected to be available. And if we take Greenwood's judgement, that becomes an argument for reducing the range of missions undertaken, for re-examining the attachment to certain doctrines and weapon systems, for re-ordering and reducing the British military establishment.

But the argument must go further. Until the 1974 defence review, reductions could be achieved largely through clipping imperial wings, but after that review's concentration onto the European and Eastern Atlantic theatres, there is no place where the cuts could be so easy. The problem is that within the British state there is no identifiable mechanism for defining where and how the basic re-ordering should be carried out and then doing it. Existing political and strategic assumptions are a barrier to resolving the major dilemmas. Between those assumptions, the commitment to maintaining military industrial capacity, the apparently equal balance of power between the three services expressed in their roughly equal shares of the total budget, and the range of choice between the Labour government's policy in the late 1970s and the Conservatives' approach, there is no room to find the solution. As technological progress continues, forcing up equipment costs, the dilemma intensifies; there are no significant peripheral commitments left to ditch, and while economic growth may pick up from the level of the mid-1970s it is unlikely to be enough to answer the problem. If the over-riding theme of this review of defence policy has been the policy's failure, there is no reason to expect anything better of the 1980s on the present showing.

This is not to say it would be impossible to find a solution. It would be possible to plan for, say, a ten per cent increase in annual spending; this would increase the proportion of GDP spent on defence quite sharply, from around five per cent to around seven per cent after five years, on the optimistic assumption that GDP grew at about three per cent annually, taking the defence share of GDP back up to the levels of the mid-1950s. This might require a combination of cuts in other public spending, private consumption and civil industrial investment. This in itself would require a change in the political balance in Britain and the jettisoning of many assumptions about the welfare state at a time when, by all accounts, unemployment would be rising. If this level of resources could be made available, one presumes it would be possible to strengthen Britain's forces in ambitious ways while sustaining the necessary levels of spending on the less visible aspects of the military establishment. Alternatively, in concert with a smaller increase in military spending, a decision to sink at least some elements of nation-statehood into a wider unit, as the Europeanists urge, might in the long run permit the British state to lop off some of the commitments now regarded as irreducible, but once again political change is a prerequisite. Thirdly, there is the possibility of thoroughly rejecting current defence orthodoxies and effecting fundamental changes in policy, challenging the basic assumptions of the present including the commitment to NATO.

The point about each of these possibilities is that they demand a major degree of political and social change. One way or another, for good or bad, a defence policy for the 1980s which does not repeat the dismal story so far would demand a reworking of some of the basic social and political structures and assumptions underpinning the British state.

Notes

1. *Statement on the Defence Estimates 1978*, Cmnd 7099 (HMSO, London, 1978), p. 10.
2. *Statement on the Defence Estimates 1979*, Cmnd 7474 (HMSO, London, 1979), p. 42.
3. Ibid., Annex C.
4. *Defence: Outline of Future Policy*, Cmnd 124, para 2, reprinted in *Brassey's Annual 1957* (William Clowes, London, 1957).
5. L.W. Martin, *British Defence Policy: The Long Recessional*, Adelphi Paper 61 (IISS, London, 1969), p. 2.
6. D. Greenwood, 'Defence and National Priorities Since 1945', in J. Baylis (ed.), *British Defence Policy in a Changing World* (Croom Helm, London, 1977), pp. 195-6.
7. *Supplementary Statement on Defence Policy 1967*, Cmnd 3357, part III, para 3, in *Brassey's Annual 1967* (William Clowes, London, 1967).
8. 'Implementation of the £110 million Cut in the 1976/77 Defence Budget (D.59)', Memorandum by the Ministry of Defence, SCOE 87, in Minutes of the Defence and External Affairs Sub-committee of the House of Commons

Expenditure Committee, 30 March 1976, HC 236-iv (HMSO, London, 1976).

    9. Martin, *The Long Recessional*, p. 21.

    10. *The Government's Expenditure Plans, 1978-79 to 1981-82*, vol. II, Cmnd 7049-II (HMSO, London, 1978), p. 3.

    11. *World Armaments and Disarmament: SIPRI Yearbook 1978* (Taylor & Francis, London, 1978), Table 6A4.

    12. S. Pollard, *The Development of the British Economy 1914-1967*, 2nd edition (Edward Arnold, London, 1969), Chapter 8.

    13. 'Defence Cuts 1977-78 to 1979-80 (D.63)', Memorandum by the Ministry of Defence, SCOE 87/1, in HC 236-iv.

    14. D. Greenwood and D. Hazel, *The Evolution of Britain's Defence Priorities 1957-1976* (University of Aberdeen, 1978), pp. 16-18.

    15. D. Greenwood, *The United Kingdom's Current Defence Programme and Budget* (University of Aberdeen, 1978), p. 58; this balance is reflected in the approximately equal proportions of the budget allocated to each service.

    16. The Labour Party Defence Study Group, *Sense About Defence* (Quartet, London, 1977); M. Kaldor, D. Smith and S. Vines (eds), *Democratic Socialism and the Cost of Defence* (Croom Helm, London, 1979).

    17. *The Guardian*, 19 October 1978.

    18. *The Bahamas Meetings*, Cmnd 1915 (HMSO, London, 1962).

    19. *Statement on the Defence Estimates 1978*, Cmnd 7099 (HMSO, London, 1978), para 205; *Annual Defense Department Report FY 1978* (US DoD, 1977), p. 148.

    20. A.J.R. Groom, 'The British Deterrent', in Baylis (ed.), *British Defence Policy in a Changing World*, p. 153; see also Groom, *British Thinking About Nuclear Weapons* (Frances Pinter, London, 1974).

    21. See I. Smart, *The Future of the British Nuclear Deterrent: Technical, Economic and Strategic Issues* (RIIA, London, 1977); the Ministry of Defence refuses to give a precise date for when *Polaris* will cease to be operational, saying only that the force 'can remain in service into the 1990s' – 'Nuclear Weapons Systems', Memorandum submitted by the Minister of Defence, in *Sixth Report from the Expenditure Committee Session 1978/9: The Future of the United Kingdom's Nuclear Weapons Policy*, 348 (HMSO, London, 1979), pp. 2-3; one estimate concludes that *Polaris* can remain operational 'throughout this century' – F. Hussein, 'Options for the UK's Future Nuclear Weapons Policy', in *The Future of the United Kingdom's Nuclear Weapons Policy*, pp. 187-9 and 203; if Hussein is correct, then the decision on replacement can be put off until 1987 or later.

    22. For these points I am indebted to the research of Robin Cook: see R. Cook, 'Buy a new H-Bomb – the Easy Way', *New Statesman*, 12 January 1979; see also, Cook and D. Smith, *What Future in NATO?*, Fabian Research Series 337 (Fabian Society, London, 1978), and Cook and Smith, 'The Reason Why Not', in *The Future of the United Kingdom's Nuclear Weapons Policy*.

    23. Chapman Pincher, *Inside Story* (Sidgwick & Jackson, London, 1978), p. 306.

    24. *The Guardian*, 1 November 1979.

    25. M. Gowing, *Independence and Deterrence*, 2 volumes (Macmillan, London, 1974), vol. I *Policy Making*, especially pp. 179-85.

    26. Smart, *The Future of the British Nuclear Deterrent*, Appendix VIII.

    27. J. Bellini and G. Pattie, *A New World Role for the Medium Power: The British Opportunity* (RUSI, London, 1977), especially Chapter 6.

    28. 'The Cruise Missile', *Flight International*, 1 October 1977.

    29. See *World Armaments and Disarmament: SIPRI Yearbook 1975* (MIT

Press, London, 1975), Chapter 11; also R. Burt, 'The Cruise Missile and Arms Control', *Survival*, January/February 1976.

30. 'ALCM' and 'SLCM', *Market Intelligence Report* (Defense Market Survey, Greenwich, Ct, 1978).

31. Smart, *The Future of the British Nuclear Deterrent*, Appendix VIII.

32. D. Ball, 'The Costs of the Cruise Missile', *Survival*, November/December 1978.

33. *Flight International*, 11 December 1976, 17 September 1977, 18 February 1978; *The Guardian*, 22 July 1978.

34. *International Herald Tribune*, 24 October 1978, 25 October 1978; *The Guardian*, 28 December 1978.

35. R. Evans and R. Novak, *International Herald Tribune*, 18-19 February 1978.

36. For example, *Department of the Air Force Report to the 95th Congress* (for FY 1978) (US DoD, 1977), pp. 29-30.

37. 'Keeping the Boeing B-52 Operational until the End of the Century', *Interavia*, December 1978.

38. *Flight International*, 23 July 1977; *Aviation Week and Space Technology*, 27 March 1978.

39. The estimated total is made up of 10,000 at British Aerospace working on the airframe and some components, 6,000 at Rolls-Royce on the aeroengine, 8,000 in a large number of companies on avionics and equipment, and a further 12,000 workers employed 'indirectly': Roy Mason, Secretary of State for Defence, *Hansard*, 31 March 1976, col 1334.

40. *Flight International*, 18 February 1978.

41. These estimates are based on the rule of thumb that in a modern aerospace project 35 per cent of the total outlay is for production, 15 per cent for research and development (R&D) and 50 per cent for operation and support (O&S). The MoD has estimated that R&D costs are increased by 25 per cent as a result of collaboration, to a total of which Britain was committed to find 42.5 per cent; R&D costs for the main version of *Tornado* have been estimated with this in mind. The air defence version is a British only project, so R&D costs are not affected by collaboration, but an estimated 65 per cent of the main version's R&D costs were applicable to the air defence version R&D bill which was estimated to account for that. (See the Minutes of the Defence and External Affairs Sub-Committee of the House of Commons Expenditure Committee for 27 April 1976, HC 236-v) (HMSO, London, 1976). O&S costs are not reduced by collaborative R&D or previous R&D experience, so in each case O&S costs were estimated using a notional R&D figure to express what R&D would have cost without collaboration or previous experience. Elsewhere, the additional costs of R&D resulting from collaboration have been calculated at +30 per cent (W.B. Walker, 'The Multi-role Combat Aircraft (MRCA): A Case Study in European Collaboration', *Research Policy* 2, 1974) so that I am content that my own estimates, while necessarily approximate, are not uncharitably high.

42. Cmnd 124, paras 12-17 and 23.

43. 'The Royal Air Force in the 1980s', *Air Extra*, July 1977; the concept of low-level strategic bombing was first developed in 1952 in the Ministry of Supply: D. Wood, *Project Cancelled* (Macdonald & Jane's, London, 1975), p. 149.

44. The narrative here is based on Wood, *Project Cancelled*.

45. Here the narrative is based on 'Panavia Tornado', *Market Intelligence Report* (Defense Market Survey, Greenwich, Ct, 1978).

46. B.O. Heath, 'Cooperation: Europe and Tornado', in *New Directions for NATO*, transcript of an *Aviation Week and Space Technology* Conference, 26-27 June 1978.

47. See Walker, 'The Multi-role Combat Aircraft (MRCA)'; for a list of contractors see D. Smith, 'The MRCA Tornado: a Case Study of Potential for Conversion and Diversification in the Aerospace Industry', in *idem* (ed.), *Alternative Work for Military Industries* (Richardson Institute, London, 1977).

48. *MRCA Fact Sheet*, no. 1 (Panavia, Munich, October 1973).

49. 'Panavia Tornado', *Market Intelligence Report*.

50. *Statement on the Defence Estimates 1977*, Cmnd 6735 (HMSO, London, 1977), para 317a.

51. See *Hansard*, 18 March 1976, cols 1627-53; also *The Sunday Times*, 19 September 1976.

52. *The Sunday Times*, 19 September 1976 and 3 October 1976.

53. *Flight International*, 21 May 1977.

54. *Flight International*, 9 December 1978; as an aside it may be noted that there is no evidence that this delay in entry into service results from the Labour government's reductions in planned defence spending although they were expected to reduce the rate of delivery by 'up to one-third': *Statement on the Defence Estimates 1976*, Cmnd 6432 (HMSO, London, 1976), Chapter I, para 64.

55. U. Albrecht, B. Luber and P. Schlotter, 'Das Ende des MRCA?', in *Ein Anti-weissbuch* (Rowohlt, Hamburg, 1974), p. 83.

56. W.D. White, *US Tactical Air Power: Missions, Forces and Costs* (Brookings Institution, Washington, DC, 1974), p. 56.

57. 'Europe's New Generation of Combat Aircraft', *International Defense Review* 4, 1975.

58. Cmnd 6735, para 224.

59. HC 236-v, Q505.

60. G. Pattie, *Towards a New Defence Policy* (Conservative Political Centre, London, 1976), p. 20.

61. *The Guardian*, 15 August 1977.

62. *Flight International*, 13 August 1977.

63. *The Sunday Times*, 9 October 1977.

64. *Flight International*, 19 November 1977.

65. W. Flume, 'Neues Taktisches Kampfflugzeug', *Wehrtechnik*, June 1977; 'AST 403', *Market Intelligence Report* (Defense Market Survey, Greenwich, Ct, 1977).

66. *Flight International*, 16 September 1978; 'McDonnell Douglas AV-8B', *Market Intelligence Report*, 1978; *Flight International*, 22 August 1977.

67. *Statement on the Defence Estimates 1979*, Cmnd 7474 (HMSO, London, 1979), para 201.

68. *The US Sea Control Mission: Forces, Capabilities, and Requirements* (Congressional Budget Office, Washington, DC, 1977), especially pp. 36-40; the figure for Soviet submarines generally in the Atlantic is there taken from R.G. Weinland, 'The State and Future of the Soviet Navy in the North Atlantic', in M. McGwire and J. McDonnell (eds), *Soviet Naval Influence: Domestic and Foreign Dimensions* (Prager, New York, 1977), p. 411.

69. See the 1969 speech by Dennis Healey, Secretary of State for Defence, quoted by M. Kaldor, 'The ASW Cruiser: a Case Study of Potential for Conversion in the Shipbuilding Industry', in Smith (ed.), *Alternative Work for Military Industries*.

70. The delay was due to design changes and industrial problems: *The Guardian*, 4 May 1977.

71. *Jane's Fighting Ships 1977-1978* (Macdonald & Jane's, London, 1977), p. 493.

72. Cmnd 7474, para 306a.

73. B. Moynahan, 'The Last Gunboat', *The Sunday Times*, 11 December 1977.

74. 'Sea Harrier', *Flight International*, 2 September 1978.

75. *Second Report from the Expenditure Committee Session 1975-1976: Defence*, HC 155 (HMSO, London, 1976), Minutes, pp. 74-5, Q222 and 223.

76. 'Britain's Navy prepares for Sea Harrier', *Interavia*, December 1978.

77. HC 155, p. 75, Q223.

78. Ibid., p. 74, Q222.

79. I. Mcgeogh, *Command of the Sea in the Seventies*, quoted in Kaldor, 'The ASW Cruiser'.

80. Cmnd 7474, para 201; Cmnd 5976, Chapter I, para 25b.

81. The basic guide to the development of new counter-insurgency techniques is C. Ackroyd, K. Margolis, J. Rosenhead and T. Shallice, *The Technology of Political Control* (Penguin, Harmondsworth, 1977).

82. C. Barnett, *Britain and Her Army 1509-1970* (Penguin, Harmondsworth, 1974), p. 493.

83. Conditions for ordinary soldiers were graphically described by P. Toynbee, *The Guardian*, 6 March 1978.

84. T. Davies, 'The Private Hell of a Private Soldier', *Observer*, 4 March 1979.

85. *The Diaries of a Cabinet Minister*, vol. 3 (Hamish Hamilton & Jonathan Cape, London, 1977).

86. Cmnd 7474, Annex B.

87. T. Geraghty, *The Sunday Times*, 24 October 1976.

88. Engine problems also delayed *Chieftain*'s entry into service for four years: *Tanks and Fighting Vehicles* (Salamander, London, 1977), pp. 58-9.

89. Ibid., pp. 58-9 and 134-5.

90. E. Luttwak and D. Horowitz, *The Israeli Army* (Allen Lane, London, 1975), Chapter 6.

91. *RUSI and Brassey's Defence Yearbook 1978/9* (Brassey's, London, 1978), p. 212, gives the following data: for the US XM-1, a combat weight of 58 tons, top road speed of 72kph (45mph) and 56kph (35mph) cross-country; for the FRG's *Leopard II*, a combat weight of 54.5 tons, top road speed of 68kph (43mph) and 55kph (35mph) cross-country; *Tanks and Fighting Vehicles*, pp. 138-9 and 244-5, gives lower weights – 52 tons for XM-1 and 50 tons for *Leopard II*.

92. *The Guardian*, 14 September 1978; *The Sunday Times*, 17 September 1978.

93. *The Sunday Times*, 7 November 1976, and *Hansard*, 9 November 1976, cols 206-7; by the time MBT 80 is produced, *Chobham* armour or a close equivalent will be protecting the newest tanks of the FRG, USA, USSR, Israel, possibly Iran and possibly France.

94. *The Guardian*, 2 February 1979; *Financial Times*, 6 February 1979.

95. *Building a Chieftain Tank and the Alternative Use of Resources* (Vickers Shop Stewards Cttee, Newcastle, 1978).

96. Lord Chalfont, *The Times*, 6 March 1978.

97. *The Times*, 9 December 1977.

98. *The Guardian*, 20 February 1978.

99. *The Times*, 19 April 1978.

100. *The Times*, 27 April 1978.

101. *The Times*, 4 May 1978.

102. *The Times*, 16 November 1978.

103. *The Times*, 2 May 1978.

104. *The Sunday Times*, 24 September 1978.

105. *The Times*, 15 April 1978; *New York Times*, 17 April 1978.

106. D. Fairhall, *The Guardian*, 6 December 1977.

107. *The Guardian*, 29 March 1979 and 30 March 1979.

108. *The Guardian*, 11 January 1978.

109. *The Times*, 10 January 1978.

110. *Tenth Report from the Expenditure Committee Session 1977-78: British Forces Germany*, vol. I, HC 563-I (HMSO, London, 1978), pxxvii, para 42.

111. *The Guardian*, 11 January 1978.

112. *The Guardian*, 29 June 1979.

113. See D. Cortwright, 'Soldiers Rising: Impressions of the NATO Armies', in T. Nairn (ed.), *Atlantic Europe? The Radical View* (TNI, Amsterdam, 1976), and M. Binkin and J. Record, *Where Does the Marine Corps Go from Here?* (Brookings Institution, Washington, DC, 1976), pp. 61-4.

114. D. Greenwood, 'Defence Programme Options to 1980-81' and 'Postscript', in Kaldor, Smith and Vines (eds), *Democratic Socialism and the Cost of Defence*.

6 COSTS AND TECHNOLOGY

Of central significance in the British state's inability to match desired military capability to available resources is the consistently increasing cost of providing the desired capability. Cost increases in military equipment have been far sharper over the past thirty years than the norm in the civil economy. It has been calculated that while the US commodity price index rose by 235 per cent between 1945 and 1974, the US F-111 medium bomber costs about 16,750 per cent more than a comparable World War II aircraft, and that the funds that would have purchased 100,000 fighters in 1945 would, after adjusting for inflation, purchase only 1,000 of the most sophisticated current US fighter aircraft.[1] The 385 copies of *Tornado* to be procured for the RAF will cost slightly more than the entire production of *Spitfire* fighters before and during World War II, while the cost per ton of comparable warships has increased since 1945 by between a factor of ten and a factor of fifteen.[2] As we saw in Chapter 5, the next British tank, the MBT-80, is expected to cost £1 million each compared to about £300,000 for the current *Chieftain*.

Cost increases of this magnitude outpace inflation, growth in Gross National Products, and growth in most states' military budgets. Norman Augustine has shown that if trends prevailing since the 1920s continue for a few more decades, by the year 2036 the entire US military budget would be able to afford but one aircraft; if this precious item were shared between the services on alternate days of the week, enough funds would accrue to replace it approximately once every fifteen years. Similar prognoses apply to other major items of equipment.[3] This calculation is, of course, based on simple extrapolation of current trends and does not amount to a prediction, but it is a graphic illustration both of the tenacity of the tendency for costs to increase and of the mounting problems it poses for military planners.

Underlying these cost increases is the drive to produce ever more sophisticated, complex and capable weapon systems with greater speed, armour, firepower, range, better navigation and communications. Costs express the resources devoted to and utilised in the development and production of equipment; technological improvement over previous equipment requires more resources – people, machinery, materials, plant – per unit of equipment. The drive for continued improvement is itself the result both of a series of specific decisions by states and of the philosophy and organisation of military technology.

Related to the problem of increased costs from one generation of weaponry to the next is the problem of costs increasing as development of a weapon system proceeds. Because of the greater openness about costs in the USA, largely a result of the system of Congressional committees, more is known about the problem of cost over-runs in the USA than in Britain or most other states. Despite reformed management techniques at the end of the 1960s, following such embarrassments as the huge over-run on the cost of the Lockheed C-5A *Galaxy* heavy transport aircraft, this remains a serious problem in the USA in the 1970s with barely any major projects costing at the end what was estimated at the outset.[4] This problem has a number of causes. Corporations have shown a habit of 'buying in' to a contract by making a consciously low bid with an ambitious design specification, which is almost bound to lead to increased costs as development work progresses; managers of military projects are more usually concerned to maximise performance than to minimise costs, so that if problems are encountered in development the tendency is to solve them almost regardless of cost. A common habit is adding on additional capabilities as a project progresses: for example, the General Dynamics F-16 started life as a low-cost lightweight fighter specialised for air combat, but has since then expensively metamorphosed into a ground attack aircraft as well so that it could be sold to four West European states (Belgium, Denmark, the Netherlands and Norway).[5] On the other hand, the reverse side of the cost over-run coin, there is a habit of reducing capabilities in order to keep costs within bounds: this happened with the American B-1 bomber before it was cancelled in 1977, and occurred, as we have seen, with *Tornado*, both with the adoption of a less ambitious main weapons computer and with the effective dropping of the air superiority and close support roles in 1970.

Even with the best management techniques, however, there are awesome problems in forecasting costs in projects which involve technological innovation. When new techniques and materials are required to solve particular problems or provide a particular mix of performance characteristics, the contractors and the government department must enter uncharted waters. One study, utilising rough measures of technological advance, demonstrated that the greater the advance embodied in any project, the less likely final costs were to conform to first estimates.[6] Cost estimates are based on experience with previous comparable weapon systems; the greater the advance in the new project, the less comparable it is with previous ones, and therefore the less predictable are the costs.

The determination to provide technological improvements in succeeding generations of equipment therefore underlies both the problem of cost over-runs and the problem of cost increases across generations. There is an ingrained tendency to seek the most sophisticated solution to any problem, even when cheaper and simpler alternatives are available and sophistication is inappropriate. For example, it has often been argued that NATO should place greater emphasis on rocket artillery to supplement field guns and howitzers as a way of saturating an area with artillery fire to block enemy attacks or weaken defences. The WP has made a major investment in this form of artillery. Its advantages are said to be its relative cheapness, easy operation and relatively undemanding maintenance, its ability to be mounted on almost any wheeled or tracked vehicle, including commercial lorry chasses, and its fast rate of fire. Rocket artillery lacks the finest accuracy, but this is of little importance when the intention is to saturate an area. NATO states have now begun to show an interest in rocket artillery, but appear to be opting for expensive carriers for the batteries of rockets and for precise accuracy;[7] the effect will be to sacrifice quantity and ruggedness for unnecessarily high performance and greater costs.

Taking the most sophisticated path is hardly surprising given the way in which technology has increasingly been used to substitute for people in the armed forces of the industrialised states. William White has cited a series of figures showing the effects and development of this process of 'technological substitution'. During World War II about 36 per cent of US Army personnel were direct combat troops; by the Korean War this proportion had shrunk to 33 per cent, and by 1973 it was just 22 per cent. In the US armed forces as a whole in the mid-1970s, only 16 per cent of personnel served in direct combat roles, whereas during the American Civil War just over a century earlier this figure was above 90 per cent. Rough measures show that the amount of fire-power brought to bear in warfare has sharply increased proportionate to personnel: in World War II, 0.2 tons of munitions were expended for every man-year of the USA's entire war effort; during the Korean War the rate was up to 0.5 tons, and for the years 1966-71 in South-east Asia it was 1.3 tons. The increase is even sharper if tons of munitions expended are compared not to the whole war effort but to man-years of actual exposure to combat: World War II shows one ton per man-year of combat, while the Korean War shows eight tons per man-year, and at the height of the US war in South-east Asia the ratio was 26 tons per man-year.[8] Thus, the amount of fire-power brought to bear on the battlefield has ceased to be a direct function of the number of service personnel directly engaged in combat. There is a greater reliance on a decreasing number of far more powerful pieces of equipment. At the peak of World War II the USA produced approximately 50,000 aircraft, 20,000 tanks and 80,000 artillery pieces in a single year; in 1974, with a total defence budget of about the same magnitude in real terms, the USA managed 600 aircraft, 450 tanks and no artillery pieces.[9] Technological sophistication and technological substitution are parts of the same process.

The problem for military planners is not only that increased costs mean less pieces of equipment to provide the overall capability desired, but that increased sophistication does not necessarily mean increased effectiveness. This was recognised, though only transiently, in the American decision to develop the F-16 as a low-cost specialised fighter aircraft; it was recognised with greater permanence in the development of the USA's A-10 attack aircraft, designed primarily for use against tanks, with heavy armour and a speed no more than that of World War II fighters, and a main armament of a 30mm cannon (though this has been needlessly complicated by adding on various missiles); it was, fleetingly, recognised in the proposal that the British AST-403 be a low-cost fighter.

One problem which will be increasingly encountered in aircraft is 'electron overload', a consequence of the close proximity of numerous electrical circuits with different functions. The difficulty of achieving perfect insulation means that one circuit could be activated by the charge from another. On more than one occasion aircraft have accidentally fired missiles, possibly because of this problem; the loss of an F-14 aircraft off a US aircraft carrier in 1976 near Scotland was caused by one engine firing independently as the aircraft moved forward for launching, and this may have been due to the same problem. Relatively small aircraft, such as *Tornado*, packed with complex electronics, could be especially prone to this problem; when a *Tornado* crashed in the Irish Sea in June 1979, this may have been due to the pilot's error, but the fact that a similar crash occurred in 1978 with a *Buccaneer* acting as a 'test-bed' for *Tornado*'s avionics suggests that the cause of both crashes might have been an electronic rather than a human failure.[10] In general, the more complex a system is the more likely it is to break down, even when all components are properly manufactured, and the more components there are the greater the chances of one or more of them being imperfect. System failure such as this can be tolerated if the force as a whole is large enough to sustain a few breakdowns with only marginal impairment to its overall effectiveness, but the lower the numbers, the more important any single failure becomes.

The effectiveness of the force as a whole also suffers if sophistication pushes costs up, and therefore pushes numbers down, but the weapon systems remain vulnerable to opposing systems. As we shall see, the proliferation of highly accurate and relatively cheap anti-aircraft and anti-tank missiles severely challenges the survival potential of even the most sophisticated aircraft and tanks, which should therefore be available in greater numbers, but cannot be because of cost as a result of sophistication.

As a general process, technological substitution is not limited to the military; we see it in industry, agriculture, the service industries, housework, the provision of health facilities, education and almost all aspects of industrialised societies. It is part of the condition of life in highly technological societies, but it seems to go further in military industry and activities than elsewhere, because the drive to get increased performance even if higher cost is the outcome is so much stronger. Ferranti, having designed a microprocessor to MoD specifications for use in aircraft, is now concerned that MoD might after all not require the product, leaving it with a microprocessor that is uncompetitive in the commercial market; in the USA some of the leading manufacturers of microprocessors are determined to resist Pentagon blandishments to develop them to specialised military requirements because the products will not be commercially viable, but the Pentagon appears to insist it needs microprocessors and integrated circuits with far higher capabilities for processing data than are now available in the USA.[11] Although a slackening in the civil market for microprocessors might attract these companies into work for the Pentagon,[12] it is clear that even in electronics, the most rapidly innovative of technologies in the recent past, there is a qualitative difference between civil technology and what the military wants.

Military Industrial Capacity

Military rivalry between NATO and the WP is commonly seen as a form of technological rivalry, in which NATO's perceived technological superiority provides an advantage off-setting the WP's numerical advantages in some types of equipment. Within limits this is a quite valid view, and it is certainly reasonable to qualify any quantitative assessment of the military balance by a qualitative assessment, although, as I argued at the beginning of Chapter 4, this still fails to provide a comprehensive assessment of the comparative effectiveness of each side's forces. It is, however, important to be aware that there are limits to the validity of this view, that the constant striving for technological improvements does not always provide stronger military capability, that there are times when a cheaper and simpler option makes more sense. It is, moreover, important to understand this view within its historical context, as the product of highly industrialised and technologically skilled societies and, what is more, as a relatively recent product. British naval supremacy over the French in the eighteenth century owed nothing to warship design, in which Britain was generally agreed to be inferior, but stemmed both from the existence of a highly proficient body of skilled naval officers and from the superior strategic perspective of British naval policy.[13] It was not until well into the second half of the nineteenth century that modern industrial skills were applied in any systematic way to the development of warfighting abilities, with the appearance of breech-loading and then repeating rifles, more accurate artillery, machine guns, iron-clad warships and finally the first tanks of World War I. And it was not until World War II that technological rivalry and superiority as such came to take a central place in views about military strength, with the development of radar, navigation and bomb-aiming techniques, anti-submarine warfare techniques and finally the atomic bomb. The failure of American armed force to achieve its goals in Vietnam against an adversary with far less technologically advanced forces is a strong reminder that technological superiority does not hold all the answers in all situations.

The basis for pursuing military-technological rivalry is the maintenance of a large and specialised military-technological infrastructure, which not only provides the ability to maintain the rivalry, but encourages the strategic perspective that this is a central aspect of military rivalry and generates the momentum of technological improvement. Maintaining this infrastructure is a matter of state policy in both NATO and the WP,[14] although in both, whether the basic motive is analysed in terms of profit motive or bureaucratic interest or commitment to the state's goals, the personnel and institutions which constitute the infrastructure have their own interest in its maintenance. At the core of this infrastructure, the key personnel and institutions, are the research and development teams of, in NATO states, specialised military industrial corporations or specialised sections of more diversified corporations. To be kept in existence, these teams must be kept in business, which means they must always have new projects to work on to replace completed projects; since the rationale for any new project is that it be an improvement on its predecessor, the commitment to maintaining the ability to pursue military-technological rivalry means a commitment to a constant process of technological improvement. It is, obviously, important also to maintain the ability to produce sophisticated equipment to high quality standards, but in general production workforces can be treated in more cavalier fashion than the research and development teams. As projects reach completion, laying off production workers is more common and less damaging to the technological infrastructure than dispensing with development technicians and scientists, largely because production skills are less specialised and less costly to provide.

The capacity to develop and produce weapon systems can be understood as the scale of resources devoted to a project in a given period.[15] As one development project is succeeded by another more demanding and more complex, greater resources are required in order to complete it in the same amount of time. The expansion of capacity in this way can be limited by extending the development period, but the need to materialise the project as operational equipment within a reasonable time restricts the degree to which the expansion of capacity can be limited in this way. The aerospace industry shows a clear demonstration of the expansion of capacity and extension of development periods over time: in 1915, the first Handley Page military aircraft took 50 weeks for development by a team of six; development of *Halifax* bombers in the eve of World War II took 118 weeks for a team of 71; a modern combat aircraft can take about ten years for development by a team of about 400; the number of 'design weeks' has thus gone from 300 to 8,380 to about 200,000.[16] In the absence of extending the development periods, industrial capacity would realise its theoretical tendency to expand infinitely; even with extended development periods, it expands impressively.

The cost of sustaining a viable military-technological infrastructure can therefore be understood as the cost of sustaining an ever-active and ever-expanding industrial capacity, an overall cost which is expressed in the cost increases of weapon systems over their predecessors. If a state is committed to maintaining this infrastructure, it must therefore seek a way to limit the increase of the cost of capacity, while simultaneously supporting the momentum of technological improvement. It must develop policies to counteract or compensate for the expansion of capacity even while it must continue to foster the expansion of capacity by placing new development and production contracts with the industry. There is a variety of such policies; in Britain's case the main ones have been reorganisation of the industries, reducing the numbers of aircraft procured and the numbers of types produced, cancellation, exports and various forms of collaboration with other NATO states.

In 1946 there were 23 major airframe manufacturers in Britain, and nine major aeroengine companies; by 1974, mergers, business failures and direct government intervention had whittled them down to six airframe companies and one aeroengine manufacturer, Rolls-Royce, a nationalised corporation.[17] In 1977 three of the six airframe companies were nationalised and amalgamated as British Aerospace; a fourth, Short Brothers, was 98 per cent state owned, and a fifth, Westland, specialises in helicopters and has no British competitor. Also in 1977 the main shipbuilding companies were nationalised and amalgamated as British Shipbuilders. The thrust of this dual nationalisation of 1977 can be seen almost entirely in terms of the need to reorganise and rationalise industrial capacity, in the civil sector of the industries no less than the military, to avoid duplication of industrial effort and resources. With this measure, the reorganisation of the industries virtually reached its logical limits at a national level; further rationalisation of these industrial resources must involve either completely abandoning a significant proportion of capacity to other uses, or international collaborative reorganisation, or both.[18]

As the number of corporations is whittled down, so also are the number of types of the same category of equipment. The result, since the services only reluctantly if at all agree to abandoning major missions, is the development of multi-role weapon systems such as the ASW Cruiser, *Tornado* and AST-403. At the same time, the increasing cost of especially multi-role but also specialised weapon systems leads to a reduction in the overall numbers procured and a parallel reduction or restriction on the growth of production capacities.

In the British aerospace industry, as Derek Wood's history shows, cancellation has been a forceful presence, but Wood's tendency to see this as a tragic tale of missed opportunities, misjudgement and incompetence is not entirely adequate.[19] Had the projects not been developed, Britain would have lost large sections of its industrial capacity for military aviation, but had the projects been produced unsustainable production costs would have been incurred. Cancellation of a project and its replacement by another provides a way of sustaining capacity at less cost, even though at some waste. The design team which worked for BAC on the *Tornado* came in direct line of descent from three previous projects – the TSR-2, the Anglo-French Variable Geometry project and the UK Variable Geometry project – none of which survived to the production stage. Whether or not funding projects which are eventually cancelled is a deliberate policy is not clear, but that it functions as technique for maintaining development capacity at lower cost is, and the UKVG project is an example of a development which seemed intended merely to bridge a gap rather than produce an aircraft. However, there are clear limitations to this technique, not the least being that it erodes morale in the development teams and prevents them from assessing the success of their efforts, even if a prototype flies before cancellation; it also prevents the production workforce from learning new techniques with new materials incrementally, thus lengthening the 'learning period' when a new project does at last survive through to production, and restricts the accumulation of experience.

The fourth way of coping with the problem of expanding capacity is through the export of armaments, a trade which saw a boom during the 1970s, especially to the Middle East. The major boost for the British arms export effort came with the establishment of the Defence Sales Organisation in the MoD in 1966.[20] Apart from earning useful foreign exchange and, in the case of exports to some Middle Eastern states, helping absorb the petro-dollars released by the oil price increases since 1973, the main advantage of exporting arms is that it helps to sustain military industrial capacity, especially production capacity, without cost to the national budget; effectively, it transfers abroad the cost of sustaining capacity. The state may not make a profit on a deal and may even lose money, but the decisive advantage lies in the contribution exports make to keeping the domestic military industry operating, and it seems that this is coming to be freely acknowledged.[21] That this trade absorbs a scarce international surplus which should be used to tackle problems of starvation, disease and deprivation appears to be of less importance both to the industrialised exporting states and to the major importers than the advantage each gains from it. But while Britain, fourth in the arms sellers' league just behind France and well behind the USA and the USSR,[22] has evidently benefited like its competitors from the 1970s' boom, it would seem that the boom is beginning to dry up. This is largely because the main purchasers have either over-ordered or at least have ordered up a full inventory, which in most cases they do not possess the trained personnel to operate properly. The dethronement of the Shah of Iran poses particular problems for the British tank industry, as we have seen, and should be an object lesson on the risks of a policy whose success depends on the fate of an unpopular dictator. New large weapons importers may yet emerge — for example, China — but, other objections to the arms trade aside, it provides no stable basis for arms production policies in NATO.

The inadequacies of these four ways of responding to problems of capacity expansion have led NATO states to turn increasingly to a further method, collaborative development or production of major weapon systems. The benefit in terms of the cost of the final product of collaborative ventures is now doubted even within the industry,[23] but more important is the difficulty West European states face in sustaining industrial capacity on the scale needed to produce the most sophisticated equipment. It is not in the unit cost of finished products that the advantage is felt, but in the overall cost of sustaining capacity. Collaboration is possible in a variety of forms – co-development, with or without co-production, licensed production of all or part of a weapon system – and there have been many arguments that it should go further, towards establishing international weapons procurement agencies instead of each state having its own procurement policy, and towards a multinational West European arms industry. Such proposals are seen to be attractive within the context of unity in NATO or the European Community, and their political context and meaning will be discussed in Chapter 7; their immediate economic and industrial context is the need to find some response to the continuing problem of capacity expansion, the need to find a way of sharing development costs as sharp cost increases continue from one generation of weaponry to the next. Collaborative projects and proposals to extend the principle and put it on a more permanent footing can be seen as an international continuation of the rationalisation and reorganisation of industry at a national level, but the consequent need to co-operate with other states about policy central to the state's identity and existence gives the process a further and far-reaching political dimension.

The Revolution in Accuracy

Over the past decade there has been a revolution in conventional weaponry which has both the potential to provide some relief from the problem of spiralling costs and, on the other hand, could exacerbate those problems. It is based on the improvements in accuracy provided by a wide variety of precision-guided munitions (PGM); although PGM also utilise laser and thermal guidance, as a category they are based on electronic technology, the most innovative field in the recent past, now replacing aerospace, automotives, ordnance and shipbuilding, the products of previous cycles of industrial innovation, as the dominant and fastest advancing military technology. Of various definitions proposed for PGM, the most tenable is that offered by James Digby, that a PGM is a guided munition whose chance of striking the target at full range when unopposed is greater than 50 per cent;[24] as Dibgy points out, by this definition Japanese 'kamikaze' aircraft in World War II functioned as PGM, as did dogs laden with explosives used by Soviet troops to attack German tanks in the same war. The term usually applies to light anti-tank, anti-aircraft and anti-ship missiles, but might also apply to longer range weapons such as cruise missiles.

Although the implications of PGM did not come to be widely realised until the 1970s, the technologies of precision guidance have been emerging since the late 1950s: design studies on *Swingfire*, a wire-guided anti-tank missile now in service with the British army, began in 1958;[25] full development on *Redeye*, an American anti-aircraft PGM, began in 1959 after in-house research by the Pentagon starting in 1956.[26] The American war in South-east Asia spurred development of some types of PGM and provides the classic example of the effectiveness of air-to-ground PGM: between 1965 and 1968, US aircraft made 600 sorties against the Thanh Hoa Bridge, losing twelve aircraft in the process, but in 1972 the bridge was destroyed in one raid by eight aircraft equipped with laser-guided bombs. That other great modern military testing-ground, the Middle East, provided further lessons when, in 1967, the Israeli destroyer, *Elat*, was sunk by an anti-ship missile fired from a light Egyptian boat, and in the 1973 war when Israel's previously dominant air and tank forces received severe shocks at the hands of Egyptian forces equipped with PGM. One of the most striking advantages of PGM is cost: used against tanks and aircraft, the missile can cost a fraction of one per cent of its target.

Conclusions about the operational impact of PGM partly derive from the Vietnam and, especially, 1973 Arab-Israeli wars, but care is required in applying those conclusions to the very different terrain, weather conditions and military forces in Europe. The performance of PGM is reduced in conditions of poor visibility, and counter measures are available against PGM and their operators, such as stronger armour, smoke-screens, electronic jamming and heavy artillery fire. The attraction of cheapness can be over-stated: for example, although the US TOW anti-tank missile sells at about $8,000 with $36,400 for the missile-launcher ($42,000 for helicopter-borne launcher),[27] the vehicle on which the launcher is mounted can cost considerably more. Overcoming the limitations of PGM, and especially the lightness of their warheads, will be one factor tending to push costs upwards. Already PGM are undergoing a steady process of technological improvement and sophistication: first-generation anti-tank PGM were wire-guided and controlled by the operator throughout their flight to the target; second-generation versions, although still wire-guided, receive commands automatically from a computer as long as the operator keeps his sights on the target; third-generation models, now in development, will dispense with wire-guidance, needing simply to be launched at the target on which they will home in by themselves, correcting the flight-path as required.[28] These automatic anti-tank PGM are known as 'fire and forget' weapons, or 'shoot and scoot'.

Despite the fact that the obsession with technological sophistication has already taken over, anti-tank PGM, even including the cost of the launching vehicle if they are mounted (and some types are man-portable), should retain a major cost advantage over tanks, and the same should hold for anti-aircraft PGM. Adding capabilities to tanks and aircraft to provide some counter to PGM will push their costs up even faster, and it is generally the case that improvements in a mature technology are more expensive and require more additional capacity and time than improvements in a relatively young technology. Moreover, PGM will retain the decisive improvement that if a target is within the maximum range and can be tracked throughout the necessary aiming process, it can be hit;[29] for many targets, hitting them means putting them out of action. As a result, 'It will become much less desirable to concentrate a great deal of military value in one place or in one vehicle';[30] sophisticated weapon systems such as tanks and aircraft are precisely 'concentrations of a great deal of military value', becoming distressingly vulnerable to cheap missiles fired in most cases from much cheaper weapon platforms. The corollary of this is that small units can now deploy far more hitting power: for example, Steven Canby has argued that single infantry companies equipped with PGM could have a greater anti-tank capacity than entire battalions before 1970.[31]

Indeed, the major impact of PGM on land is to challenge the battlefield superiority of tanks, and therefore to provide infantry with greater defensive strength against tank-led offensives; the immediate relevance of this to the European theatre will not escape anybody who has listened to the constant moaning of NATO commentators at the size of the WP's tank inventory. The potential of anti-tank guided weapons (ATGW) was revealed in the Sinai battles of the October 1973 Arab-Israeli War, and much debate about ATGW since then has hinged upon differing interpretations of the events of that war. The Israeli army, perhaps the foremost modern exponent of tank warfare, had developed a doctrine which permitted tanks to advance free of the constraint of being accompanied by infantry, whose role was to follow the offensive and 'mop up' remaining pockets of resistance. Although dramatically successful in the 1967 Six Day War, it was almost disastrous in 1973 when the Egyptian army held back its tanks and led the offensive with 'tank-hunting' teams of infantry equipped with first-generation Soviet ATGW; in counter-attacks, Israeli tanks then suffered heavily against Egyptian infantry dug into strong defensive positions. It was only when the Egyptian army attempted to follow up with a second offensive, combined with the effect of a daring Israeli counter-offensive across the southern end of the Suez Canal, that the initial Egyptian advantage was neutralised.[32]

Because tanks have been regarded as the essential core of land offensives, the erosion of their authority by infantry equipped with ATGW offers attractive possibilities for defensive forces, and holds the potential for developing forces deployed for strictly and clearly defensive purposes. This does not mean that PGM, whether carried by soldiers, on vehicles, in helicopters or fixed-wing aircraft, could not be used in offensives; precision guidance will be absorbed into every branch and mission of armed forces and used by forces on the offensive to increase their hitting power. But the specific threat of ATGW to tanks and the possibility of small dispersed units operating a mobile defence in depth, able to slow the momentum and absorb armoured offensives, suggest that the advent of PGM offers more advantage to the defence than the offence.[33]

There have been a number of arguments against this vision.[34] It has been noted that the operators of PGM will be vulnerable to counter-fire, especially because of the longish flight-time of ATGW (up to 30 seconds for some first-generation types over a range of two kilometres) during which the operators of first- and second-generation types must continue to track the target. But it is virtually impossible to spot ATGW in flight — speeds range from 300 kph to 1,000 kph for TOW[35] — and equally hard to spot where an ATGW was fired from unless the eye happens to be looking at the exact place at the moment of firing. ATGW can also be designed to make detection of the launching point harder: TOW has a two-stage motor, the second stage only firing when it is well clear of the launcher so that the puff of smoke when that happens is positively misleading as to the operator's location; *Swingfire* can be fired by an operator situated up to 100 metres from the launcher. Operators can also use natural cover and dig themselves into fox-holes. Thus it is not precise fire from tanks to which PGM operators would be vulnerable, but 'area fire' by artillery intended to saturate an area which, if ATGW are operated in dispersed units, would be quite large. This kind of artillery barrage can be responded to in kind, which makes the comparative ranges of artillery and its accuracy important; current artillery has ranges up to about 20 kilometres, with greater ranges, up to about 30 kilometres, possible with new types such as the British-German-Italian FH-70 howitzer and with new guided artillery shells.[36] Aircraft, rocket artillery and medium-range missiles will also have a role here. There is no reason to believe that the offence's artillery and other supporting fire-power must be more effective than the defence's.

It has also been argued that electronic counter measures mounted on tanks and perhaps on accompanying armoured vehicles could jam and mislead ATGW; it is hard to see how wire-guided ATGW could be vulnerable to such measures,[37] although automatic third-generation ATGW might be. Providing tanks with the capability for electronic warfare would make them even more expensive, and easily-mounted smoke-releasing devices would be cheaper and possibly more effective though dependent on weather conditions. More importantly, the development of stronger armour along the lines of the British-developed nylon-titanium *Chobham* armour would provide greater protection against all types of ATGW warheads. As yet, the WP has not deployed tanks with this kind of armour, but can be expected to, forcing ATGW warheads to be heavier, needing larger missiles at more cost. But although *Chobham* armour can offer greater protection, it will not make tanks invulnerable even to current ATGW, and the armour would also need to be mounted on infantry-carrying vehicles if tanks were not to become swiftly isolated from their supporting infantry. A further argument is that one weakness of some kinds of ATGW is that while the impact of their warheads would kill the crew, the tank itself could be repaired and put back in action.[38] This, however, assumes a very large reservoir of trained tank-crews together with an efficient infrastructure for repairing tanks in battlefield conditions and, in the best of cases, could still not prevent the offensive's momentum from being lost.

Until some new technological development, therefore, the large-scale deployment of PGM in ground forces must be concluded to be more advantageous to the defence than the offence, asymmetrically favouring infantry and other anti-tank units more than armoured forces. There is at present no alternative to the tank to form the core of major offensives; were a WP offensive ever to occur, tanks can be expected to be the major component of combined arms teams.[39] Weaponry which helps neutralise the effectiveness of tanks therefore provides crucial capabilities to defensive forces in their major task; the propaganda vision of hordes of Soviet tanks rolling westwards through Europe at least has the merit of concentrating the mind in the right place. While ATGW operators, whether on foot, in vehicles or in helicopters, are not going to have an easy time of it, neither are tanks.

It is not clear, however, that NATO forces are capable of adapting to take full advantage of the new possibilities. At present, in the WP as well, the tendency appears to be grafting new technologies onto old doctrines rather than thoroughly rethinking those doctrines. There is general acceptance of the need for mass deployment of ATGW: for example, TOW entered service in 1970, and reached a production figure of 100,000 in late 1975 and a figure of 200,000 missiles produced in mid-1978;[40] by late 1978 nearly 200,000 ATGW had been delivered to NATO.[41] But continued moaning about the WP's tank numbers is accompanied by at least token efforts to match WP forces category-by-category — NATO's tank forces have also shown a net numerical increase since the start of the 1970s.[42] Moreover, ATGW are increasingly mounted in batteries on vehicles or carried in helicopters, sacrificing some of the advantages of easy concealment, dispersed deployment and low cost, and turning ATGW units themselves into targets of high value. ATGW open up new perspectives for land warfare and the defensive deployment of ground forces, but it is far from certain that military blinkers can come off for long enough for those perspectives to be seen; indeed, as ATGW remorselessly grind on to more sophisticated and expensive third- and further-generation types, it may be that the chance has already been lost.

PGM have three distinct consequences for air forces: aircraft equipped with PGM will have greater hitting power against targets on land or sea or in the air; however, they will be more vulnerable to precision-guided surface-to-air missiles (SAM); and improvements in artillery range together with precision accuracy for surface-to-surface missiles, including the deployment of tactical cruise missiles, may erode the rationale for using aircraft in some missions. In sum, aircraft may find it harder to get to their targets but easier to destroy them once there, while against some targets aircraft may no longer be needed.

The example of the Thanh Hoa Bridge shows how increased accuracy of air-to-ground munitions can result in more effective air power. Apart from the laser-guided bombs used in that case, other methods of precision-guidance include radio command from either the aircraft launching the missile or an accompanying one, TV-guidance from a camera in the missile's nose, inertial navigation and, against radar installations, weapons which home in on radiation.[43] For air combat, the accuracy of air-to-air missiles has been improved primarily by radar guidance and infra-red homing systems which pursue the heat from the target aircraft's engine.[44] A related development on the American F-16 fighter is known as HUDWAS – standing for Head-up Display With Automatic Simulation; built by the British Marconi-Elliott company, this system superimposes on the pilot's view of the target a simulated display of the path shells from his cannon will take, adjusting immediately to show the effects of changes in speed and direction of either the target or the pursuing aircraft: it is claimed that as long as the end of the simulated path touches the target, the pilot cannot miss.[45]

However, the key question is the survivability of manned aircraft not only against opposing fighters and interceptors, but against ground-based air-defence systems using precision-guided SAM. The longer the range of the mission, the deeper the strike into enemy territory, the more enemy air space must be flown through in the face of dense and well-organised anti-air defences; unless nuclear weapons are used, and even with precision-guided air-to-ground weapons, this feat must be performed again and again. In general, rates of loss of two per cent (that is, twenty aircraft lost per 1,000 sorties flown) have been thought prohibitively high, enough to curtail or force outright cancellation of missions,[46] and those rates will probably be well surpassed against precision-guided SAM. On missions in the immediate vicinity of the battlefield, SAM carried in vehicles or fired from a man's shoulder together with anti-aircraft guns with fast rates of fire will create a particularly hostile environment for manned aircraft; here, as NATO exercises have shown, losses will also be inflicted by SAM operated by friendly forces. In the 1973 October War, Egyptian SAM created a virtual air defence barrier around their ground forces; Egyptian SAM were eventually destroyed in one place only, and that was done by Israeli ground forces. As one commentator noted, 'This presents a paradox: the purpose of NATO air power is to support ground forces; but if ground forces have to defeat the enemy's ground forces first, what is tactical air power for, except for neutralizing enemy air power?'[47]

In missions in close support of ground forces, manned aircraft act as a kind of long-range artillery; improved artillery accuracy and longer ranges erode the rationale for using costly aircraft in this way, while over slightly longer ranges, terminal guidance for ballistic missiles and the development of medium-range cruise missiles could also diminish the need for manned aircraft.[48] Advocates of manned aircraft in these roles stress their ability to react quickly to the demands of an emergency, to seek out their own targets rather than have them provided as artillery and surface-to-surface missiles require, although some types of aircraft would have their target designated for them with lasers by ground forces; it is argued that the fast moving environment of a future war requires the flexibility manned aircraft provide.

This may be so, but suggests the need for an air force performing a relatively limited range of missions which artillery and missiles lack either the range or the accuracy to carry out. A more substantive defence of continuing the full spectrum of manned aircraft missions depends in general upon their ability to surmount the threat from SAM by deploying electronic counter measures (ECM), on attacking aircraft or on specialised 'electronic escort' aircraft or from the ground. The problem here is that ECM will be confronted by electronic counter-counter measures (ECCM) and, baffling though the initials may be, the future operational value of manned aircraft partly depends on a competition between ECM and ECCM in which the latter start with a decided advantage.[49]

The main form of ECM is based on active or passive jamming of enemy radar so that attacking aircraft are not spotted until it is too late. Active jamming works either by deceiving enemy radar by returning false echoes, or by cluttering up their screens with so much 'noise' that the true radar echo cannot be detected or identified. Applying the latter method over a wide range of frequencies can be ineffective because it may generate too little power to jam any single frequency, while concentrating on a single frequency can be countered by the radar hopping from one frequency to another across a broad range and emitting pseudo-random noise which makes it hard for ECM operators and their computers to decode which frequency is in use. For both 'broadband' and 'spot' jamming, the power reaching the enemy radar must be greater than that of its returning radar echo; it is difficult for ground-based ECM to achieve this if the enemy radar is detecting objects at shorter range, while if the jamming is done from an aircraft it must carry the full range of ECM equipment and be able to generate more power than is available to the enemy's ground-based radar, which is a difficult and costly prospect. ECM which work by deception depend upon identifying the enemy radar's pulse rate and simulating it to return a false echo, but pulse rates can be varied as easily as frequencies, which provides another decoding task for ECM.

Applying active jamming against SAM involves similar problems, and although radar on SAM or with the ground units which launch the missiles are unlikely to vary frequencies over such a broad spectrum, the time available for decoding and jamming by ECM would be minimal.[50] If SAM are command-guided rather than radar-guided, ECM attempting to interrupt the radio signal must get between the missile and the ground-based command unit since the missile's receiver will be angled back to receive commands; the most likely way of doing this is for ground forces to overrun the command units, which raises the paradox about the role of tactical air power that emerged from the 1973 Arab-Israeli war. SAM which home in on the heat of the aircraft's engine are immune to such ECM, and no solution to this threat has apparently been identified apart from the technique used by Israeli pilots in 1973 of flying so that their exhaust trails crossed, creating a hot patch of air that attracted the heat-seeking SAM which exploded harmlessly; however, this demands high flying skills and split-second timing, and could be countered by phased launching of groups of SAM.

There is a further problem with active jamming, since its signals can be intercepted and a bearing taken to reveal the source which, if the source is an attacking aircraft, reveals what the whole point of ECM is to conceal. The problem with passive jamming is that it is a hit-and-miss affair, likely to jam friendly as well as enemy radar. 'Chaff' — strips of reflecting material such as tinfoil cut to a size corresponding to the enemy radar frequency and scattered in the air — can now be countered by hopping from one frequency to another, while making the reflectors into transponders to throw enemy radar emissions back is more promising only if it can be made to avoid interfering with friendly radar.

In short, for every form of ECM about which information is publicly available — and in a field such as this that is a particularly important qualification — there is an appropriate and relatively straightforward form of ECCM. This does not mean that ECM will be utterly ineffective, just as the new accuracy of SAM does not mean attacking aircraft will be unable to operate at all, but it does mean that ECM have failed to provide a panacea to the threat of precision-SAM. The main response at the moment to ECCM appears to be computerising ECM to decode ECCM more quickly and handle more data at one time; this may erode a little of the advantage ECCM have, but provides no lasting basic answer. The most obvious way to deal with the threat posed by SAM is to attempt to destroy SAM units, radar installations and command posts rather than electronically out-wit them, but whether this is attempted with ground or air forces or both it will be extremely difficult and costly of both equipment and personnel. A more promising solution, if air forces could unhitch themselves from loyalty to the current range of manned aircraft missions, would be to reassess the roles of air power and see what can be jettisoned or reduced.

The difficulty of using manned aircraft in close support of ground forces and improvements in artillery suggest that this air mission could receive less attention. This would also reduce the requirement for air

superiority aircraft which are needed partly to keep enemy fighters off
the backs of close support aircraft; air superiority also protects ground
forces from enemy aircraft, but ground units can be equipped with
SAM to perform much of this task themselves. It may still be important
to have air power available to aid units thrown off balance by an enemy
offensive or to help in swift exploitation of local successes; for this, the
wiser course would be to produce cheaper, rugged and specialised aircraft using familiar and relatively straightforward technology, rather
than continually trying to push forward the frontiers of technology with
projects like *Tornado*. Although they are equally vulnerable to SAM,
the ability of helicopters as anti-tank weapon systems also vitiates the
rationale for fixed-wing aircraft, and helicopters can reduce their vul-
nerability by operating techniques which show only the smallest target
for the shortest period of time – British *Lynx* helicopters carrying TOW
ATGW will have the sighting equipment in the roof permitting them to
stay close to the ground or trees. Similarly specialised aircraft could be
used to hinder the movement of enemy forces, supplies and reinforcements – the interdiction mission – until the accuracy of medium-range
missiles increases. Longer range interdiction, such as attacking airfields,
and long-range strike missions face the problems of deep penetration of
enemy air space against well-organised defences consisting both of SAM
and interceptor aircraft. If the hyper-expensive American B-1 bomber,
cancelled by President Carter in 1977 but still capable of re-emerging in
the 1980s, is the future model for long-range strike aircraft, it would
seem to make more budgetary sense for a state like Britain simply to
opt out of the role. With *Tornado* going ahead, however, the RAF has
no intention of doing that: long-range strike is the status mission and it
will hold on to it against all-comers; indeed, like most air forces it will
resist any argument that technological change should result in pruning
its missions, and will seek to justify itself with new, marginal and costly
sophistications to the same kinds of weapon systems it now operates.

At present, the implications of PGM at sea are neither as clear nor
apparently as profound as on land or in the air. The example of the
sinking of the Israeli destroyer, *Elat*, in 1967 demonstrates that precision-
guided anti-ship missiles make large surface vessels as vulnerable to
much smaller surface craft as they have long been to submarines and
aircraft. The successful firing of a missile by the US Navy from a type
of hovercraft moving at 60 knots, and reportedly capable of speeds up
to 80 knots, appeared to open up the possibility of naval tactics based
on small craft able to engage larger vessels on a hit-and-run basis.[51] But
the main interest in the US Navy seemed to be in developing a larger

frigate-sized version of the vessel (about 3,000 tons) which seems to lose the main advantage of the prototype, and the project's future is uncertain.[52] Precision-guided anti-ship missiles are now widely deployed by NATO and WP naval forces, and small vessels would be more vulnerable to them than larger and sturdier ships. As long as there is an interest in deploying navies to express global power, it is unlikely that small vessels would become the main component of large navies; the US Navy continues to be structured around large aircraft carriers, while the USSR is introducing smaller *Kiev* class carriers, and the Royal Navy awaits its complement of mini-carriers in the form of the ASW Cruisers. For navies which concentrated on less ambitious tasks, the development of fast hovercraft and hydrofoils may hold more promise, especially if they were supplemented by land-based aircraft. But for Britain, such a perspective presupposes major changes in force structure, naval doctrine and strategy.

Technological Exotica and Technological Advance

PGM raise the prospect of increased defensive conventional strength at reduced cost. On the face of it, NATO's declared defensive purposes leave it strategically well placed to take advantage of PGM, developing defensive deployments able to absorb even the most massive armoured offensive in Europe without needing to increase military spending; strategic changes along these lines might, in the context of other political and military steps, contribute to reducing tension between NATO and the WP by reducing the emphasis on weapon systems and force structures applicable for offensives. On the face of it, the British state could avoid the need to develop and produce the costly MBT-80 tank by opting to structure ground forces around infantry equipped with PGM. Institutional resistance in both the military and industry are likely to block such change.

Greater demands are already being placed on PGM, introducing greater sophistication which will not only increase costs but raise questionmarks about their reliability. So far, ATGW and precision-guided SAM have been characterised by easy operation, high reliability and undemanding maintenance, but this is already on the way out. What seems to attract the military is not the possiblity of dispersed units deploying for in-depth defence, but the concept of the electronic or automated battlefield; this emerged in the Vietnam War when the USA attempted to establish a barrier of sensors to detect infiltration by the National Liberation Front forces, and grew into a formal army research programme to develop sensors and fast communications into a centrally controlled battlefield command system.[53] Such a system could realise the vision of the future described by General Westmoreland, the former US Army commander in Vietnam, when he foresaw battlefields 'on which we can destroy anything we can locate through instant communications and the almost instantaneous application of highly lethal firepower'.[54] This will serve to emphasise even further the perception of military rivalry as technological competition, and despite the changes it seems to foresee for the future, it will both directly and indirectly cement both military and industry into their present technological philosophies and institutional patterns.

In the absence of institutional and doctrinal reforms, far from permitting increased defensive strength at reduced cost, PGM will provide a rationale for building all kinds of technological extras into existing weapon systems, thus actually exacerbating cost problems for the armed forces as a whole. And the strengthening of defences will produce one often unconsidered consequence, that if and when offensives are launched they will need to be even more powerful and destructive, which will effectively mean widespread and early use of chemical and nuclear weaponry.

The forward march of military technology is never particularly welcome; it may on occasion display attractive possibilities, but the nature of the institutions which generate and utilise the technology ensure that its advance normally means more lethal warfare and, after the first benefits of reduced costs when a breakthrough is made to a new technological route, the familiar pattern of increasing costs.[55] Military technology is now developing in ways which only a few years ago would have seemed pure science fiction. The US Army is developing infra-red sensors for detecting enemy forces which, it is said, are so sensitive 'they can detect the heat given off by a 1-meter block of ice half way across a continent'.[56] Lasers, which have so far been used to mark targets and aim weapons, may shortly become weapons in their own right: aircraft have reportedly been shot down by high-energy lasers in American trials.[57] The development of 'hunter-killer' satellites able to destroy enemy reconnaissance satellites means that a future major war will include warfare in outer space.[58] The Pentagon is running an exploratory development programme on a self-initiated anti-aircraft missile which, in one form, could be delivered to the vicinity of an enemy airfield where it would wait until an aircraft was preparing to take off, at which point it would launch itself and automatically home in on the aircraft to destroy it.[59]

Unless the advance of military technology can be constrained, such military exotica and other similar projects will become operational systems. Limiting the advance of technology will mean breaking with current military perceptions and institutions, developing both defence policy and industry in different forms. If this proves impossible, yet more lethal weapon systems will develop requiring ever greater resources. The irony is that by no means all of these super-sophisticated products will increase military effectiveness, let alone contribute to security. If no basic steps are taken to reshape military industry, the problem of expansion of its capacity will remain, and in the case of Britain and other West European states must lead either to intolerable economic burdens or to a collaborative international reorganisation of the military industrial and technological effort. This would not be a permanent solution to the problem of capacity expansion, but it would mean a refocussing of strategic decision into a forum outside the nation-state, becoming a vehicle for the development of supra-national power. The question of the organisation and control of military technology is becoming a decisive one in the future political and economic development of Western Europe and NATO.

Notes

1. Senator Proxmire, quoted in *Aerospace Daily*, 30 March 1976.

2. M. Kaldor, 'Defence Cuts and the Defence Industry', in D. Smith, (ed.), *Alternative Work for Military Industries* (Richardson Institute, London, 1977).

3. N.R. Augustine, 'One Plane, One Tank, One Ship: Trend for the Future?', *Defense Management Journal*, April 1975.

4. See *Defense Monitor*, October 1976; on the C-5A see R.F. Kaufman, *The War Profiteers* (Doubleday, New York, 1972), especially pp. 184-200.

5. See *Flight International*, 23 October 1976.

6. R. Perry *et al.*, *System Acquisition Strategies*, R-733-PR/ARPA (Rand, Santa Monica, Calif, 1971).

7. 'Artillery-rocket Launchers', *Armies and Weapons*, February/March 1978.

8. W.D. White, *US Tactical Air Power: Missions, Forces, and Costs* (Brookings Institution, Washington, DC, 1974), pp. 4-6.

9. Augustine, 'One Plane, One Tank, One Ship'.

10. See *New Manchester Review*, 29 June 1979; *Flight International*, 30 June 1979.

11. *New Scientist*, 11 January 1979; *Business Week*, 27 November 1978.

12. On current showing, such a slackening seems unlikely in the short term, with sales in 1978 by US computer firms up by 20 per cent over 1977, and a further 13-15 per cent increases expected for 1979: *Financial Times*, 6 February 1979.

13. See A.T. Mahan, *The Influence of Sea Power upon History 1660-1783* (Hill & Wang, New York, 1957).

14. On the USSR's policy in this respect, see A.J. Alexander, *Decision-making in Soviet Weapons Procurement*, Adelphi Paper 147/8 (IISS, London, 1978).

15. See M. Kaldor, *European Defence Industries – National and International Implications* (University of Sussex, Brighton, 1972), p. 7: 'To put it formally, development capacity equals development costs divided by the time taken for development . . . (P)roduction capacity equals unit production costs times the number of weapons divided by the time taken for production.'

16. Ibid., p. 9.

17. D. Wood, *Project Cancelled* (Macdonald & Jane's, London, 1975), Appendices 1 and 2.

18. See Kaldor, 'Defence Cuts and the Defence Industry'.

19. Wood, *Project Cancelled*.

20. On the Defence Sales Organisation, see *State Research Bulletin* 6, June/July 1978.

21. See L. Freedman, *Arms Production in the United Kingdom: Problems and Prospects* (Royal Institute of International Affairs, London, 1978), pp. 29-31.

22. Precise figures on the arms trade are virtually unobtainable; figures from the US Arms Control and Disarmament Agency do not tally with those of the Stockholm International Peace Research Institute, and both bodies' figures for Britain differ from those provided by the Ministry of Defence.

23. *Flight International*, 29 October 1977.

24. J. Digby, 'Precision Weapons', in J.J. Holst and U. Nerlich (eds), *Beyond Nuclear Deterrence: New Aims, New Arms* (Macdonald & Jane's, London, 1977), p. 158.

25. 'Swingfire', *Armies and Weapons*, February/March 1978.

26. 'Redeye', *Market Intelligence Report* (Defense Market Survey, Greenwich, Ct, 1975).

27. T. Gervasi, *Arsenal of Democracy* (Grove Press, New York, 1977), p. 191; 'TOW' stands for Tube-fired, Optically-tracked, Wire-guided.

28. 'Anti-Tank Weapons', *Military Technology* April 1978; *Jane's Weapon Systems 1978* (Macdonald & Jane's, London, 1978), p. 31.

29. Digby, 'Precision Weapons', p. 161.

30. J. Digby, *Precision-guided Weapons*, Adelphi Paper 117 (IISS, London, 1975), p. 4.

31. S. Canby, *The Alliance and Europe: Part IV Military Doctrine and Technology*, Adelphi Paper 109 (IISS, London, 1974), p. 24.

32. For a narrative of the war see Parts II and III of E. Monroe and A.H. Farrar-Hockley, *The Arab-Israeli War October 1973: Background and Events*, Adelphi Paper 111 (IISS, London, 1974); on the evolution of Israeli tank doctrine see E. Luttwak and D. Horowitz, *The Israeli Army* (Allen Lane, London, 1975), Chapter 6; the tactical conditions in the Sinai did not prevail in the Golan heights where attacking Syrian tanks suffered heavily against Israeli tanks in defensive positions – see M. Dayan, *The Story of My Life* (Sphere, London, 1976), p. 516 – and some analyses of the effects of ATGW have gone astray by apparently failing to account for this difference.

33. See the useful summary and weighing of the arguments in J.J. Mearsheimer, 'Precision-guided Munitions and Conventional Deterrence', *Survival*, March/April 1979.

34. For representative examples see the reports of two seminars held at the Royal United States Services Institute: *The Future of the Battle Tank in a European Conflict* (RUSI, London, 1974); *Tactical Employment and Comparative Performance of Ground- and Air-launched Anti-tank Weapons* (RUSI, London, 1976).

35. *Jane's Weapon Systems 1978*, pp. 31-44; Gervasi, *Arsenal of Democracy*, records a lower speed for TOW, 368 mph (589 kph), but *Jane's* also records a speed of 950 kph for the Franco-German HOT ATGW.

36. The normal range of the FH-70 would be 24 kilometres, extended to over 30 kilometres with special ammunition: *Jane's Weapon Systems 1978*, pp. 378-9; see *idem*, pp. 45-6, on the US *Copperhead* Cannon-launched Guided Projectile, designed to provide terminal guidance for artillery using laser-guided shells homing onto targets designated by aircraft or remotely piloted airborne vehicles; *Copperhead* apparently grew out of a US Army research programme begun in 1972 intended to provide 'a first-shot first-hit capability for both rockets and cannons': 'Terminal Homing', *Market Intelligence Report*, 1975.

37. The makers claim that the British *Swingfire* is immune to electronic counter measures: *Jane's Weapon Systems 1978*, p. 41.

38. C.I. Hudson, 'New Conventional Munitions', in *New Conventional Weapons and East-West Security Part I*, Adelphi Paper 144 (IISS, London, 1978), pp. 49-50.

39. See P.A. Karber, 'The Soviet Anti-tank Debate', *Survival*, May/June 1976.

40. *Tactical Employment and Comparative Performance*, p. 1, and *Flight International*, 29 July 1978.

41. *Armed Forces Journal*, January 1978.

42. See Tables 4.1 and 4.2 in Chapter 4, above.

43. *Jane's Weapon Systems 1978*, pp. 135-60.

44. Ibid., pp. 161-73.

45. Gervasi, *Arsenal of Democracy*, p. 57; it is known as a 'Head-up Display' because the pilot need not look down to see it.

46. White, *US Tactical Air Power*, p. 69; Canby, *Military Doctrine and Technology*, p. 37.

47. Canby, *Military Doctrine and Technology*, p.37.

48. In medium-range missions, it could be possible to operate cruise missiles from weapon platforms that evade at least some of the cost constraints on long-range versions discussed in Chapter 5, above: see D. Ball, 'The Costs of the Cruise Missile', *Survival*, November/December 1978.

49. There is a useful outline of ECM and ECCM techniques in *RUSI and Brassey's Defence Yearbook 1975/6* (Brassey's, London, 1975), pp. 297-303.

50. When the British *Rapier* SAM operates in its radar-guided mode, it is the narrowness of the radar beam which reportedly permits it to function well in severe ECM conditions: 'Rapier – the Mature Low-level SAM', *International Defense Review* 1974, no. 4.

51. *The Guardian*, 19 April 1976.

52. 'Surface Effect Ships', *Market Intelligence Report* (Defense Market Survey, Greenwich, Ct, 1978).

53. 'Automated Battlefield', *Market Intelligence Report*, 1975; J.P. Bulger, 'Tactical Sensors for the Army', *National Defense*, January/February 1976; M.T. Klare, *War Without End* (Random House, New York, 1972), Chapter 7.

54. Address at the annual luncheon of the Association of the United States Army, 14 October 1969, reprinted *Congressional Record*, 16 October 1969.

55. As a counter-example, at least potentially, the use of graphite thread to replace metal in aircraft components could reduce weight and costs while increasing structural strength and durability: *International Herald Tribune*, 14 November 1978.

56. N.R. Augustine, 'New Technology for An Army of Opportunity', *National Defense*, November/December 1975.

57. *The Economist*, 4 December 1976.

58. Stockholm International Peace Research Institute, *Outer-space – Battlefield of the Future* (Taylor & Francis, London, 1978), Chapter 8.

59. 'SIAM', *Market Intelligence Report*, 1978.

7 RIVALRY AND ALLIANCE

Analysis of NATO is complicated by the fact that its member states both co-operate and compete with each other. While they combine in organising military power, declare that an attack upon one is an attack upon all and insist on the need for unity against the common enemy, they nevertheless pursue all kinds of conflicts with each other, over substantial as well as peripheral issues. In fact, one of the central and definitive characteristics of NATO is that its member states are both allies and rivals: NATO is constructed upon a dichotomy between its members' need for the cohesion of alliance and the inevitability of their mutual rivalry.

NATO's cohesion has never been watertight — most notably France in the 1960s and Greece in the 1970s withdrew from its military organisation — but to the extent that there has been cohesion, it has largely been assured by American leadership. Indeed, NATO cohesion and US hegemony have been virtually the same thing; rejecting the one has meant rejecting the other. Under American leadership in the late 1940s and early 1950s, it was possible to leave behind some of the forms of rivalry of previous decades, but continuing conflicts of interest and the unevenness of economic development in Western Europe and the USA meant that, even as they profited from a more stable international system, West European states consistently bit the hand that fed them their cohesive diet. In the 1970s, as this international system faces a profound crisis, the decline in American leadership, which partially reflects the growing strength of Western Europe (though much else besides), has begun to result in major challenges to the current form of NATO cohesion.

Rivalry between NATO states can be seen as the modern version of inter-imperialist rivalry whose classic period was in the years leading up to World War I. Analyses of inter-imperialist rivalry deriving from that period stress that it tends towards inter-imperialist war, and rivalry tending towards war is itself seen as a defining characteristic of imperialism.[1] Clearly, the modern form is very different: the greater internationalisation of capital, the emergence of powerful non-capitalist states and strong national liberation movements in colonised countries, the memory of the economic anarchy of the 1920s and 1930s and the capacity of the USA to be the organising agent combined to create the conditions

180

for closer cohesion between the capitalist states. But this did not eliminate the well-springs of rivalry between the states of NATO. Over the
past decade in particular there have been sharp conflicts of interest over
oil and energy, trading and monetary policy, especially with the collapse
of the US-created Bretton Woods international monetary system in
1971, and over the response to the general international economic crisis
of the 1970s. These cannot be dismissed as peripheral or insignificant
disagreements: they concern conflicting interests over key aspects of
the functioning of the international system and of individual domestic
economies.

The pursuit of rivalry by NATO states has been mediated through
co-operation and each part of the dichotomy between their cohesion
and their rivalry is equally important. This has created in NATO a kind
of unstable equilibrium, the reconciliation of irreconcilables, in which
rivalry and co-operation are mutually limited. As economic crisis poses
the states with major challenges and intensifies the issues which separate
them, a unified response becomes more important even as it becomes
more difficult. Although 'crisis' is an over-used term, it is fair to see the
crisis of the 1970s, which will extend well into the 1980s and possibly
beyond, as having similar dimensions to the crises of the 1920s and
1930s and of the 1870s.[2] In both previous cases, the outcome of crisis
was major change and upheaval in the internationalist capitalist system;
indeed, crisis can be seen as a mechanism of change and renewal. If it is
right to see the current crisis in a similar light, then one should expect
the coming years to be a period of major international reorganisation
which, for NATO, means a reworking of the unstable equilibrium of
rivalry and cohesion, an alteration in the terms of both sides of the
dichotomy. It is therefore no surprise that current commentaries on
NATO, its problems and its future contain a multiplicity of proposals
for different types of reorganisation in the alliance. In these commentaries the basic issues concern the possibility of a new relationship
between the USA and Western Europe, the prospects for the European
Economic Community (EEC) and the condition of relations between
West European states.

American Decline and West European Unity

The basic challenge to the current form of equilibrium in NATO lies in
the decline of American leadership, in the USA's inability to fulfil the
same kind of hegemonic organising role it fulfilled from the end of
World War II until the early 1970s (though already with decreased effect
in the 1960s). This decline is visible in a number of ways, not least in

the widespread scorn with which President Carter and the cavortings of the US Congress are viewed. However, as I argued in Chapter 3 in relation to the problems of US foreign policy, the difficulties are neither confined to nor ultimately caused by an occasional ineptitude in foreign policy or misjudgement in domestic economic policy.

Table 7.1 compares the development of the American economy with that of the current members of the EEC between 1953 and 1976.[3] The change in the relative gross national and domestic products over time is quite remarkable: the combined product of the current EEC states in 1953 amounted to but 45 per cent of the US product, while by 1977 it amounted to 84 per cent. This represents a change not in real purchasing power but in real economic power, reflecting both the much faster West European growth rates and the weakness of the dollar in the 1970s.

Table 7.1: Gross National Products, 1953, and Gross Domestic Products, 1977, of the USA and Current Members of the EEC (in US$ billion)[a]

	1953	1977
Belgium	8.23	79.2
Denmark	3.82	46
Eire	1.44	9.4
Federal Republic of Germany	35.02	516.2
France	42.97	380.7
Italy	20.52	196.1
Luxembourg	0.33	2.8
Netherlands	6.38	106.4
United Kingdom	47.94	244.3
TOTAL	166.65	1581.1
United States of America	369.72	1878.8
RATIO	0.45	0.84

a. The fact that 1953 data are for gross national products and 1977 data are for gross domestic products is of little significance given that it is the ratio which is of interest.

Sources: 1953: *OECD National Accounts 1953-1969* (Paris, 1971); 1977: *OECD Economic Surveys: United Kingdom* (Paris, March 1979).

The USA's relative decline still leaves it with a larger gross domestic product than the EEC's combined total: it is important to retain a perspective on American decline and challenges to US hegemony — while the process is well advanced, it does not mean that within NATO there is another single state as powerful. A similar picture emerges from data on expenditure for research and development which provide a rough indication of relative technological strength; in 1963, expenditure in capitalist countries apart from the USA (and therefore including others, most notably Japan, not now in the EEC) amounted to 40 per cent of American expenditure, whereas by 1973 the figure had changed to 92 per cent.[4] These data do not reveal the source of the expenditure, only where it was spent, but despite this important qualification the broad trend is clear.

This relative decline has been developing over a long period: it had already been noted in the early 1960s,[5] and the rest of the decade provided further evidence of the increasing economic strength of, especially, the Federal Republic of Germany (FRG) and Japan and their capacity to challenge the USA's economic power.[6] In 1971, when the USA suffered its first deficit in annual trade, the US Department of Commerce pointed out that whereas American productivity growth had exceeded both Western Europe's and Japan's for 80 years from 1870, it had begun to fall behind from 1950.[7] Through the 1970s, the domestic US economy has been affected by inflation, low rates of growth and trade deficits, although, despite parallels drawn with Britain's economic debilities, it has not yet plumbed those depths.

Business Week has summed up the consequences of this gradual process as 'a crisis of the decay of power'.[8] A wide variety of evidence exists for this view, although it must be said that many participants in the American debate rely on gross exaggeration, distortions of fact and a manichean world view which are worse than unhelpful in understanding the dimensions of relative decline. Perhaps the most telling piece of evidence was the role of the USA at the Bonn summit meeting of leading capitalist states in July 1978, where the final agreement was widely agreed to bear the hallmark of Chancellor Schmidt of the FRG, and the Carter administration was reduced to promising (vainly as it turns out) to try and reduce US imports and energy consumption, to helping pressure Japan into either exporting less or importing more and to committing itself to strengthen the dollar.[9] What is significant about this is that it is precisely at such a summit meeting that, formerly, the USA would have been expected effectively to dictate, or at least to take the lead in developing, a response to contemporary economic problems. Although a different US president might be able to project a more effective public image and appear to sustain the USA in its old role, the material basis for its former firm leadership is being eroded.

Although the USA is thus, compared to its past, relatively disadvantaged in its relations with other NATO states, within NATO itself this has not been felt to its full extent. While economically the USA, though the largest unit, is but one competitor among many and while politically it has encountered a serious problem of credibility, militarily it remains the leader of the alliance. It provides the vast majority of NATO's strategic nuclear forces and dictates strategic planning at this level; the American president remains in control of the tactical nuclear weapons deployed by West European states (except Britain and France), and NATO's tactical nuclear modernisation programme is entirely the USA's programme; in most perspectives on the defence of Western Europe, trans-Atlantic reinforcements are still considered an important element of NATO forces. Militarily, the USA is far and away the most powerful member of NATO and its armed forces in Western Europe are a major component of the basic strategic perspectives of all West European NATO states. In 1978, when Western interests required a military intervention in Shaba province in Zaire, it was Belgian and French forces which went in, an eloquent symbol of the difficulties of the USA in the direct use of armed force — but those forces needed American transport aircraft to get to Zaire, an equally eloquent symbol of the USA's still imposing military leadership on the alliance.[10]

The USA's continued strategic hegemony within NATO partially compensates for its relative economic and political decline and limits West European states' pursuit of rivalry with the USA. *Business Week*'s analysis of declining US power argued that the trend could only be arrested by policies which encourage investment at the expense of consumption and increase the resources devoted to the military as a basis for assuming 'additional international responsibilities'.[11] This seems to be a recipe for further emphasising the military counter-balance to economic and political decline, yet increasing military spending would probably absorb resources which would otherwise be used for civil industrial investment, thus, against all intention, contributing to a further weakening of the US economy.[12] As a further problem with this recipe, it remains uncertain that enough domestic political support for overseas military interventions can be developed, although arms exports to underdeveloped countries and increased military investment in NATO could continue to be important and are politically less difficult.

The USA's relative political and economic decline is also partially compensated for by West European disunity. All Europeanist rhetoric aside, Western Europe constitutes neither a single political nor a single economic entity. The directly-elected European parliament and the initiation of the European Monetary System (EMS) no less than the continued functioning of the EEC may seem to provide the possibility of generating a common response to the economic and political challenges of West European states, and the severity of those challenges may seem to demand a common response, but the difficulties of coming up with one are evidently immense. The closer EEC members get, the more scratchy their relations seem to become. We see here a particularly acute form of the mediation of rivalry through cohesion, at the root of which is the uneven economic development of Western Europe, the divergent strengths of the domestic economies, the differing requirements of both the state and capital in each country. Table 7.1 illustrates this, in Britain's decline from first to third place, in the spectacular growth of the FRG's economy, and in the dominant position held by the four largest economies (Britain, France, the FRG and Italy) jointly responsible for 85 per cent of the EEC's combined product, a dominance which is not made more comfortable for the smaller states by the fact that these four countries also account for 88 per cent of the EEC's population. The same problem was illustrated in the reluctance of Britain and Italy to join the EMS and is continually felt in disputes over the EEC's Common Agricultural Policy and other political and economic wrangles.

Uneven economic development and concomitant intra-West European rivalry complicate any analytical effort to counterpose Western Europe and the USA. Yet it can also be argued that West European states can only really pursue their political rivalry with the USA if they are capable of more unified positions; this is one of the elements underpinning the ideology of Europeanism with its aspirations to West European unity. What Europeanism cannot adequately answer is the question of how more unified positions are to be developed, for the perception of common ground among West European states is at least roughly matched by the perceptions of diverging and conflicting requirements. In the late 1940s, in the reorganisation of international capitalism, the decisive factor was not just the shared perception that greater cohesion was necessary but its combination with the capacity of the USA to provide leadership. In Western Europe, the obvious present analogue to the USA then is the FRG, the economic success story of Western Europe, now gaining political and military clout to match its economic strength, yet there is likely to be a deep aversion to West German hegemony in Western Europe.[13]

A further element in the prospects for greater unity is the USA and the chances of arresting its relative decline. At present, American policy appears to seek a more prominent role for both the FRG and Japan in sharing the burdens of organising the international system, and the USA has encouraged both the formation of the EEC and its moves towards greater unity. Yet this presents something of a paradox. In part, the USA can be seen as demanding that the FRG and Japan accept the responsibility that should go with their power and develop policies based on sharing in hegemony rather than on narrow self-interest, while its encouragement of the EEC could be seen partly as a continuation of its post-1945 policies of wanting a strong Western Europe to stand against the Soviet threat, and partly as an awareness of the opportunities for free movement of capital provided by the EEC where American capital is heavily invested. Yet this also means the USA effectively strengthening its rivals, ceding aspects of international leadership and the advantages that has provided, while encouraging in Western Europe the formation of a political entity able to challenge American power more strongly. The US administration looked benignly on the creation of the EMS, yet this was also diagnosed, with some justice, as the formation of a monetary bloc against American capital, the antithesis of the old dollar-based Bretton Woods system which emphasised the free international movement of capital, and as stemming from West European lack of confidence in American economic leadership.[14] Indeed, the very process of ceding aspects of hegemony, with its erosion of a single organising centre, virtually invites the formation of alternative power centres which must inevitably be competitive, even if, for the sake of the continued functioning of the international system, that competition must still be mediated through co-operation. At the same time, visions of West European unity must be complicated by the continuing strength of American capital in the West European countries, no less than by the habits of and attachment to alliance with the USA. The delicate balance of rivalry and competition allows for no simple programme for transition to political unity in Western Europe.

If Western Europe is regarded as a single entity, there is a sharp discrepancy between the USA's relative economic and political decline against Western Europe and its continued strategic hegemony over Western Europe within NATO. This discrepancy defines a focal point for rivalry within NATO between the USA and Western Europe; a major issue in the development of NATO in the 1980s is the extent to which Western Europe can reduce the scale of this discrepancy to take a role in NATO more accurately reflecting the general economic and political balance between it and the USA. But to do that, West European NATO states must function in unity, and the degree to which intra-European rivalry can be superseded defines a further major issue for NATO's future.

Stated in terms of polar opposites, the alternatives for the British state in this context boil down to accepting American leadership or commitment to West European unity; at bottom, the choice must be between these alternatives – they are not compatible. If the British state commits itself to West European unity, the question arises of the terms of that unity, and the basic issue here is whether the FRG would be the organising and leading force or whether a more diversified power bloc would be possible. In practice, neither pole represents a goal which can be thought of as attainable in pure form and movement towards either expresses a tendency which need not be thought likely to fulfil itself. But escape from the contrary attractions of these two poles would be conceivable only in the context of major social and political change, not only in Britain but also throughout Western Europe. Harking back to former political independence in international affairs offers no realistic prospects to the British state as it is now constituted.

Consequently, British defence policy, like the defence policies of all West European NATO states, is caught between these two poles, is pulled by both at the same time. The rival tendencies express themselves within defence policy, and they do so particularly acutely in issues revolving around major weapons procurement decisions. The further consequence of this is the ability of all West European states to move in both directions at the same time in their procurement policies. The growing importance of industrial collaboration in the provision of military equipment, and the sharpness of the problem of capacity expansion to which collaboration is a countervailing response, was discussed in Chapter 6. Here we are dealing with issues of central concern to the identity and integrity of nation-states, the ways in which they equip their armed forces. For states such as Britain, France, the FRG and Italy which have sought a degree of self-reliance in their procurement policies by sustaining military industry, the issues as self-reliance becomes less tenable are the forms in which their identity and integrity are to be compromised; they constitute a central element in the future trajectory of those states and in the possible development of a new form of unstable equilibrium in NATO.

Standardisation and Industrial Collaboration

As the 1970s proceeded, there were increasingly widespread statements of concern about NATO's industrial inefficiency; the problem is largely one of duplication of effort by several national military industries which results in NATO as a whole producing several weapon systems for each mission. One analysis states that in Central Europe NATO deploys 30 types of anti-tank missile, 6 types of short-range missile and 5 medium-range types, 23 types of combat aircraft, 40 types of heavy artillery and 7 different main battle tanks.[15] The list could go on to record yet more duplications: no weapon system is produced for use by all NATO states, and even when we account for genuinely different conditions in which the systems are to be used and for the retention of older types alongside new acquisitions, the picture is still remarkable.

At the root of this duplication is the fact that NATO is a combination of separate states whose independence is in part expressed through their independent weapons procurement policies and independent armed forces with their own particular structures and operating doctrines, and in some cases through the determined maintenance of independent military industrial capacity. The consequence of industrial duplication is widely seen as a strategic problem: NATO, it is argued, would get a greater output of equipment and thus more military strength for the same input of expenditure if this duplication was eliminated. In the context of widespread concern and often alarmism at the condition of the military balance in Europe the interest in eliminating duplication is easily understood. The point has perhaps been put most explicitly and trenchantly by General Johannes Steinhoff, former Chairman of NATO's Military Committee:

> NATO must finally recognise that its member countries cannot keep up the strength of their forces if they continue to believe that their defence as an element of their national sovereignty can thereby support a continual policy of power and prestige, or even an industrial policy.[16]

The point here, of course, is that if the basic concern were to reduce a perceived military disadvantage against the WP, the measures which must be taken cannot be thought of as simply technical adjustments to NATO states' procurement policies; they demand fundamental change in the way the states approach the question of weapons procurement.

In debates on this problem, a series of catchwords has emerged summarising the possible approaches to a solution. 'Standardisation' describes a process in which NATO states, by more closely co-operating in development, production and procurement of military equipment, would move towards the adoption of standard equipment throughout the alliance; we would see, rather than French aircraft, British tanks and German artillery, *NATO* tanks, aircraft and artillery. For this, common, or at least compatible, procurement and development procedures would be required along with standard tactical doctrines to govern the deployment of standard equipment. Along with this process would go 'integration', usually taken to mean the closer co-ordination of NATO states' forces by developing common or compatible procedures in such fields as communications and logistics, further integrating military command structures and co-ordinating national procurement programmes, especially their time-tables, and operational requirements. Clearly, standardisation and integration are linked processes; the advantages are seen in terms of longer production runs of equipment which would reduce unit costs and permit a greater total procurement of equipment, a more efficient overall research and development programme and more efficient and capable military forces for the alliance as a whole.

Both processes thus set out far-reaching ambitions, and both have less ambitious counterparts (which some commentators appear to use more or less interchangeably). A more modest version of standardisation is 'interoperability' which would still require closer co-operation in development, production and procurement so that, for example, a British artillery unit which ran out of ammunition could be refurbished by its Dutch neighbours while a German aircraft could land at a Belgian airfield and be refuelled and rearmed, receive minor repairs and a maintenance check, and even be turned round and sent off on a further mission. If integration of NATO's various armed forces were not possible, the more modest goal of 'harmonisation' might be, for this would maintain the separate identity of national forces while attempting to eliminate inconsistencies between them.

The attraction of standardisation has owed much to the view that this provided the best context for industrial collaboration. There are a variety of possible forms for collaboration, including one state purchasing the licence to produce equipment to a design developed in another and co-production deals in which states purchasing equipment from abroad participate in its production. The most ambitious form is when co-operation begins at the earliest stage, in the definition of operational requirements, and proceeds through initial design work and full-scale development, such as in the case of the *Tornado*. But collaboration, even from the earliest stage, can produce different weapon systems because of modifications preferred by individual states or armed services; with *Tornado* the British and Germans used different contractors for key parts of the aircraft, such as the main weapons computer, while the Franco-German *Alpha Jet* is virtually two different aircraft which will be used in two different roles. Much of the problem here stems from the insistence of states and corporations on maintaining their own production and assembly facilities and from the difficulty of reconciling different and stubbornly supported operational requirements and tactical doctrines. This has been diagnosed as a major obstacle preventing collaborative projects from reaping the expected benefit of cost-savings; within the British aerospace industry it is now recognised that collaboration does not necessarily mean cheapness.[17] It was thought it could be circumvented through a comprehensive effort at removing such national distinctions and aiming at standard equipment and doctrines through as much of the alliance as possible.

A report from the US House of Representatives Armed Services Committee, sceptical of the terms in which the debate has been set, argues that

> Standardization has emerged as the special province of civilian, industrial and administrative military leadership, while interoperability has been the principal concern of military commanders.[18]

However, although there is some truth in this argument, interoperability cannot be seen as a purely military concern. While it is clearly less ambitious and more concerned with the problems of military functioning than with those of industrial policy, what it really does is transpose the issue of standardisation and collaboration from the level of the weapon system as a whole to the level of its components and support equipment. It neither eliminates the need for one form or another of industrial collaboration nor does it avoid the problems of reconciling differing tactical doctrines or government procurement policies and schedules. The increasing attention given to interoperability towards the end of the 1970s may reflect awareness of the problems of such an ambitious project as standardisation and integration, but interoperability provides no easy way out.

In fact, during the 1960s and 1970s NATO has gone through a process of destandardisation. The development of the French military industry, followed by the FRG's and, to a lesser extent, Italy's, diversified the sources for military equipment. At one time, especially in the more sophisticated items of military equipment, NATO forces were relatively standardised because they largely bought American products and a smaller number from Britain. The development of independent procurement policies and the greater attention of these states to the maintenance of independent military industrial capacity has accompanied moves towards greater political independence from the USA, even when American companies have been involved in the production of the equipment. In the French case, the development of military industry was part and parcel of the development of an independent foreign policy under de Gaulle's presidency and of the decision to emphasise this by withdrawing from the NATO military command in 1966. Destandardisation has reflected intensifying intra-NATO rivalry.

Standardisation and industrial collaboration can be seen as a dual strategy to change the organisation of the military market and the organisation of military production in NATO. Whatever the terms used, and whatever the specific form of the processes, an effort to move away from duplication of industrial effort and the resulting weapon systems must involve overcoming the rivalry which is the source of that duplication. But if there is to be standardisation in the future it cannot be like standardisation in the past, equivalent to the USA's domination of the supply of equipment in NATO. The difficult question in advocacies of standardisation and interoperability is who is to design and make the standard weapon systems or components, whose doctrinal preferences are to be jettisoned or how differing doctrines are to be reconciled, and how the arrangements will be made. While standardisation and collaboration demand greater cohesion between the states involved, they also involve intensified competition and rivalry in which the stakes include the survival of major industrial capabilities. Industrial and military cooperation actually intensifies industrial and military competition; NATO's collaborative weapons projects contain miniature versions of the basic NATO dichotomy between cohesion and rivalry, and can be seen as the seeds of alternative possibilities for a new unstable equilibrium.

The Two-way Street

Although West European arms production has grown in the past two decades, the flow of armaments across the Atlantic remains almost entirely from the USA to Western Europe — as Roy Mason, formerly British Defence Secretary, put it, 'a few solitary pedestrians walking down the sidewalk one way, and a mighty motorcade ten times larger going the other way'.[19] The expansion of West European military industrial capacity has made this an increasingly sore point in intra-NATO relations, and the 1970s saw a growing chorus demanding a two-way street in the trans-Atlantic arms trade, a West European share of the domestic American arms market.

This is not, however, a purely West European proposal; the most influential advocacy, which did much to stimulate West European thinking, came from a report to the US Department of State and Defense by Thomas Callaghan who, starting from the argument that US security interests require a strong West European military industry, proposed a programme establishing targets for reciprocal arms sales between Western

Europe and the USA together with complementary development projects.[20] He argued that after twelve years such a programme would have produced definite progress towards compatible military doctrines throughout NATO, standard or interoperable equipment and a rationalised military marketplace. Basic to the programme would be American willingness to import more West European products and the formation of a single West European arms agency to co-ordinate reorganisation of military industry.

While Callaghan stressed the USA's strategic interest in his programme, other views have stressed the USA's commercial interest. Thus a report to the Pentagon in 1976 argued that unless the USA bought West European equipment, it would find itself increasingly excluded from the West European arms market,[21] and Robert Komer, the senior adviser in the Pentagon on NATO affairs, has baldly stated,

> Either we're going to give the allies a somewhat bigger share of our market or they're going to increasingly go for their own equipment, even if ours is better and cheaper. It's as simple as that, because we do the same thing.[22]

There are, however, a number of different versions of the two-way street. Under Mason's interpretation, it means the USA surrendering some of its independence in military procurement to accommodate West European products.[23] As US Defense Secretary, James Schlesinger endorsed the principle, but insisted that the only basis on which the USA could buy West European equipment was the competitiveness of the products;[24] there would be no artificial aid for West European states even, presumably, if this resulted in them copying American protectionism as Komer fears. This view has been abrasively supported by a report from the House Armed Services Committee which argues that the European version of the two-way street is a blatant political device for strengthening its arms industry at American expense; indeed, this report rejects the orthodox view that there is now a one-way street by balancing against US military exports to Western Europe not only US imports of equipment but also the dollars spent by US military personnel in Western Europe.[25] Harold Brown, the current US Defense Secretary, retains the insistence on competitiveness, but in rather less intransigent form,[26] which may be as much a difference in personal style as a difference in substance, but could also reflect a lesser confidence in the superiority of all things American. Mason also agreed on the need for competitiveness as the basis for the USA to buy from Western Europe, and from this argued the need for West European industrial reorganisation as a way to approach the economies of scale available to the US industry.

However, with military equipment the concept of competitiveness is decidedly tricky. It is hard to sustain in the face of a record of cost over-runs and the difficulties of accurately estimating costs for projects involving technological advance,[27] but it is rendered almost worthless by differences in military doctrines. A purchaser selecting between, for example, the British *Chieftain* and German *Leopard* would select on the basis of the preference for the doctrine of tank warfare embodied in one tank's capabilities over the doctrine embodied in the other, at least as much as on the basis of comparative cost; in essence, the choice would depend on whether the purchaser's military ideology more closely resembled British or West German military ideology. The competition insisted upon by Schlesinger and others is thus a political and ideological competition, not a commercial one. In order to buy European the Pentagon would have to think European; West European states tend to buy American because they have tended to think American.

The insistence upon competitiveness modifies the basic thrust of Callaghan's report and is clearly some way from Komer's perspective, for in both the intention is precisely to provide artificial aid to West European military industry, in the former case for strategic reasons and in the latter for long-term commercial ones. Moreover, the Callaghan report's proposal for complementary rather than competitive development projects on the two sides of the Atlantic seeks to link and co-ordinate the industries, whereas the insistence on competitiveness implies at least two separate entities linked only by their competition to equip the same alliance.

Under Schlesinger's influence, however, a different version of the two-way street was also proposed, focussing on aerospace, and going further towards building a military bridge across the Atlantic by suggesting that Western Europe could depend on American designs and development and simply participate in production.[28] The model for this was the General Dynamics F-16 fighter, a maximum of 348 of which are to be bought by Belgium, Denmark, the Netherlands and Norway. Under the agreement signed in June 1975 the four West European states will pro-duce a total by value of ten per cent of parts of the first 650 American copies, 40 per cent of their own and 15 per cent of further export copies, while Belgium and the Netherlands will each assemble a maxi-mum of 174 West European copies. In addition to 650 copies in which there will be some West European components, the USA ordered a further 738 in December 1976 which will be entirely US-produced.[29]

The F-16 project is a revealing illustration of this version of the two-way street: it involves West European states depending on American technology, participating as junior partners in only a part of the overall process which produces an aircraft. All the main F-16 contractors are American bar one, the British Marconi-Elliott, and the companies working on the project in the four countries are merely sub-contractors. When the project finishes, they can be expected to seek further work, and having adapted themselves to American procedures for this project they will probably press for participation in another American project. Their prospect is to become foreign subordinates of American military industry.

It is the issue of technological dominance, dependence and independence which ultimately distinguishes the meaning of the various forms of the two-way street. At one pole, following the F-16 model, it would be an instrument to promote West European military technological dependence on the USA; at the other, following Mason, it would strengthen West European military industry at the expense of the American industry and the USA's independence in weapons procurement. The former strengthens US strategic hegemony in NATO, the latter undermines it.

NATO's dualism of rivalry and cohesion can be seen lurking beneath the surface in such competing versions of the two-way street. In practice in collaborative projects this same dualism is expressed in bargaining over the terms of co-operation. Bargaining is usually intense and capable of producing labyrinthine arrangements for contracts, sub-contracts and work-sharing. The resolution of disputes owes more to economic and industrial strength than to any spirit of unity. For *Tornado*, for example, the prize contract for the airframe, the centre-fuselage, went to the German MBB even though it had no experience in swing-wing technology while the British BAC had four years of development projects and research experience going back to 1945. This decision stemmed from the strength of the FRG's economy, and the FRG's consequent ability to place a large order for *Tornado* without which the project could not have been viable; in fact, the FRG soon reduced its order, because the basic design specification stemmed from British design work which effectively excluded two roles in which the FRG was interested.[30] Equally to the point in MBB getting the centre-fuselage was that Rolls-Royce won the prime aeroengine contract on a virtual walk-over because it so dominates the West European aeroengine industry with an output greater than that of its West European competitors combined;[31] there had to be some plum for the FRG, whereas Italy, with a smaller order, got no plums at all. The need to reorganise the West European aerospace industry is widely accepted, and collaborative projects such as *Tornado* provide the arena for competition over the terms of that reorganisation, a competition in which the prize could be leadership of a multinational West European aerospace sector.

Trans-Atlantic collaboration reveals similar bargaining, but with a different focus for the competition. During the 1970s the USA has been tempting the rest of NATO with a package deal to produce the Airborne Warning and Control System (AWACS); the proposal was to provide airborne early warning and surveillance through a fleet of Boeing E-3A *Sentry* aircraft (modifications of the Boeing 707 airliner) operated by a multinational force, with costs shared and participation in production to off-set the European states' financial contributions. Since 1976, at American initiative, the USA and FRG have been attempting to collaborate in fulfilling their respective requirements for main battle tanks, and it has been widely assumed that bargaining over the two projects between the USA and the FRG was closely linked.[32]

AWACS grew out of a US Air Force programme begun in 1962; the prime contract was awarded in 1970, and in the same year NATO initiated studies on a new airborne early warning system which by 1975 focussed on AWACS and the E-3A. The US Air Force AWACS began operations in October 1978, patrolling the seas between Britain, Iceland and·Greenland.[33] In both production and deployment the NATO AWACS fleet was to be a symbol of unity in action, but agreement on the details of financing and off-set production was hard to come by. In March 1977, for a variety of reasons which included a dire need to replace its own obsolete early warning aircraft and the FRG's reluctance to participate in AWACS on the terms offered, Britain withdrew from AWACS and announced it would develop the *Nimrod* anti-submarine aircraft for early warning.[34] But Britain had an interest in the US-FRG tank project, having participated in early studies until it decided it could not afford a new tank so soon, and still intending to compete for the contract for the tank gun.

In January 1977, after competitive trials, the US Army decided that the American prototype tank, the Chrysler XM-1, now named the *General Creighton Abrams*, was superior to the FRG's *Leopard II*, and amid recriminations that the trials were rigged the FRG withdrew from full collaboration, leaving open the possibility of producing standard parts for the two tanks, including the gun,[35] and thus shifting from producing a standard tank to producing interoperable tanks. In the gun competition in December 1977, the German smooth-bore 120mm gun was selected by the US Army in preference to the British rifled 120mm gun, and in January 1978 a provisional order was placed for the German product to equip the second batch of XM-1s from the early 1980s. There was apparently little difference in the quality of the two guns' performance but the FRG's was more advanced in development,[36] which actually suggests that the British gun would eventually be superior in performance. The different designs reflect different doctrinal preferences, with smooth-bore guns generally providing weightier fire-power but less accuracy than guns with rifled barrels, although the British are also developing shells of a type which, hitherto, only smooth-bore guns have been able to fire, with the intention of using it with rifled guns. However, the crucial difference between the competitors was that Britain had withdrawn from the AWACS project and offered no immediate market for tank engines; having provisionally awarded the gun contract to the FRG, the USA probably expected reciprocity in the form of the contract for the tank engine plus the FRG's participation in AWACS. If the FRG disappointed it, the USA would still have the option of cancelling the gun contract. Perhaps as a further sweetener, in spring 1978 the USA placed its first substantial order for West European military vehicles with a $100 million contract for trucks and other vehicles from the FRG.[37] Although it does not yet seem as if agreement has been reached on the tank engine,[38] in December 1978 the FRG's agreement was decisive in securing a Memorandum of Understanding to produce a NATO AWACS fleet of 18 E-3A *Sentrys* at a total cost of $1,800 million.[39]

This type of reciprocity can hardly be thought of as fair exchange. The USA has little industrial investment in tank guns, and its current M-60 tank is armed with a British-designed 105mm gun; this is one of the ways in which the decision to use a German gun on the XM-1 can be 'sold' to Congress.[40] On the other hand, were the FRG to equip *Leopard II* with a US-designed engine, it would thereby undermine the continued viability of its substantial capacity to develop and produce tank engines. It is true that as the main West European participant in AWACS, likely to stump up about 25 per cent of the cost, the FRG can expect a large slice of the co-production work and the benefit of being the main site for AWACS basing,[41] but the significance of AWACS goes beyond the purely economic.

With the example of the F-16 we have seen how collaboration in production could be used to foster technological subordination; AWACS could have a similar function for the USA but with added dimensions. NATO's infrastructure for Command, Control and Communications (C^3) is widely regarded as inadequate, in need of thorough overhaul to eliminate idiosyncratic national differences and incompatibilities which hamper communications between units of different nationality. At the heart of C^3 is early warning and surveillance, AWACS' mission. Thus in the event of reorganisation of C^3 AWACS is a foot in the door for American technology and capital providing opportunities for further lucrative contracts for systems compatible with AWACS and future American-led co-production schemes. It offers the USA the chance to shape the whole of NATO's C^3 according to American technology, American forms of organisation, strategy and world view. C^3 can be thought of as the brain and central nervous system of a modern military apparatus: American domination of it would provide potent levers for future influence in NATO.

In trans-Atlantic co-operation, then, the prize in the competition is situated in Western Europe; should the USA manage to sell a succssion of projects on the lines of F-16 and AWACS, it will be developing a strategy to foster dominance in the West European military marketplace and strengthen hegemony in NATO, compensating for its relative decline and making it less likely that a unified West European political formation will be a stronger competitor. For the USA the prize is West European dependence, but for Western Europe the prize is no higher than its own independence. A project like *Tornado* can be seen as a way of avoiding technological dependence on the USA, as can the FRG's abrupt withdrawal from full collaboration in the tank project, but not as a way of breaking into the American procurement market, let alone fostering US technological dependence on Western Europe. The *Roland* surface-to-air missile, produced by the Franco-German consortium Euromissile and procured by the USA might be thought of as a counterweight to projects like the F-16 and AWACS. But whereas the FRG offers *Roland* as evidence that the street is already two-way,[42] a more acid French view noted that instead of opening the door to a $1,500 million market by importing *Roland*, the USA merely purchased the licence to produce it (paying royalties of 6.5 per cent, declining to 5.5 per cent as mass production starts).[43] Even so, the USA is producing a system of West European design, but this is still not equivalent to the F-16 for not only will the US *Roland* be completely produced in the USA by Hughes Aircraft Corporation and Boeing, and not only does it show a number of design changes from Euromissile's original, there has even been talk of selling to Norway, which expressed interest in 1976, and other countries in competition with Euromissile's product.[44]

The political meaning of superficially similar co-operative projects can thus be very different. Similar differences are evident if the problem, almost always encountered in collaborative projects, of incompatible procedures is considered. This can surface in anything from different management and accounting practices, different ways of writing design specifications, different ways of estimating the cost, contrasting hierarchies and organisation in development teams to different intellectual traditions and thus approaches to solving problems. The Pentagon has remarked upon the difficulties with *Roland* of transferring West European designs to American production facilities,[45] while the F-16 provides a number of entertaining examples of the difficulty of reconciling West European and American practices.[46] But while with *Roland* the designs are adapted and the production procedures left almost untouched, with the F-16 there has been a sharp struggle between the Pentagon and General Dynamics on one side and the West European states and subcontractors on the other, in which there is some American compromise but more West European change.

It is not hard to see why the two-way street appeals to West European states and military industrial corporations: it seems to offer a way of increasing the market for West European military products and stimulating West European unity within a continuing NATO alliance, an apparent synthesis of Europeanism with the Atlanticist emphasis on the unity of NATO as a whole. But, even if the House Armed Services Committee sees the two-way street as a West European plot,[47] it is clear that it could instead be an instrument to strengthen US strategic hegemony by intensifying technological dominance in key areas. Because of its emphasis on West European co-operation, the two-way street can seem like a concept from the ideological scaffolding of Europeanism, but it is a concept of some variety defining an arena of rivalry within NATO.

A central issue here is that of the transfer of technology. In general, one benefit of industrial collaboration is thought to be a transfer of technology from the more to the less capable partner(s). Equally generally, one side complains that it is simply giving away technological know-how and getting nothing in return, while the other complains that it is not receiving any important technology. Two points need to be brought out here. First, a genuine transfer of technology would provide the recipient with control over that technology, the ability independently to duplicate and develop it further; simply producing or assembling parts to pre-established designs is not necessarily going to give an industrial enterprise control over the underlying technologies. What counts is if it can build a research and development capacity, for it is there that technological control and independence reside. Secondly, technology is more than just technique: it is a way of working, a set of procedures and institutions, a way of thinking and approaching problems, which provide models of organisation, behaviour and thought to the participants and to others who observe the process and its products. Technology embodies social relations and functions as an ideological model, a particularly strong one because of its genuine achievements. Thus, while an incomplete transfer of technology which does not give the recipient control of the technology (for example, AWACS and the F-16) may foster dependence on the supplier, a genuine transfer of technology may, for example, 'Americanise' a West European corporation or industrial sector, resulting in an ideological penetration which could in the long term strengthen US interests.[48]

This need not always be the case. For example, Westland, the British helicopter manufacturer, developed a great deal of its expertise through a series of licences from the US firm of Sikorsky, producing helicopters to Sikorsky designs. It has since gone on to develop and produce its own helicopter based on a Sikorsky helicopter, and switched its focus of co-operation from the USA to France in the mid-1960s, undertaking development and production of a trio of civil and military helicopters (*Lynx*, *Gazelle* and *Puma*) with Aerospatiale.[49] In the future Westland may work with MBB of the FRG and Agusta of Italy as well as with Aerospatiale,[50] but co-operation with Sikorsky has served its purpose of establishing an independent helicopter development capacity and is unlikely to be repeated. Thus, the 'Americanisation' of West European industries might simply make them more able to undermine the American lead in that industrial sector, but this process of ideological penetration and co-operation is one of the most important long-term consequences of military industrial collaboration, whether through co-operation with the USA it leads to 'Americanisation' or through co-operation within Western Europe it leads to 'Europeanisation'. It is not only in industry that these effects are felt, but within states themselves, in the administrative sections who oversee the projects and in the military who operate the final product; here it amounts to a kind of ideological subversion from within which, if the process were 'Americanisation' would constrain the possibilities for rivalry with the USA but, if it were 'Europeanisation', would strengthen them.

Finally on the two-way street, it should be added that it provides room for tactical manoeuvre in intra-West European rivalry. The decision by four states to purchase the F-16, for example, can be seen as a way of signalling that closer West European cohesion on terms laid down by a permutation of Britain, France, the FRG and Italy will not be automatically accepted. The USA can function as an alternative power centre to hold against any developing West European power centre, whether it be the FRG alone or with other states. The option of not participating in a West European project and instead joining an American project could be used as a threat to gain better terms, or could be taken up in order to get better terms in a future project. Britain is especially well placed for such a tactic with a strong aerospace component sector which is already doing a fine trans-Atlantic trade and an aeroengine sector which is dominant in Western Europe. From the discussion so far it should be clear that the tactic carries risks of subordination to the USA, but it nevertheless has its attractions.

Beyond *Ad-hoc* Collaboration

There is no doubting either the increasing momentum of collaboration in weapons production and procurement in NATO or the seriousness with which the issues are treated. Table 7.2 gives a summary of the impetus of collaboration in Western Europe from the early 1960s. The table lists only the major projects and excludes 'one-off' licences between single states, but the basic trend of increased emphasis upon collaboration is unmistakeable even though the table gives no overall picture of the West European states' procurement policies. Procurement independently or by straightforward import remains significant, as do projects involving the USA, but the general pattern revealed by the table is for West European states to collaborate with each other and, as between Belgium and Britain (vehicles), Britain and France (helicopters) and France and the FRG (light missiles), an important part has been played by package deals covering co-operation on a series of systems.

But despite the general momentum of collaboration, and despite the urgings of numerous commentators and states' declarations of intent, the problem of duplication remains. There may be a number of reasons for the snail-like progress towards standardisation and interoperability. A major argument in favour of standardisation is the military disadvantage NATO's chaotic procurement is thought to produce in the face of the orderly Soviet-dominated standardisation of the WP; slow progress to standardisation may reflect a surreptitious perception that the military balance is really not as bad as it is cracked up to be, a speculation made more attractive by the arguments in Chapter 4. The military dividends of standardisation and interoperability would be of greatest benefit in a long war where replacement of equipment would be of major importance; the swift destructiveness of a nuclear war would make standardisation and interoperability militarily irrelevant, and

Table 7.2: Collaborative Weapon Systems Operated or Under Development by West European NATO States, 1977[a]

Date[b]	Name	Type	States	Comment
1959 O	Hawk	SAM	USA, Belgium, France, FRG, Italy, Netherlands	US leadership
1962 O	F104-G	Combat aircraft	USA, Belgium, FRG, Italy, Norway, Netherlands	US design; co-production under licence by Belgium, FRG, Italy and Netherlands
1962 P	Super Frelon	Helicopter	France, Italy	Collaborative with some participation from Sikorsky of the USA
1964 D	HOT	ATGW	France, FRG	Collaborative
1965 P	Puma	Helicopter	France, UK	Collaborative
1967 O	Ikara	SAM/ASW	Australia, UK	Initial design Australian; joint project on UK modification
1968 O	Martel	AGM	France, UK	Collaborative
1968 O	Transall	Air transport	France, FRG	Collaborative
1968 P	Jaguar	Combat aircraft	France, UK	Collaborative
1968 D	Tornado	Combat aircraft	FRG, Italy, UK	Collaborative, UK/FRG leadership
1968 D	Sea Wolf	Shipborne SAM	Netherlands, UK	Collaborative
1969 D	Sea King	Helicopter	UK, US	Independent UK design developed from earlier Sikorsky helicopter
1970 D	E-3A	AWACS	US, NATO	US design, NATO participation in production
1971 P	Gazelle	Helicopter	France, UK	Collaborative
1971 P	Lynx	Helicopter	France, UK	Collaborative
1971 P	Striker	AFV	Belgium, UK	UK design
1971 P	Scimitar	AFV		
1972 P	Roland	SAM	France, FRG	Collaborative
1972 P	Milan	ATGW		
1972 D	F-16	Combat aircraft	USA, Belgium, Denmark, Netherlands, Norway	US design, West European agreement on purchase and co-production signed 1975
early 1970s O	Atlantic	Reconnaissance	Belgium, France, FRG, Italy, Netherlands	French leadership

Date	Name	Type	States	Comment
1973 O	Chinook	Helicopter	US, Italy	US design
1973 O	Mirage F1-C	Combat aircraft	Belgium, France	French design
1973 O	Scorpion	AFV	Belgium, UK	UK design
1973 O	Sea Sparrow	SAM	USA, Belgium, Denmark, FRG, Italy, Netherlands Norway	US leadership
1974 P	Skyflash	AAM	UK, US	UK modification of US design
1974 D	RS-80	Rocket artillery	FRG, Italy	Collaborative, UK withdrew in 1975
1975 O	Otomat	ASM	France, Italy	Collaborative
1975 P	Alpha Jet	Trainer/ combat aircraft	France, FRG	Collaborative
1976 O	Spartan	APC	Belgium, UK	UK design
1977 O	VFW-614	Air transport	Belgium, FRG, Netherlands	FRG leadership
1977 P	FH-70/ SP-70	Artillery	FRG, Italy, UK	Collaborative, SP-70 is self-propelled version, entering production later
1977 D	BK-117	Helicopter	FRG, Japan	Collaborative
1977 D	—	ASM	France, FRG, Netherlands, Norway, UK, US	Initial studies on joint requirement after MoU signed in 1977
1977 D	ASMD	SAM	FRG, USA	Initial studies

a. The list of weapon systems is not complete although the main ones are included, nor, it should be added, does it by itself indicate what emphasis is placed on collaborative development and production projects — it is indicative only. See text.

b. The date given for each system is when it entered operation (indicated by 'O' after the date), or when it entered production ('P') or when development began ('D') (although the definition used for this last dating is not crisp and varies from one system to another).

Glossary

AFV	Armoured Fighting Vehicle
AGM	Air-to-ground missile
APC	Armoured Personnel Carrier
ASM	Anti-ship missile
ASW	Anti-submarine warfare
ATGW	Anti-tank guided weapon
AWACS	Airborne Warning and Control System

MoU   Memorandum of Understanding
SAM   Surface-to-air missile

Sources: The basic sources were *Jane's All The World's Aircraft* and *Jane's Weapon Systems* (Macdonald & Jane's, London, annual), for several years in the 1960s and 1970s; use was also made of T. Gervasi, *Arsenal of Democracy* (Grove Press, New York, 1977) and various articles and other reference books.

awareness of this may provide another quiet brake on progress in that direction. NATO planners are also likely to be concerned that standardisation is all very well with successful weapon systems, but where there are design weaknesses or consistent malfunctions the effect would simply be to equip the whole alliance with mediocrity or worse. The ability of NATO states to agree all-round three per cent annual increases in military spending shows that a different response to perceived military weakness is possible, and this response avoids the problems of standardising doctrines throughout NATO forces. Finally, although collaboration is made necessary by the expansion of industrial capacity, industrial competition makes systematising the process much harder; the root cause of the problem of duplication is an obvious hindrance to its solution.

A further problem is that so far there has been no adequate institutional framework. Establishing one could of itself do nothing; it would have to be fused with the political determination and capability to see the process through. But if NATO is to move beyond *ad hoc* collaborative projects, and whatever the political meaning of the movement was, an appropriate institution for co-ordinating the process is essential.

The USA is currently encouraging what might be termed semi-institutional arrangements with other NATO states, in the form of Memoranda of Understanding (MoUs) which commit the signatories to and set out the principles for reciprocal procurement purchases. To date, the USA has concluded MoUs with Britain, Canada, France, the FRG, Italy, the Netherlands and Norway.[51] The practical effect of these, however, is hard to see. The MoU with Britain commits the two states

> to the end that defense equipment production and procurement efforts of the two countries be administered so as to assure the maintenance of a long term and equitable balance in reciprocal purchasing of defense equipment.[52]

Thus it implies a major effort and co-ordination, but it is neatly hedged with the qualification that the agreement applies only to purchases the two parties decide it applies to and not to all indiscriminately, so if practical agreement on specific projects is not forthcoming it need never apply at all. Not only is the MoU thus internally deprived of significance, but it is also not binding on the US government since no MoU has been ratified by the US Congress.[53]

What matters is not nice-sounding agreements but the establishment of actual institutions. This has long been recognised; in 1975 NATO's Eurogroup, which was founded in 1968 to co-ordinate the European 'presence' in NATO and consists of all NATO European states except France, asserted the need for new West European organisational arrangements with the aim of getting weapons procurement beyond 'the constraints of narrow national markets'.[54] It could not be more clearly put, for the only thing which can get beyond 'narrow national markets' is an international market, and this brings us again to Callaghan's proposal that at the West European end of the two-way street there should be a single West European weapons procurement agency.[55] This proposal was repeated in a report from the EEC Commission on the West European aerospace industry which, it was asserted, would vanish in the face of American competition unless multinational aerospace corporations were formed under the EEC's aegis with a single weapons procurement agency to assure a co-ordinated market for their military products.[56] The same proposal was included in the report of Leo Tindemans, the Belgian prime minister, on European union in December 1975 and was yet more solidly repeated in the 'Klepsch report' to the European Assembly in 1978.[57]

A candidate for providing the basis of a single procurement agency would be Eurogroup itself, but this had the fatal weakness that France would not join. Accordingly, in February 1976 a new body was established, the Independent European Programme Group (IEPG), formally independent from both NATO and the EEC and, crucially, including France together with all the European states in NATO (Portugal joined only in November 1976) under the chairmanship of Italy. The British government stated that the aim of the IEPG was to avoid industrial duplication, increase standardisation and interoperability, ensure the maintenance of a strong West European technological base 'and to strengthen the European factor in the relationship with the United States and Canada'.[58]

The Klepsch report argued that IEPG, which is at present a more or less informal body, should have a permanent secretariat and form the main institutional part of the single West European procurement agency; either the EEC Commission or the EEC Council, or both, should be represented in the IEPG along with the participating states and the EEC

Commission should represent EEC member states in negotiating with the USA about the trans-Atlantic arms trade.[59] But in these proposals the report betrays itself, for the IEPG is supposed to be as independent of the EEC as it is of NATO and on this basis includes non-EEC members of NATO (Norway, Portugal, Greece and Turkey) whereas the Klepsch report straightforwardly sees the IEPG as a vehicle to West European unity alongside the EEC. Indeed, the report is permeated with that 'Euro-nationalism' which is also found in, for example, the EEC Commission report on West European aerospace mentioned above. Figure 7.1 outlines the Klepsch report's proposed structure for a West European procurement agency; it will be seen that, based on a strengthened IEPG, it is structurally linked to the EEC but not to NATO. If implemented, and if we assume as conditions for its success the requisite political determination and standardisation of military doctrines, the proposal would establish a distinct West European unified presence within NATO based on an institution outside NATO. It effectively means, and requires, a West European defence policy. This, of course, leaves a question mark hanging over the geographically peripheral European states which are members of NATO but not (yet) the EEC.

Figure 7.1: Possible Structure of West European Arms Procurement Agency

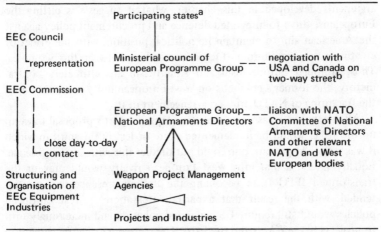

a. Belgium, Britain, Denmark, France, the FRG, Greece, Italy, Luxembourg, the Netherlands, Norway, Portugal, Turkey.
b. This appears to be inconsistent with the proposal (*Two-way Street*, p. 52) that EEC-members in the IEPG should be represented by the EEC Commission in negotiations with the USA and Canada.

Source: Adapted from *Two-way Street* (Brassey's, London, 1979), Part IV/4, p. 95.

The relation of the procurement agency to the USA is another open question. In a much quoted study, Roger Facer argued that a broad policy of West European collaborative procurement 'does not involve a renunciation of other ways of obtaining equipment';[60] this is so, but there is little doubt that, as conceived within the ideological framework of the Klepsch report, the emphasis of the procurement agency's policy would fall on West European collaboration independent of the USA. Indeed, although Facer's formulation is an attempt to reconcile Europeanism with Atlanticism, he argues that it is ultimately 'the political argument which sustains the case for a new initiative' for more efficient collaboration in procurement in Western Europe, and this is the political argument of West European integration,[61] that is, of Europeanism, not Atlanticism. A similar attempt to reconcile the two opposites comes from David Greenwood who argues that the 'core countries' of NATO Europe should force the pace towards defining a 'distinctly European' theory of defence and providing the equipment for it; this would fall short of a wholly independent West European defence effort, yet provide greater independence from the USA and would actually reinforce the US commitment to the defence of Western Europe.[62] Since the USA would presumably wish to maintain the influence in NATO and Western Europe which is provided by its military presence in Europe, Greenwood's logic has some force to it; rereading it in the light of the arguments developed in this chapter, what it suggests is pitting the Europeanist drive to integrated defence and procurement policy against the American aim to maintain its political position, with the effect of creating a new equilibrium of forces somewhere between the two poles. Thus, although Europeanism and Atlanticism are ultimately contradictory, the former's emphasis on West European unity need not imply the fracturing of NATO, but a rearrangement of it.

All this, however, assumes that the Klepsch report's proposal to vamp up the IEPG would be implemented more or less in the spirit in which it was made. At present, one could not predict this with any confidence. Equally likely is that intra-West European rivalry would prevent the transformed IEPG from becoming the unified presence that was intended, with the result that a partial integration of West European policies would still require US-generated cohesion and increasingly turn to projects like AWACS and the F-16. The consequent rearrangement in NATO might be expressed as an Atlanticist and incomplete integration of West European defence and procurement.

Particularly instrumental here, and important stumbling blocks on the Europeanist path, are continued acceptance of the US strategic nuclear 'umbrella' and reliance on US reinforcements. If moving out from under the American umbrella were to mean developing a West European nuclear force, this would require the full supporting system of targeting satellites as well as the development of a West European missile industry, presumably based on British, French and West German technology and industry. Replacing the role of American reinforcements in West European defence would, presumably, require increased forces and arms spending. The alternative, of which there is no sign within orthodox thinking, is the development of strategic and tactical doctrines which would break completely with present NATO doctrines rather than take the same doctrines and simply substitute West European for US forces. As long as West European defence is seen to depend on US nuclear forces and reinforcements, an integrated independent policy is a mirage, and in the absence of completely new doctrines, turning that mirage into reality would be extremely costly.

Earlier I discussed the discrepancy between the USA's relative political and economic decline and its continued strategic hegemony within NATO. The arguments in this chapter suggest the possibility that this discrepancy will be narrowed in the 1980s by a more cohesive West European presence which would nevertheless fall short of the full Europeanist vision. But the arguments have also suggested the pitfalls along the way towards this comparatively modest destination and the potential for a strengthening of American hegemony. Out of this, I have no desire to try and gaze into a crystal ball and make predictions; what is evident is that NATO is currently poised between two contradictory poles, both of which exert a strong attraction on NATO states' policies. The general development of the international political and economic crisis, including factors outside this chapter's discussion, will both condition and be conditioned by developments in this aspect of intra-NATO relations; like previous crises, it will produce a reorganisation of the international system, including a rearrangement in NATO on the basis of a continuing dichotomy between its members' cohesion and rivalry.

Whatever the form and political meaning of the outcome, it seems likely that we shall witness a new internationalisation of the process of armament; whether or not a West European supra-national state were to emerge, the decisions which equip West European armed forces will increasingly be inter-state decisions setting up collaborative projects. In the case of *Tornado* I referred to the difficulty of cancelling such projects, and the proliferation of collaborative projects will repeat this difficulty many times over while the establishment of an institution such as a single West European procurement agency would elevate the problem to a new level. This will erode what little democracy there now is in defence policy, undermining even the limited present forms of parliamentary and public accountability. It could be argued that were a supra-national state to develop in West Europe, this problem would be countered by the development of supra-national parliamentary forms, and it might even be argued that the directly elected European parliament will already be able to provide democratic accountability. But in the short-term the problem is that the activities of states collaborating in weapons procurement cannot be controlled or even called to account by the European parliament, while the IEPG, if transformed along the lines of the Klepsch report and Figure 7.1, is structurally linked to the EEC but not controlled by any EEC institution; the European parliament might be able to sack the EEC Commission, even if it cannot do much else, but it cannot sack the IEPG. And in the long-term the problem is both that the West European supra-national state is an uncertain prospect and that its own susceptibility to even limited democratic accountability is, at best, a matter for wishful thinking. The creation of new international institutions of armament is therefore an uncomfortable prospect, one that is made even less appealing because the key arguments legitimating them derive from distorted perceptions and presentations of the Soviet military threat. Institutions created out of a quasi-cold war ideology should not be attractive to anybody concerned about the impact and consequences of a continued and possibly intensifying arms race.

Notes

1. See the discussions and evaluation of these theories in G. Arrighi, *The Geometry of Imperialism* (NLB, London, 1978), especially pp. 14 and 91.

2. For an ambitious overview of the 1970s' crisis see M. Kaldor, *The Disintegrating West* (Allen Lane, London, 1978).

3. Over the same period, Japan went from a gross national product of $19.56 billion in 1953 to a gross domestic product of $691.2 billion in 1977: *OECD National Accounts 1953-1969* (Paris, 1971) and *OECD Economic Surveys: United Kingdom* (Paris, March 1979).

4. Derived from J. Annerstedt, 'Technological Dependence: a Permanent Phenomenon of World Inequality?', mimeo, 1978 (paper given at International Workshop on Technological Dependence, Bonn, November 1978).

5. Thus M. Dobb cites an article in *Westminster Bank Review*, November 1961, in *Studies in the Development of Capitalism* (Routledge & Kegan Paul, London, 1963), pp. 389-90.

6. See especially B. Rowthorn, 'Imperialism in the Seventies – Unity or Rivalry?', *New Left Review* 69, 1971.

7. See S. Melman, *The Permanent War Economy* (Simon & Schuster, New

York, 1975), p. 83.

8. 'The Decline of US Power', *Business Week*, 12 March 1979.

9. For the text of the meeting's communique see *The Guardian*, 18 July 1978; on the 'atmospherics' of the meeting see *The Guardian*, 17 July 1978, and *International Herald Tribune*, 19 July 1978.

10. See P. Mangold, 'Shaba I and Shaba II', *Survival*, May/June 1979.

11. *Business Week*, 12 March 1979.

12. See R. Smith, 'Military Expenditure and Capitalism', *Cambridge Journal of Economics*, vol. 1, no. 1, March 1977.

13. For a review of the FRG's history see G. Minnerup, 'West Germany Since the War', *New Left Review* 99, 1976.

14. *Business Week*, 12 March 1979; *International Herald Tribune*, 31 July 1978.

15. 'Standardisation: the Key to NATO's Survival', *Market Intelligence Report* (DMS, Greenwich, Ct, 1977).

16. General J. Steinhoff, quoted in J. Tuthill's Preface to G. Tucker, *Towards Rationalising Allied Weapons Production* (AIIA, Paris, 1976).

17. *Flight International*, 29 October 1977.

18. *NATO Standardization, Interoperability and Readiness*, Report of the Special Subcommittee of the Committee on Armed Services, HASC no. 95-101 (US House of Representatives, 1978), p. 10.

19. R. Mason, 'Britain's Security Interests', *Survival*, September/October 1975.

20. T.A. Callaghan, *US/European Economic Cooperation in Military and Civil Technology* (Ex-Im Tech, Arlington, Va, 1974); also, *idem*, 'A Common Market for Atlantic Defence', *Survival*, May/June 1975.

21. R.A. Gessert *et al.*, *NATO Standardization and Licensing Policy – Exploratory Phase*, OAD-CR-167 (General Research Corporation, McLean, Va, 3 volumes, 1976), vol. 1, pp. 16-17.

22. Quoted in *NATO Standardization*, HASC no. 95-101, p. 17.

23. Mason, 'Britain's Security Interests'.

24. Cited in D.C.R. Heyhoe, *The Alliance and Europe: Part VI The European Programme Group*, Adelphi Paper 129 (IISS, London, 1976/7), p. 8.

25. *NATO Standardization*, HASC no. 95-101, especially pp. 1-2, 18, 20-1, 25-7.

26. Press conference with Harold Brown, 6 May 1977, reprinted in *Survival*, July/August 1977.

27. See the discussion of these issues in Chapter 6, above.

28. *Annual Defense Department Report FY1977* (US DoD, 1976), p. 187.

29. See *Status of the F-16 Aircraft Program*, Report to Congress by the Comptroller-General of the United States (General Accounting Office, Washington, DC, 1977); *Flight International*, 23 April 1977; *Air International*, November 1977.

30. *Tornado* was more fully discussed in Chapter 5, above.

31. *The European Aerospace Industry: Position and Figures*, SEC (76) 2657 (Commission of the European Communities, May 1976).

32. *Aviation and Marine*, July 1977; *The Economist*, 7 December 1977 and 28 January 1978.

33. *Department of the Air Force Report to the 96th Congress* (US DoD, 1979), p. 27; on the evolution of AWACS see also 'Boeing E-3A Sentry', *Market Intelligence Report* (DMS, Greenwich, Ct, 1979), and 'Can NATO afford AWACS?', *International Defense Review*, 1975 no. 5.

34. See *The Economist*, 2 April 1977.

35. *Aerospace Daily*, 18 January 1977, and *Washington Post*, 8 March 1977.

36. *New York Times*, 1 February 1978.

37. *Armies and Weapons*, May 1978; a similar sweetener was used to tempt

Belgium into the F-16 deal with an order for 16,000 machine guns to equip US tanks including XM-1: see 'Machine Guns', *Market Intelligence Report*, 1979.

38. The engine was agreed by the USA and FRG to be a candidate for standardisation, but the FRG stated stringent requirements for the engine if it were to be a gas-turbine engine: *Department of Defense Consideration of West Germany's Leopard as the Army's New Main Battle Tank*, Report to Congress by the Comptroller-General of the United States (GAO, Washington, DC, 1977), p. 12; the US Army has now selected the AGT-1500 tank engine, developed by Avco of Connecticut ('XM-1', *Market Intelligence Report*, 1979) but it now seems unlikely that the FRG will adopt this for *Leopard II*, at least for the first batch, without major modifications: see W.J. Spielberger, *Von der Zugmaschine zum Leopard 2* (Bernard & Graefe Verlag, Munich, 1979), especially pp. 245-6, 251 and 296-7.

39. *International Herald Tribune*, 7 December 1978; *Flight International*, 16 December 1978.

40. *New York Times*, 1 February 1978.

41. *Flight International*, 26 November 1977.

42. *White Paper 1975/1976; The Security of the Federal Republic of Germany and the Development of the Armed Forces* (trans) (Federal Ministry of Defence, 1976), p. 63.

43. Ingenieur-General Cauchie, 'French Armaments Policy and Interoperability', in *A European Armaments Policy Symposium, Paris 3-4 March 1977: Official Record* (WEU, Paris, 1977), p. 22; on the royalties, 'SHORADS', *Market Intelligence Report* (DMS, Greenwich, Ct, 1978).

44. *Armed Forces Journal*, December 1975; 'SHORADS', *Market Intelligence Report*, 1978.

45. *Annual Defense Department Report FY1978* (US DoD, 1977), p. 170; see also 'Technology Transfer and the US Roland Missile', *Interavia*, November 1978.

46. L. Kraar, 'General Dynamics Struggles to Build a Plane for All Nations', *Fortune*, February 1977.

47. *NATO Standardization*, HASC no. 95-101.

48. These issues are more usually discussed in the context of relations between industrialised and underdeveloped states; see my 'Trans-Atlantic Cooperation and Conflict in Military Technology', in D. Ernst (ed.), *The New International Division of Labour, Technology and Underdevelopment — Consequences for the Third World* (Campus Verlag, Frankfurt aM, and Praeger, New York, forthcoming).

49. 'Franco-British Antelope', *Air International*, December 1977.

50. *Flight International*, 29 October 1977.

51. *Department of Defense Annual Report Fiscal Year 1980* (US DoD), p. 215.

52. *Memorandum of Understanding between the Government of the United States and the Government of the United Kingdom of Great Britain and Northern Ireland relating to the Principles Governing Cooperation in R&D, Production, and Procurement of Defense Equipment*, signed 24 September 1975, and Annex I, signed 2 April 1976, Section A:1.

53. *NATO Standardization*, HASC no. 95-101, p. 1.

54. Eurogroup Communique, 5 November 1975, printed in *Survival*, January/February 1976.

55. Callaghan, *US/European Economic Cooperation in Military and Civil Technology*.

56. *Action Programme for the European Aeronautical Sector*, EEC Commission Report to Council, 10 October 1975.

57. The Tindemans report was submitted to the EEC Council on 29 December 1975; for the Klepsch report see *Two-way Street* (Brassey's, London, 1979).

58. *Statement on the Defence Estimates* 1977, Cmnd 6735 (HMSO, London,

1977), para 151.

   59. *Two-way Street*, pp. 48-52.

   60. R. Facer, *The Alliance and Europe: Part III Weapons Procurement in Europe – Capabilities and Choices*, Adelphi Paper 108 (IISS, London, 1975), p. 46.

   61. Ibid.

   62. D. Greenwood, 'Politics, Economics, and European Defence', in *RUSI and Brassey's Defence Yearbook 1975/6* (Brassey's, London, 1975), pp. 120-3.

8 SECURITY IN DISARMAMENT

The accumulation of weapons, particularly nuclear weapons, today constitutes much more of a threat than a protection to the future of mankind. The time has therefore come to put an end to this situation, to abandon the use of force in international relations and to seek security in disarmament.[1]

One could assume that the authors of these sentences are moved by the recognition that in a nuclear war there would be no victors in any meaningful sense, and perhaps also by the realisation that the accumulation of weapons absorbs resources which are thereby denied to other uses including the alleviation of misery in poorer countries. It appears that the authors assert the impossibility of marginal change affecting this situation by proposing a radical reform of the international system to exclude the use of force. The quotation happens to come from the Final Document of the United Nations Special Session on Disarmament in 1978, and it ought to give special cause for hope that the Document was approved by representatives of 148 states.

Yet it is not very fashionable these days to talk of disarmament, perhaps because of a widespread understanding that the prospects for disarmament are rather dim, whatever states' representatives declare at the UN. The irony is that the 1970s was marked out in advance by the UN as the Disarmament Decade; in fact, it has been a decade of unremitting armament. Military competition between NATO and the WP has not slackened, new technologies have been applied to military ends, the international trade in arms saw an unprecedented boom, and the ability to develop nuclear weapons seeped through the international system to more states than the five who openly acknowledge possession of nuclear weapons.[2] During the 1970s neither the threatened nor the actual use of force showed any sign of disappearing from the international arena. If one examines the defence policies of most states, including all those in NATO and the WP, it is extraordinarily difficult to identify any way in which considerations of disarmament have had an effective impact on policy or strategy. Armament is a central concern of states, disarmament merely peripheral.

In this chapter I do not intend to offer a major analysis of why disarmament and its less ambitious cousin, arms control, have failed to make significant headway, nor to discuss in detail the numerous fora in which disarmament and arms control negotiations are pursued.[3] Instead, what follows will consider in outline existing approaches to disarmament and arms control and suggest a different approach.

General and Complete Disarmament

To disarm is an irregular verb with no first person singular and only a future tense.[4]

It may seem a banal thing to point out, but the characteristic of disarmament is a reduction of military forces and capabilities, which might occur as a product of multilateral agreement or unilateral decision. Despite plenty of negotiations, the definition of 'to disarm' given above has stood the test of time.

It might therefore seem simply wasted effort to discuss General and Complete Disarmament (GCD), a technical term usually taken to mean the multilateral reduction of arms to levels adequate only for domestic policing and maintaining internal order together with a contribution to a UN force, carried out under strict and effective international control.[5] Yet in the 1950s and early 1960s there were high hopes, now hard to recall, for GCD. In 1955 the USSR accepted a western draft of a treaty of GCD and the world seemed close to comprehensive disarmament until the USA withdrew from all its previous negotiating positions.[6]

It is fascinating to speculate on how history might have been different had the treaty been signed, ratified and implemented. The USA could not have fought in Vietnam and the USSR would have had tanks neither for Hungary in 1956 nor Czechoslovakia in 1968; wars in Bangladesh, Biafra, the Middle East, the Horn of Africa and on the China-Vietnam border would not have occurred. Indeed, this speculative rewriting of history creates a world which is virtually unrecognisable, and by itself it is enough to suggest how unrealistic the hopes for GCD were.

The basic thrust of GCD is the elimination of armed force as a factor in inter-state relations. It is immediately evident that this would mean a decisive change in the nature of most states' foreign policies, in the way in which they pursue their international interests, and in the very substance of those interests. It would also mean profound ideological change, abandoning hostile and competitive concepts of states' security and relinquishing the concept of armed force as a basic constituent of security. Equally, economic change is entailed, a reallocation of the vast proportion of the resources now devoted to military preparations, opening new possibilities for the use of technological and industrial skills.

Parenthetically, it can be added that reallocating economic resources is not quite the problem it is often made out to be; a growing and increasingly confident body of literature exists which demonstrates the possibilities for converting military industry to other uses in the context of either GCD or more limited arms reductions. There are problems to be overcome, but they are short-term and surmountable and the results of the effort would be entirely beneficial.[7] The basic problems of GCD are not economic in a narrowly technical sense but political and social, for it demands radical change in the international system, and therefore in the states which constitute that system, and therefore in the societies those states rule.

It is but one of many ironies of the subject of disarmament and arms control that treaty commitments bind the British state and many others to allegiance to the concept of GCD. The 1963 Partial Test Ban Treaty announces that 'the speediest possible achievement of an agreement on general and complete disarmament' is the 'principal aim' of the parties to it; the Nuclear Non-proliferation Treaty, first signed in 1968, binds parties under Article VI to negotiate their way to GCD; the preamble to the Biological Weapons Convention, first signed in 1972, states that the parties are 'determined to act with a view to achieving effective progress' towards GCD, and the agreement on military use of techniques for environmental modification, signed in 1977, says that the signatories wish to contribute to halting the arms race and bringing about GCD.[8] A visitor from another planet might well be astonished to read these and other solemn and binding international agreements and yet see increasingly destructive arsenals; the visitor might think the contrast was the work of either fools or scoundrels, and possibly both.

The sad reality is, of course, that these treaty commitments are little more than a ritualistic genuflection towards a nearly forgotten altar; our visitor would soon see that they are taken seriously only in small circles of advocates of disarmament, and would probably conclude that in practice the commitments are neither solemn nor binding. None of the states which have duly signed and ratified those treaties is genuinely committed to the kind of radical social and political transformation embodied in the concept of GCD.

It might be argued that emphasising the radicalism of GCD is both tactically mistaken, since it is unlikely to attract states which would have to be transformed, and wrong in principle. But an effort to posit a 'non-radical' version of GCD runs into immediate problems. The question of the level of force necessary to maintain 'internal order' is difficult since, to begin with, the definition of internal order is unclear.

For example, the British government might say that army operations in Northern Ireland are simply a matter of maintaining internal order, but there are other governments with an equal vote in the international community which see those operations as colonial warfare. Nor is it clear that internal order is always desirable since in many cases, starting with South Africa, it entails buttressing repressive and offensive regimes. In such cases in particular, the equipment required to maintain internal order might include helicopters, aircraft, tanks and other heavy equipment. In large territories such as the USA or USSR, larger forces might be required to maintain internal order than in smaller ones, while states with a shaky political and social consensus, or a recent history of upheaval, might also argue for more forces to maintain internal order than would seem reasonable in, for example, Scandinavian social democracy. If the concept of GCD manages to assume that things would be the same apart from the absence of armed force as a factor in international relations, it nevertheless faces major problems of definition which are not simply technical difficulties but reveal the political weakness of that assumption.

A further problem in the way GCD is often viewed is that it is thought of as a single event; the GCD treaty itself might take a period of years to implement, but signing and ratifying the treaty itself is seen as a single occurrence. It may be more useful to envisage disarmament as a process, to be made up of small but definite steps which could gather their own momentum, a process which culminated in a GCD agreement rather than began with it. Of course, it would hardly be simple to develop such a process in current circumstances, but it might offer more immediate potential for progress than expecting states to take such a revolutionary step as GCD in one go.

Arms Control

The problem which this idea of disarmament as a process attempts to address is that GCD is not in any effective sense on the international political agenda. But the immediate difficulty with it is its resemblance to the rationale usually offered for piecemeal arms control agreements and negotiations.[9] Arms control differs from disarmament by not necessarily implying reductions in forces; the aim is to deploy less military power than would be possible, usually by mutually agreed constraints, or to limit certain aspects of military activities by banning particular categories of weaponry, limiting the geographical area in which certain arms may be deployed, or by restraining such activities as nuclear testing. As an overall process, arms control is often viewed as a step-by-step approach to disarmament, therefore seeming little different from the idea of disarmament as a process, but the problem is the lack of evidence that the practice of arms control in the 1960s and 1970s has actually resulted in stepping towards disarmament.

Modern arms control theory and policies essentially date from the late 1950s when hopes for GCD began to crumble, but arms control has been with us a long time, starting perhaps with the 1868 St Petersburg Declaration which banned certain 'arms which uselessly aggravate the sufferings of disabled men, or render their death inevitable'.[10] Here there is no rhetoric about GCD, no aspiration to remove force from international affairs; instead, warfare is accepted as part of international politics and the aim is simply to outlaw especially hellish weaponry.

There is a very obvious moral ambivalence in the Declaration and in all arms control which singles out specific weapons and types of warfare as particularly brutal and attempts to ban them while leaving other weapons and types of warfare unaffected. The uncomfortable principle of such an approach appears to be that warfare can be morally acceptable if it conforms to certain standards; that is, killing people is not always wrong — it depends how it is done. The principle is clearly problematic, but refusing to discriminate between different types of weaponry and warfare is equally uncomfortable. Some weapons have especially gruesome effects, as a Kurdish victim of napalm has testified:

> The entire left hand side of my body, including my face, was severely burnt in the attack. I have no left ear. The muscles in my left arm were damaged, thus limiting the range of movement in the arm. Burns from the napalm have destroyed the thumb and fingers on my left hand and therefore the hand is useless.[11]

New incendiary weapons based on triethyl aluminium, affectionately known as TEA, will render napalm obsolete, for whereas napalm burns only those actually spattered with the jelly, TEA releases a spasm of heat so intense it will cause third degree burns on anyone exposed to the fireball.[12] It is morally reasonable to say that such forms of warfare should not be permitted, and this need not mean active encouragement or even passive acceptance of other forms of warfare.[13] Arms control can be a useful practical expression of this certainly complex moral position.

Arms control agreements of this kind need have no pretensions to being harbingers of GCD, although the extension of moral discrimination to other forms of warfare would be an essential part of building support for a disarmament process. A prime example of arms control with higher ambitions is the Partial Test Ban Treaty, signed in 1963 shortly after the peaceful resolution of the Cuba missile crisis of 1962, which banned nuclear tests in the atmosphere, under water and in outer space. Coming just after a particularly dangerous international crisis, it was the first practical result of what was widely seen as a new spirit in US-Soviet relations which expressed a shared interest in survival, in staving off the nuclear holocaust and in constructing a safer international system. The treaty foresaw a complete test ban to follow, an end to the arms race, nuclear disarmament and ultimately GCD. In fact, by 1963 both the USA and USSR had perfected the technology of nuclear testing underground and this has been able to continue without hindrance; a comprehensive ban on testing has yet to be agreed.

The Partial Test Ban was negotiated remarkably quickly, in just a few weeks, after five years of negotiations on a comprehensive ban had stalled on the issue of how compliance to the treaty was to be verified. The USA insisted that seismological techniques were inadequate to ensure that no tests took place clandestinely underground and that a small number of 'on site' inspections were necessary each year to resolve ambiguous seismological results, finally settling on seven inspections a year as the minimum required; the USSR initially rejected the need for inspections, but finally agreed to three a year. And upon the unwillingness of either side to move its position and the consequent inability to reconcile two arbitrary numbers, the negotiations foundered and a partial ban was the result.[14] The USA and USSR were thus able to calm public fears about the radioactivity produced by atmospheric nuclear tests without hampering their nuclear weapons development programmes; indeed, both have increased the rate of nuclear testing: by the end of 1977 the USA had conducted a total of 626 nuclear tests, 333 since the Partial Test Ban, and the USSR a total of 371, 207 since the Partial Test Ban.[15] Elizabeth Young's description of the treaty as 'the first international Clean Air Bill', and useful as such, is now widely accepted although her judgement that 'as an arms control measure it was almost useless' is too charitable: it was utterly useless, and positively harmful precisely because it did calm public opinion.[16]

One lesson of this episode is that states will often agree to ban things they no longer believe are essential or which they have no interest in doing. The 1971 Sea Bed Treaty prevents states from placing nuclear weapons or other weapons of mass destruction in or on the seabed, the ocean floor or the subsoil, but does not limit the activities of nuclear-armed submarines patrolling just above the seabed;[17] it is now common to liken this treaty to an agreement in which states agree not to bolt their aircraft to the ground. Similarly the 1967 Outer Space Treaty prevents states from placing nuclear weapons or other weapons of mass destruction in orbit, on celestial bodies or in outer space by any other means, and also prohibits military manoeuvres, bases and weapon tests on the moon or other celestial bodies;[18] unfortunately it does nothing to prevent the development and deployment of satellites able to destroy other satellites, which is the most likely form of outer space warfare, nor does it stop non-mass destruction weapons from being placed in orbit.[19] The only arms control treaty which has involved actual disarmament is the Biological Weapons Convention which took effect in 1975, but even here it has to be recorded that bacteriological or biological warfare was coming to be regarded as unreliable and impracticable. Should this type of warfare regain adherents in either the USA or the USSR, it is sadly the case that the Convention suffers from loose wording and inadequate verification procedures and contains, like many arms control treaties, a clause permitting states to withdraw if their 'supreme interests' are jeopardised.[20]

It is not only the record of arms control agreements which generates scepticism about their claims to be part of a disarmament process; the motivation for entering arms control negotiations often has very little to do with disarmament as such. Since October 1973 representatives of NATO and the WP have met in Vienna to discuss reductions of forces stationed in Czechoslovakia, Poland, East and West Germany, Belgium, Luxembourg and the Netherlands. For NATO, these talks were to be a way of removing numerical imbalances between NATO and WP forces and thus eliminating a perceived military disadvantage; disarmament by NATO was not an issue. But perhaps more important was that participation in the talks could be used to reduce pressure from within US Congress led by Senator Mansfield for bringing home American forces in Europe; in Western Europe the talks have had a similar effect, stalling debate on issues like the appropriate size of the British Army of the Rhine or of NATO's force of tactical nuclear weapons. The talks have effectively frozen the *status quo* without showing signs of producing genuine force reductions. Among the issues unresolved is the current size of WP forces, the very starting point for negotiations on reductions, and perhaps symbolic of the lack of progress has been the two sides' inability to produce a short title for the talks to replace the cumbersome 'Mutual Reductions of Forces and Armaments and Associated Measures in Central Europe' with its unprepossessing acronym of MUREFAAMCE; while the WP has referred to them as Mutual Force Reductions (MFR),

NATO's preference is Mutual and Balanced Force Reductions (MBFR).

The question of motivation is also important in understanding the Strategic Arms Limitation Talks (SALT), the US-Soviet negotiations on strategic nuclear forces which began in 1969. Henry Kissinger has stated that the USA at that time was facing a disadvantage in strategic forces and that the purpose of SALT was to gain time for American force improvements by getting agreement from the USSR on mutually freezing the overall force levels, a goal he argues was met by the 1972 SALT agreements (known as SALT I) which placed limits on anti-ballistic missiles and on sea- and ground-launched offensive strategic missiles.[21] Kissinger's argument about the USA's strategic nuclear disadvantages is supported neither by his statements at the time nor by an examination of the evolution of strategic nuclear forces; developments in US warhead technology in the late 1960s permitted the deployment of several independently targetted warheads on each missile, confronting the USSR with a disadvantage, and Sonnenfeldt and Hyland have argued that a principal Soviet motive in SALT has been the desire to use SALT to block such 'drastic advances'.[22] A further motive for both sides was probably the need to do something to fulfil Article VI of the Nuclear Non-proliferation Treaty, signed in 1968, which obligated the parties to negotiate in good faith towards ending the arms race and securing nuclear disarmament and GCD. But although SALT might thereby have seemed a part of a disarmament process, the effect of SALT I was to freeze the total of nuclear missiles at the levels of 1972, permitting increases in the numbers of warheads and their accuracy. SALT was effectively co-opted to the service of orthodox conceptions of national security.

In 1977, the Carter administration seemed set to try and introduce disarmament into the negotiations on SALT II, but as the debate on SALT II built up in the USA, advocates of the treaty increasingly pitched their arguments at the level of normative assumptions about national security, and decreasingly at the level of disarmament. One commentator, an official in the Arms Control and Disarmament Agency, argued that the SALT II agreements made public in May 1979 were clearly disadvantageous to the USSR, and thus one-sidedly beneficial to US security.[23] In one sense, it is quite reasonable to view arms control in this way, and more sensible than devoting extra resources to building up US strategic forces, but any relationship arms control might then have with disarmament is purely accidental and it does little or nothing to help change attitudes as a preparation for actual disarmament agreements.

Table 8.1: The SALT II Agreement

	Maximum levels under SALT II[a]	Possible force levels 1985			
		Delivery vehicles		Warheads*	
		USA	USSR	USA	USSR
MIRVed ICBM	820 ⎫	464	820	1690	4820
	⎬ 1200				
MIRVed SLBM	? ⎭ ⎫	736	352	7360	1060
	⎬ 1320				
Bombers carrying cruise missiles	? ⎭	120	0	2400	0
unMIRVed ICBM	? ⎫	504	360	1510	1080
	⎬ 2250				
unMIRVed SLBM	?	0	624	0	1870
Other strategic bombers	?	225	90	900	180
Total delivery vehicles permitted under SALT II	2250				
Total estimated force levels 1985		2049	2246	13860	9010
Actual force levels 1979**		2058	2500[b]	9200	5000

a. Figures shown are maxima in those categories; question marks indicate that the total for that category is not limited as long as cumulative totals are not exceeded (thus, MIRVed ICBM plus MIRVed SLBM must not exceed 1,200, but within that total the only limit is that MIRVed ICBM must not exceed 820).
b. The figure given comes from the Pentagon although the *International Herald Tribune* gave a figure of 2,344.

Glossary

ICBM	Inter-continental Ballistic Missiles
MIRVed	Equipped with Multiple Independently targetted Re-entry Vehicles (MIRVs) — that is, with multi-warheads in which each warhead has its own target.
SLBM	Submarine-launched Ballistic Missiles.

Sources: *International Herald Tribune*, 10 May 1979 except:
* My estimate on the basis of the previous two columns, using sources and estimating methods noted for Table 4.7 in Chapter 4, above, with totals rounded to ten;
**Department of Defense Annual Report Fiscal Year 1980 (US DoD, 1979), p. 71.

This is not to say that SALT is a process which ought to be jettisoned or that ratification of SALT II by both sides is not important. As Table 8.1 shows, under the agreement signed in June 1979 the USSR at least has to reduce its total of nuclear delivery vehicles, although it will not be prevented from increasing its total of nuclear warheads.[24] The important thing about SALT is that it institutionalises each side's interest in survival and suggests a shared concern for some minimal degree of sanity in their force planning. Without obligations under SALT agreements, there is little reason in principle why either side should not have 3,000 nuclear delivery vehicles or more. Moreover, SALT II initiates some restraints in future nuclear weapons development, a principle which might be developed and expanded both in SALT III and other arms control negotiations. SALT II involves no disarmament, since the number of nuclear warheads will increase, but that does not mean it is valueless.

If SALT III expands to include the issue of US nuclear forces in Europe which can also attack the USSR but have hitherto been excluded from SALT, it is likely that the West European members of NATO will seek participation, which will also introduce the issue of Soviet nuclear weapons capable of destroying West European but not American targets. This would result in an extremely complex set of issues, and at this stage it is far from certain that it could be possible to arrange these issues into a manageable negotiating agenda, nor that the extra participants from NATO would generate a single negotiating position. The SALT process could be endangered without any compensating benefit being gained. Indeed, it would probably generate issues of difference and disagreement between the two sides which would not be difficult were they not the subject of negotiations; this has already happened in SALT II, but with more complex issues in SALT III the result could be more serious.

The future shape and scope of SALT, then, cannot be taken for granted; at this point, it would seem wisest to delay the start of SALT III until the negotiating issues have been identified on each side and it is clear that there is a mutual will to negotiate on those issues. Yet the desire to keep momentum in SALT is more likely to lead to a premature start to SALT III.

The failure of SALT to produce actual disarmament measures has led some to conclude that arms control is not compatible with disarmament. In fact, it remains the case, as Donald Brennan argued at a time when the concept of arms control was emerging, that disarmament is among the options in arms control;[25] yet it is also the case that the option has been taken up very rarely, and the relationship between arms control and disarmament is more complex than Brennan implied. As a recent study put it,

Arms control . . . presupposes the continued existence of national military establishments. It does not require radical changes in the present world order, because it makes no claim to abolish war.[26]

Arms control is essentially conservative, seeking marginal change at most, and it is this basic feature of arms control which permits it to be seen as an actual obstacle to the radical change implied by GCD. In the case of SALT, it can be argued that the agreements serve to legitimate the large nuclear arsenals of both sides and their current and future nuclear development programmes simply by erecting a system of inter-state relations around the talks. But it is likely that the first steps in a genuine disarmament process would look remarkably like arms control agreements. The problem is not in the principle of negotiations on relatively limited aspects of military activities, but in the inability of arms control *as practised* to generate a process of disarmament; where change is required is in the political inputs to the negotiating fora.

Outline of a New Approach

The idea of a process of disarmament implies accepting limited progress to begin with, setting sights lower than GCD but with the long-term aspiration of achieving security through disarmament. For this to be possible, arms control agreements must be individually valuable; they must embody a practical achievement, or any declaration of the intention of the parties to the treaty to make progress to disarmament at a future date is meaningless at best and positively misleading at worst. This emphasises the importance of negotiations aimed at banning particularly brutal forms of warfare or stiffening the injunctions against indiscriminate warfare already contained in the international laws of war.[27] It also means that, despite qualifications, SALT is a valuable process because it indirectly expresses awareness of the futility of full-scale nuclear war. It suggests that the most useful negotiations are those which address fairly clear-cut issues with some potential for a fruitful outcome.

The content of agreements and negotiations, however, is simply the surface form. What matters is the political will of the participants, and a major concern here is not just the attitudes involved but also the institutions. A central problem in arms control is that it is now pursued within the limits of existing state attitudes and institutions of military security and defence policy. Although by themselves institutions would not provide the necessary alternatives to current policies on arms control, there is an urgent need for institutions of disarmament to counter the institutional weight of the process of armament. Where possible, arms control agreements could require the establishment of new institutions at national level capable of overseeing their implementation. At the same time, participation in international negotiations needs to be accompanied by unilateral disarmament initiatives. This could be most effective in cases where, even by orthodox conceptions, a particular military option made no great contribution to security; an immediate example is the issue of replacing the British *Polaris* nuclear force: replacement will be extremely expensive and of marginal strategic utility at most – doing without it would incur no cost to security and would be an important symbol for disarmament. In this way it would be possible slowly to reconstruct defence policy in the light of disarmament.

It must be emphasised that this is not presented as a simple process, a short cut on the path to disarmament, but it does have one major advantage: it starts the process of disarmament in the domestic political arena, where it must take root if there is to be any chance of success. This does not imply jettisoning multilateral approaches to disarmament in favour of unilateral ones: by definition, international disarmament is a multilateral process, but equally by definition it is, like international armament, made up of a series of unilateral processes. If there is to be progress towards disarmament, states will have to enter negotiations with more political commitment to it than they now show, and the place to start constructing that commitment is at home.

It is, of course, a long and difficult road, but there is company along the way in the form of states, mostly non-aligned and many of them among the poorer states, who seek a new international military order in which the industrialised states do not have such an overwhelming near-monopoly on force. There are two ways in which a new order could be created: one is for underdeveloped states to be better armed, and the other is for the industrialised states to reduce their forces. It is with states who seek the second path that an alliance can be formed by groups in industrialised countries who seek disarmament. It is those states who pressed for the UN Special Session on Disarmament in 1978 and they who produce the most genuine disarmament proposals. It is in their concern to avoid the consequences of the industrialised states' build-up of arms that the most promising basis for a process of disarmament is to be found. As we enter the 1980s, with prospects for disarmament discouragingly slight, an alliance between their pressure in international fora and the pressure of disarmament groups in several domestic arenas offers the strongest chance of progress.

Notes

1. *The United Nations Special Session on Disarmament, 23 May to 1 July 1978*, Cmnd 7267 (HMSO, London, 1978), p. 19.

2. The five nuclear weapon states, in chronological order of 'going nuclear', are the USA, the USSR, Britain, France and China. In 1974 India detonated a nuclear device; Israel is believed by most authorities to have a small nuclear stockpile; in 1977, satellite photography revealed preparations for a nuclear test by South Africa; approximately 25 further states either have or are close to having the ability to develop nuclear weapons.

3. For more detail on arms control and disarmament negotiations, see A. Myrdal, *The Game of Disarmament* (Manchester University Press, Manchester, 1977); N. Sims, *Approaches to Disarmament*, Revised and Expanded Edition (Quaker Peace & Service, London, 1979); *World Armaments and Disarmaments: SIPRI Yearbook* (Taylor & Francis, London, annual); for texts of arms control agreements see the publication of the Stockholm International Peace Research Institute (SIPRI), *Arms Control: A Survey and Appraisal of Multilateral Agreements* (Taylor & Francis, London, 1978).

4. Sims, *Approaches to Disarmament*, p. 6 (described by the author as 'the aphorism of an earlier generation').

5. This definition of GCD is taken from the 1961 'US-Soviet Joint Statement of Agreed Principles for Disarmament Negotiations', *Arms Control*, pp. 75-6.

6. See P. Noel-Baker, *The Arms Race* (John Calder, London, 1958), Chapter 2.

7. See, for example, The Economist Intelligence Unit, *The Economic Effects of Disarmament* (The Economist Intelligence Unit, London, 1963); *Economic and Social Consequences of Disarmament: Report of the Secretary-General* (United Nations, New York, 1962), G. Kennedy, *The Economics of Defence* (Faber & Faber, London, 1975), Chapter 9; D. Smith (ed.), *Alternative Work for Military Industries* (Richardson Institute, London, 1977); M. Kaldor, D. Smith and S. Vines (eds), *Democratic Socialism and the Cost of Defence* (Croom Helm, London, 1979).

8. *Arms Control*, pp. 77, 89, 103 and 123; the Non-proliferation Treaty took effect in 1970, the Biological Warfare Convention in 1975, and the convention on environmental modification in 1978.

9. *Arms Control and Disarmament*, Central Office of Information Reference Pamphlet 155 (HMSO, London, 1978), p. 1.

10. *Arms Control*, p. 53.

11. *New Statesman*, 8 July 1977.

12. SIPRI, *Incendiary Weapons* (MIT Press, London, 1975), pp. 101-2.

13. See M. Walzer, *Just and Unjust Wars* (Allen Lane, London, 1978).

14. B. Feld, 'Doves of the World, Unite!', *New Scientist*, 26 December 1974.

15. *World Armaments and Disarmaments: SIPRI Yearbook 1978* (Taylor & Francis, London, 1978), p. 320.

16. E. Young, *A Farewell to Arms Control?* (Penguin, Harmondsworth, 1972), p. 17.

17. *Arms Control*, pp. 90-2.

18. Ibid., pp. 78-80.

19. SIPRI, *Outer Space — Battlefield of the Future?* (Taylor & Francis, London, 1978), Chapter 8.

20. *Arms Control*, pp. 103-5.

21. 'Kissinger's Critique', *The Economist*, 3 February 1979.

22. H. Sonnenfeldt and W.G. Hyland, *Soviet Perspectives on Security*, Adelphi Paper 150 (IISS, London, 1979), p. 23.

23. D. Linebaugh, *International Herald Tribune*, 23 May 1979; see also J.M. Lodal, 'SALT II and American Security', *Foreign Affairs*, Winter 1978/9.

24. The SALT II treaty together with associated agreed statements were made available by the International Communication Agency: *Treaty Between the United States of America and the Union of the Soviet Socialist Republics on The Limitation of Strategic Offensive Arms*; under Article XIX, once ratified the treaty will remain in force until 31 December 1985.

25. D.G. Brennan's preface to *idem* (ed.), *Arms Control, Disarmament and National Security* (George Braziller, New York, 1961), pp. 9-10; also published as, *idem* (ed.), *Arms Control and Disarmament: American Views and Studies* (Jonathan Cape, London, 1961).

26. *Arms Control*, p. 51.

27. Ibid., pp. 125-37, see Articles 36 and 48-51 especially.

9 NATO AND THE BRITISH STATE

Prospects in the 1980s for making progress towards disarmament, whatever road is chosen, will be profoundly affected by the further development of NATO. The disarmament movement in Britain and in other countries may be strengthened, but the potential for positive action by a British government will be defined not only by domestic politics but also by the relation of the state to the alliance. Indeed, this relation is a key determinant establishing the possibilities for resolving the main problems of British defence policy.

Efforts at standardisation, interoperability, military industrial collaboration and the construction of a two-way street in the trans-Atlantic arms trade form the basic context in which problems of surplus industrial capacity and increasing weapons costs will be tackled. The effects of developments in these areas will be felt cumulatively; even with a unified and determined West European effort, they are unlikely to have any impact on budgetary decisions before the late 1980s although their political effects could be important before then in deciding whether it will be possible for British defence policy to resolve the long-standing dilemma between available resources and desired military capabilities. The extent to which it is possible for domestic political influences to affect defence policy will also partly depend on whether progress is made in establishing international institutions of the armament process in Western Europe; the more the focus of decision-making in weapons procurement shifts to international agencies, the greater the difficulties domestic groups will face in influencing policy.

The discussion in Chapter 7 emphasised the importance of considering the specific forms of standardisation, interoperability, collaboration and the two-way street. At issue is the future organisation of weapons production and the military market in NATO, the ways in which states equip their armed forces, and the concepts take different forms depending on the basic positions of their advocates. Together with other aspects of the political and economic relations between NATO states, which themselves both help shape and are partially shaped by developments in the military field, the way in which these issues develop in the 1980s will play a critical role in shaping the trajectory of the British state. It is therefore at the question of the relation between Britain and NATO that a discussion of future possibilities in British defence policy must begin.[1]

NATO Strategy in the 1980s

It would be inappropriate and probably not very sensible to attempt to predict the forms of NATO's strategy in the 1980s. The complex interplay of a wide range of factors, both within and without the field of defence policy, will shape strategy and it would be impossible to do justice to the subject here; in fact, a discussion which did marshall those factors and scrutinise them in detail would probably only emphasise the difficulty of making predictions in anything but the most general of forms. What is possible, however, is to try and summarise the main issues that may shape the further development of the alliance's strategic doctrines and debates.

A particular problem in considering future strategy at this point is provided by the general economic and political crisis faced by NATO states. If it is correct to regard this as a crisis of similar dimensions to those in the 1870s and in the 1920s and 1930s, then, as I argued in Chapter 7, we must expect new forms of international organisation of capitalism to emerge; as far as NATO is concerned, the decisive questions hinge on the relative decline of the USA and the prospects of some form of greater political and economic unity in Western Europe. But the emergence of new forms of organisation cannot be expected to be a simple single event occurring at a unique 'moment of truth'. Looking back to the late 1940s when most of the current forms of organisation were either established or previsaged (the EEC not being formed until the 1950s), it would be tempting to expect a similar fairly clear-cut process of organisation happening in a short period. But the particularities of that period must be noted: first, most capitalist economies emerged from World War II either in ruins or in an extremely weak condition, and secondly, the USA was an unchallenged hegemonic power among capitalist states. The relative decline of the USA, eroding its hegemony and weakening its organising capacity, without an alternative hegemonic centre having yet emerged, creates very different conditions. Steps towards new forms of organisation will likely be, as they are at the present, hesitant, often circular, usually disputed and with their direction by no means certain.

Within NATO, apart from the USA and Britain, important questions revolve around the positions of France and the FRG. For the role of France in NATO, the basic question concerns the extent to which it may be possible for the French state to throw off the shackles of Gaullism and re-engage in the alliance of which it remains a member though not an explicitly participating military component. Outside France it seems to be a shared impression that Giscard d'Estaing and the political forces he represents would like to be less Gaullist than domestic pressures force him to be. The development of a less abrasive nationalism reflects changes and contradictions within the French ruling bloc which are as yet unresolved. In military industry, France faces the familiar problem of balancing between the need to maintain independent industrial capacity and the increasing costs of sustaining that capacity; during the Gaullist 1960s it was still a major participant in industrial collaboration, especially with Britain and the FRG, and its interest in the European Programme Group formed in 1976 suggests it may want to develop that collaboration further. In the late 1970s, more attention in defence policy was given to conventional forces which, in view of the symbolism of independence embodied in its development of nuclear forces, may reflect a new emphasis on a European dimension in its defence planning, commensurate, perhaps, with a greater orientation towards NATO.[2] At present the return of French forces to NATO command seems politically impossible in France, but together with its military industrial collaboration with NATO states, steps such as its participation in NATO's strategic communications network pave the way for a closer relation between France and the alliance.[3] If France follows this path, it can be expected to emphasise the West European factor in NATO and thus to be a counterweight to strengthening American leadership.

For the FRG, the main problem can be summarised as how to be a great power without scaring everybody else into an anti-German coalition. Within the Federal Republic, the tendency appears to be to tread cautiously, emphasising the principles of alliance and West European unity, but the FRG's forceful initiative in the matter of the European Monetary System suggests a potential for leadership which may yet be more fully realised. The suspicion with which this prospect is viewed often stems from straightforward and unpleasant racial prejudices, but there is genuine cause for concern in the prospect of the FRG's harsh policies on the economy and political freedoms becoming normative in Western Europe.[4] The USSR has widely publicised its fear of the consequences of Federal German leadership in Western Europe; whether this is more than a propaganda ploy can only be established in the event, but it is quite possible that the results would be discomforting. The FRG used to be taken as an example of the success that could be achieved in an economy with only a modest armaments sector, but that is no longer possible: the FRG is a major arms producer with growing exports; this will doubtless provide further support within the FRG for policies which seek to match economic strength with military clout and political leadership.

The uneven positions of the main protagonists, and the yet greater inequality if the other West European states are brought into the picture, suggest difficulties in the development of NATO strategy in the 1980s. Cohesiveness in strategic planning may be hard to come by, leading either to no change however much dissatisfaction is expressed about the present position, or to constant shifts of emphasis and overall lack of clarity and consensus, similar to the case in the 1960s before France pulled out of the military command in 1966 and the announcement of the strategy of flexible response the following year. Either way, conceptual clarity would be lacking, even more than it is at present.

In the absence of domestic political change in the NATO countries, considerations of arms control are unlikely to be decisive in the formation of strategy. The two fora which might have an impact, and are certainly closely related to NATO concerns in Europe, are the Vienna talks on force reductions and the Strategic Arms Limitation Talks (SALT). NATO intentions in Vienna remain the removal of perceived numerical discrepancies in conventional forces by scaling down WP forces in Central Europe. The chances of achieving this are by no means high, and even were it achieved it would, at most, reduce the alarmism about Soviet military strength in the area; strategic change by NATO as a consequence of such a result from the Vienna talks is most unlikely. The possible extension of the scope of SALT III to include weapon systems not yet discussed in SALT was discussed in Chapter 8, along with the possibility that this would bring West European states into the SALT forum. Other possibilities suggested include 'EuroSALT', dealing with all nuclear weapons in Europe, in which the USA would also naturally be involved – simply an extension of SALT III called by a different name. Whatever the title, the complexities of such negotiations would ensure a long and labyrinthine process, and it is far more likely that the negotiating positions will be designed with strategic preferences at the forefront than that the negotiations' outcome will significantly affect strategic doctrines.

The extent to which the further development of detente will affect strategic planning is unclear. The broad outlines of the current strategies of both NATO and the WP were drawn in the 1960s, before the major gains of detente in Europe had been registered; detente has changed the political context of strategy without changing its content. There is plenty of room for change to reflect the different context, not least by removing the emphases on battlefield use of nuclear weapons and fast reaction, but the retrenchment in detente in the late 1970s has hardened attitudes and reduced the chances that change will be introduced. Despite this retrenchment, the basis for detente remains strong, both in shared desires to avoid a return to the dangers of the 1950s and in economic interests, with the USSR still requiring western technology while western business is glad of opportunities to enter the Soviet market. If NATO states continue to be alarmed by Soviet policy in Africa, this may constitute a pressure on detente although it does not affect its basis. Meanwhile a different pressure on detente, the pseudo-alliance between NATO states and China, could be eased, on the one hand, by Soviet diplomacy aimed at reducing the differences between the USSR and China and, on the other, by the strong possibility that China will reduce the ambitiousness of its modernisation plans to a level it can better afford, thereby offering a more restricted market for western business. However, if Soviet diplomacy meets no Chinese reciprocation and Chinese development plans retain their current ambitions, the Chinese question may provide a critical pressure on detente.

The development of detente itself depends in no small degree on the nature of the Soviet leadership in the 1980s. 'Kremlinology' currently seems to provide little insight into either the personnel or the politics of the leadership after Brezhnev. One is therefore tempted to speculate that continuity of policy is likely, the more so since the Soviet system appears to allow precious little scope for political innovation. But both the elevation of Khrushchev into the leadership in the 1950s and his fall from power in the 1960s were accompanied by important shifts of emphasis, not least in foreign policy and strategic planning. It would, however, require a major change for a Soviet leadership to conclude it had no further need of western technology or of relatively peaceful relations with NATO and there is no basis for supposing that this change will occur. Shifts in emphases and priorities are likely, and may lead to new tensions in international relations, yet need not preclude the continuation of the basic conditions for detente.

The Soviet response to possible changes in Eastern Europe could also be critically important. A tougher stance against oppositional forces in Czechoslovakia and Poland, even though the present stance is hardly 'soft', might be accompanied by a tighter sealing of Eastern Europe against western influence, generating increased anti-NATO rhetoric and attitudes. If such oppositional forces gain in strength and become capable of voicing general discontent in a more sustained way, the result could be a wide and intense challenge to the legitimacy of Soviet hegemony in Eastern Europe with unpredictable consequences for Soviet foreign policy. Meanwhile, one East European state, Romania, has steadily marked out an independent foreign policy during the 1970s, a process whose culmination so far was the visit of Hua Guo-Feng, Chairman of the Chinese Communist Party, in August 1978 followed a few months later by the virtual repudiation of the decisions of the WP summit meeting to increase military spending and more closely integrate WP armed forces. At present it appears that the Soviet leadership is prepared to live with this recalcitrance, and it would have to jettison its normal caution were it to attempt a forceful 'solution' to its Romanian problem. But in order to show its mettle, a new Soviet leadership might be tempted into such an adventure and, although direct NATO intervention to support the present Romanian regime is unlikely, the consequences would almost certainly include a sharp blow to the medium-term prospects of detente. It should nevertheless be emphasised that this kind of action, though possible, is not probable, despite the example of the 1968 invasion of Czechoslovakia. Crucially, the Romanian domestic system does not provide the kind of political and ideological challenge to the Soviet leadership that the 'Prague spring' did, and developments in Romanian foreign policy have not been as sudden as the Czechoslovakian reforms in 1968 appeared.

The consequences of a military adventure against Romania, which remains a member of the WP, would be small compared to the damage which would ensue from Soviet interference in non-aligned Yugoslavia in the wake of Tito's death. The Yugoslav leader's vigour continues to impress, but the stability of the Yugoslav polity without his leadership is uncertain. The situation could tempt both NATO and the WP into interventions, not necessarily military, with serious long-term consequences. Apart from the infringement of political independence which interference by both sides or either one would entail, the stability of Europe would be shaken and the risks of a military clash would be not inconsiderable. In fact, there may be room for optimism that each side would hold off for fear of the other, but rivalry between NATO and the WP within Yugoslavian politics is a possibility and a thoroughly unpleasant prospect.

The future of detente is thus uncertain, and this as much as the previous unresponsiveness of strategy makes it hard to identify any impact detente might have on NATO planning. Together with the likely insignificance of arms control as a factor for change in strategy, this emphasises the role of developments within NATO in shaping strategy in the 1980s. Here, the developments discussed in Chapter 7 in the field of industrial collaboration and weapons procurement will be crucial; if West European co-operation in these aspects of defence policy increases, the basis will exist for greater participation in the major strategic decisions. This raises the issue of the American nuclear 'umbrella' over Western Europe, a crucial expression and lever of US leadership in NATO.

In an important sense, NATO strategy is profoundly misleading. Despite the doctrine of flexible response, with its emphasis on responding 'appropriately' to aggression, and despite the emphasis of the 1970s on the need to maintain strong conventional forces, the overriding reality of NATO strategy remains nuclear deterrence. Deterrence is provided by the American strategic nuclear arsenal, and extended downwards by the largely American force of tactical nuclear weapons (TNW). But, as Chapter 3 showed, US nuclear strategy has evolved beyond 'pure' deterrence emphasising retaliation to the doctrine of limited options, attempting to stress the utility of nuclear force. At first sight, this more flexible strategy, which still retains the threat of massive destruction among its options, it a suitable match for flexible response which includes the possibility of limited use of nuclear weapons in the theatre of war. But, as I argued in Chapter 4, NATO planning on TNW has little coherence or sense, because however delicate the first use of nuclear force, massive nuclear retaliation must be expected — a nuclear defence of Europe is a swift recipe for suicide.

There is, however, a sharp contradiction between what West European states want from the US nuclear umbrella (and apparently think they are getting) and what they are actually getting. The sophistications of concepts of limited nuclear war have little attraction: what West European states have sought is a nuclear deterrent shield; the threat to use nuclear weapons to defend Western Europe makes any sense only if it constitutes the deterrent threat. For all the talk about flexible response, the heart of West European states' strategic conceptions is nuclear retaliation against Soviet aggression, retaliation carried out by the American force. But it is precisely that strategy which would embroil the American homeland in nuclear conflagration, and precisely that strategy which successive US administrations have tried to get away from since the end of the 1950s and the abandonment of 'massive retaliation'.

Here we see the seeds of a potential and long-aborted strategic crisis between Western Europe and the USA. It has a twofold basis, first in the necessarily different interests of Western Europe and the USA and, secondly, in the increased ability of West European states to express that difference forcibly thanks to their slightly greater unity and the USA's relative decline. Were this crisis to surface in the 1980s, it could thoroughly fracture the alliance's unity, possibly providing the occasion for some important measures of reorganisation within NATO. The programme of modernising TNW provides no release from this crisis because it accords with the USA's emphasis on nuclear warfighting, which the West European states are interested in only if it also means retaliatory nuclear deterrence.

However, the crisis may continue to be suppressed, either because of West European disunity, or because of unwillingness to face the costs of letting it surface. The development of a West European nuclear force to provide Western Europe's own nuclear umbrella would be a major and uncomfortable step, while the costs of investing in the infrastructure of a fully independent nuclear force would be extremely high. Nevertheless, the basis for the crisis exists, a continuing and only half-hidden source of tensions within NATO, and it must be added that the technological basis for a West European nuclear force also exists.

The Case for Disengagement

At present the British state seems firmly set on a course which will lead, under one set of conditions or another, to a closer integration within NATO. In defence as in foreign policy, the Empire has definitely ceased to offer an alternative or even complementary external focus for the state. The reduction of non-NATO non-European military deployments and eager participation in military industrial collaboration emphasise the political and military concentration on the West European arena within NATO. It would be wrong, however, to exclude consideration of the possibility of Britain's relation to NATO being defined by disengagement rather than by integration.

The first advantage of disengagement would be establishing a distance from NATO strategy, especially its nuclear strategy, and its possible consequences. Of course, nuclear fall-out respects neither national boundaries nor membership of alliances, but were Britain to adopt a non-nuclear defence policy and remove the American nuclear bases there would be a greater degree of safety in an unsafe world. The British people are not well served by reliance on American nuclear strategy, by a possible nuclear defence of Western Europe, or by the incoherence and imprecision of NATO's nuclear doctrines. Doing away with British involvement in these would be an unqualified benefit.

But what is essentially at issue here is the prospect of developing greater independence in foreign and defence policy, in contrast to the prospect now before us of diminishing independence in both. The advantages of opting for this alternative course must be seen in both domestic and international terms.

There is no immutable reason for the solutions to problems of rising costs of military equipment taking the form of military industrial collaboration, standardisation or interoperability, and integration into a West European arms procurement agency. The problem of rising costs and of the expansion of industrial capacity could be tackled by a different route, and the kind of break with present practices and conceptions which is implied by embarking on disengagement from NATO would provide the room needed for taking that route. It would be necessary to confront those attitudes which insist, first, that greater military capability must always be sought and, secondly, that it can only come from increased technological sophistication. It would be possible to seek more modest technological solutions to military problems, and the development of the technologies of precision guidance during the 1970s provides an opportunity to restructure military forces for defensive deployment in Britain. A reform of strategic concepts and force structures to capitalise on this opportunity would have to be accompanied by reform of the industrial institutions that equip the forces; denied the opportunity to participate in West European collaboration, and probably denied access to any two-way street in the trans-Atlantic arms trade, military industry would impose intolerable strains on the procurement budget unless it were reformed. Surplus capacity could be converted to other production, and diversification within military industry would provide a further institutional lever against the industry's technological momentum. To effect this, detailed and determined state intervention would be required, breaking up and reconstructing the design teams, establishing new patterns of practice and thought, directing the investment of the enterprises.

Radical solutions to the problems of cost, technology and industrial structures together with a reworking of strategy and force structure are necessary components of a policy of disengagement from NATO. But the effects of the policy would not be confined to the potential for reduced military spending and releasing industrial skills for other purposes. Its international implications can be considered by first discussing the kind of overall strategy which could be adopted.

Discussing detente in Chapter 3, I argued that its progress was undermined by nuclear deterrence with its emphasis on an inhuman threat and the perceptions of the adversary needed to legitimate the threat. For all its problems, however, deterrence of some sort is an unavoidable part of international relations, especially when the states concerned have potentially conflicting interests. We should therefore seek an alternative type of deterrence with, crucially, a greatly reduced emphasis on retaliation. This alternative could be described as defensive deterrence (contrasted with retaliatory deterrence), centred on the ability to resist aggression rather than the ability to retaliate. Very different examples of it can be found in the defence policies of Sweden, Switzerland and Yugoslavia, although none of these three states need serve as an exclusive model of defensive deterrence. It might involve three main components: a diplomacy aimed at reducing incentives to aggression, and ultimately at disarmament; a demonstrable ability to exact a high toll of any offensive forces; organising to make successful occupation of the country an unlikely prospect. In this form, the strategy presupposes the deployment of military forces, and it would be as difficult in this context as in any other to establish the necessary level of forces required. But certain military capabilities would be irrelevant, positively undesirable or needed in less strength — for example, long-range bombers and missiles, an ocean-going navy and invasion forces. Other capabilities would be given higher priority — for example, anti-aircraft and anti-shipping missiles and a highly mobile infantry force.

It is virtually impossible to conceive of NATO adopting such a strategy, but it remains an attractive alternative for Britain, well suited to Britain's geographical position which, while by no means providing the natural defence of former times, offers advantages which cannot be exploited while Britain remains so firmly committed to NATO, nuclear strategy and the Central European front.

A major aspect of such a strategy is the room it offers for diplomatic initiatives aimed at reducing the likelihood of war and furthering the process of disarmament. Together with the fact that British disengagement from NATO would constitute an historic break with the system of military blocs, it offers the potential for freeing some important log-jams in international relations, particularly in disarmament negotiations. It would, to begin with, involve unilateral disarmament measures; equally important, it would add another state to those with a concrete interest in promoting genuine measures of disarmament in the international community.

Although disengagement and defensive deterrence are in one sense less 'internationalist' than involvement in an alliance, and although they direct military attention solely to the defence of Britain, in another sense they entail a profoundly internationalist consciousness and would redefine the concept of 'national security' out of all recognition. They could not deploy the 'ultimate deterrent' of nuclear weapons, because they would seek to be free of the ultimate risk of nuclear destruction. They thus explicitly embody a sense of the risks of nuclear strategy, the awful possibility that one day nuclear weapons could be used, and correspondingly of the need to develop strategies and policies which can reduce and finally eliminate this risk. With this basic approach, it is no longer possible to accept a concept of national security which actually means the competitive international interests of a state in class-divided society; national security becomes indivisible from international safety and survival, and it comes to mean the security of the people of a nation within that international context.

Disengagement from NATO therefore offers both short- and long-term attractions; to be sure, realising them would be no simple task, and I have not yet discussed the domestic political conditions needed to make disengagement possible. But it is necessary first to consider the possible costs of disengagement as well as its benefits.

The basic cost must be seen in terms of that distance from NATO which, seen from the other side, is the most immediate benefit. That distance would leave a state with such a fragile domestic economy in a distressingly vulnerable position to potential economic retaliation from the other NATO members. Retaliation would be possible within the EEC, in the councils of the International Monetary Fund, in summit-meeting deliberations over international economic policy. It need not even be deliberate retaliation, simply a refusal to take into account the particular needs and preferences of British economic policy. Political retaliation would also be possible, an example of which might be an attempt to remove Britain from its permanent seat in the United Nations Security Council, or backing Britain's adversaries in various conflicts and disagreements.

There is a further risk that disengagement would so alarm NATO that arms programmes would be stepped up, intensifying military competition with the WP, weakening detente and further diminishing the prospects for arms control. This possibility cannot be ignored, although on the evidence of NATO's 30 years it would be hard indeed to show that British membership has prevented ambitious arms programmes or inhibited military competition.

Both this risk and the extent of retaliation would in part depend on the nature of the process of disengagement; that is, different kinds of disengagement can be envisaged. Evidently, one kind is to withdraw entirely from the alliance by abrogating the commitment to the North Atlantic Treaty and adopting a fully non-aligned foreign policy. But it is also possible to envisage a partial disengagement, in which Britain would create a greater distance between itself and NATO while remaining a member of the alliance. The fullest form of this partial disengagement would be to withdraw British forces from NATO command (following the French example of 1966), bring back all forces on the continent of

Europe, remove the American bases in Britain and opt out of joint military programmes in NATO. To ameliorate the other NATO members' retaliation, it might be possible to offer continued co-operation in, for example, communications and surveillance of the eastern Atlantic, Channel and North Sea areas, and even in some aspects of naval operations, although obviously this co-operation should not go so far that it eliminated the basic rationale for disengagement.

Because partial disengagement is a less ambitious step than opting for immediate full non-alignment, it seems more feasible in the short-term, even though the fuller step has a comforting logical consistency in it. It offers more diplomatic room for manoeuvre, a more flexible approach to international relations, and less of a sudden jolt to the other NATO members. Undertaken in pre-defined stages, the worst shock-waves could have dissipated by the time the process was complete. It would mean the first limited steps on a path which would have to include the industrial and strategic changes discussed above, leading in the end to different answers to the fundamental challenges of world affairs, and yet, modest though these first steps are, they would be a radical departure for the British state.

British Decline

It remains to consider the political conditions in Britain in which a policy of partial disengagement from NATO could be implemented, to ask whether the British state is capable of such a step. The short answer to that question is that the current form and condition of the British state effectively eliminates the option of disengagement, however partial it might be. Against this view it might be argued that France's forces are not under NATO command, that Sweden and Switzerland, two capitalist states, are both non-aligned, that Norway, with its refusal to station foreign forces permanently in its territory or base any of its forces permanently overseas, is rather less engaged in NATO than Britain is. But in Britain there is no political force comparable to the nationalism mobilised by Gaullism in support of an independent foreign policy; there is no history of non-alignment on the Swedish or Swiss model; and the British state has always regarded itself as and has always been a far more central component of NATO than is true of Norway.

A defence policy based on disengagement from NATO is possible only if there is a decisive political majority supporting the policy and the conceptions it embodies. Only then could the necessary support be generated to see Britain through the effects of possible retaliation by other NATO states. But such a political majority would not merely want to see a change in defence policy: it is impossible to conceive of majority support for radical change in defence policy unless that majority is also seeking radical change in the entire fabric of the British state, in the economy and in society. Change in defence policy would be one part of the overall transformation through which British politics and society would then be passing.

It is not that it is theoretically impossible to conceive of a more independent defence policy which does not entail social transformation as its basis, but that to do so one would have to re-write British history (to conform to a more Scandinavian pattern) and ignore current political realities. One could outline four basic options for the British state – a return to neo-Imperial greatness, non-alignment, acceptance of strengthened US leadership, or participation in the construction of a new West European polity – but for the state in its current form it is only the last two which really count. For Britain's century-long decline from its nineteenth-century pinnacle has finally led it from independent Imperial grandeur to its current delicate balance between accepting American leadership and integration into a West European unit. The basic issue for the British state is not whether or not to continue to be a member of NATO, but *how* to be a member.

There is nowhere in the British state or political establishment that can be identified as the potential source of a break from the confines of that choice, that could establish a new logic overturning the basic terms of British defence policy and opting for an independent stance. The Conservative Party, which now forms the government, and which embodies the main traditions of the state and establishment, has effectively ceased to be the party of 'nation': its new stance is as the party of Britain in Europe. In the 1970s, in a difficult turn away from its former political idiom, it came to recognise, with greater clarity than it is usually given credit for, that genuine political independence is not a realistic option for the British state as it is now constituted.

This situation is not surprising; if anything, the surprise is that it took so long for a major exponent of this position to emerge in the British political scene. For the most obvious aspect of Britain's slow decline has been the inability of successive governments to find solutions to economic debility, while the weakness of the domestic economy is counterpointed, and to some extent has been caused, by the strength of British capital abroad. This is not to repeat the argument that capital invested abroad cannot be used at home to generate industrial renewal; more important by far is that the steps which might have been taken to strengthen the domestic economy – the much argued mixture of selective import controls and currency regulation together with an industrial investment strategy — would have risked provoking a chain reaction of protectionism in the international system which would have harmed British international capital, whose not inconsiderable influence was therefore thrown against such steps. Sections of Britain's economic and corporate leaders have been, as Bob Rowthorn put it, 'effectively "de-nationalized", not through their own weakness, but through the weakness of the British state and their own home base'.[5] But this does not mean that these sections have become silent in British politics; far from it — it is their influence which ultimately developed such a ground-swell of public opinion that the 1975 referendum on membership of the EEC resulted in a massive majority in favour of staying in. The interests of these groups require the support of the British state from within the EEC, while at the same time the British state is incapable of unilateral action to solve Britain's basic economic problems. It is, at root, Britain's economic trajectory which has eliminated genuine political independence (of the kind, perhaps, advocated by opponents of British membership of the EEC during the 1975 referendum campaign) as an option for the British state.

We must, therefore, note an essential correspondence between the general direction taken by the British state and the particular direction it is taking in defence policy where it seeks West European co-operation as a response to problems of rising costs and expanding military industrial capacity. But there is a more important relation between the general and the particular, which emerges if one seeks to identify how the British state might influence developments in Western Europe and NATO, how it might carry weight in a process of reorganisation.

We can once again summarise the polar alternatives for the British state of accepting American leadership or seeking closer integration into a West European formation, noting the qualification that tendencies towards either pole need not be completely realised. To this we can add the alternative in Western Europe of accepting the FRG as the organising centre or attempting to gain a place in a more diverse organising bloc. Clearly, the British state does not have the capacity to guarantee that the particular alternative it favours will be the one to predominate, for there is a variety of other powers whose influence will also be felt, but it does have the capacity to influence events. Whichever alternative the state plumps for as the 1980s develop, and even if it favours none and seeks to maintain an unresolved balance between them all, its strongest cards are to be found in its defence policy — in the existence of a well-rounded military industry, in armed forces with the widest range of capabilities of any in Western Europe, however over-stretched that leaves them, and in its possession of a semi-independent nuclear force, however costly and ill-judged a decision to replace it in the 1980s may be. It is here, and it may be here alone, that the British state can have a decisive say in Western Europe's trajectory through the 1980s and beyond.

Various factors constrain the way in which these cards can be played. If Britain chose to stand aloof, without opting for disengagement from NATO, it would simply be left behind; the game can be played without Britain. Moreover, given present military doctrines and industrial philosophy and organisation, Britain needs collaboration to sustain its industry and equip its forces as much as any state, and this element of interdependence means it cannot control the game. And, of course, the British state, forces and industry are not immune to the processes of ideological penetration and co-operation, by Americanism or Europeanism, which accompany collaboration, just as they have not been immune to the effects of dependence on the USA in crucial military spheres. But when these qualifications are noted, it remains the case that the military field is where the British state can find its bargaining counters in the 1980s.

For those who seek reductions in British defence spending and a reallocation of resources to other uses, this offers a gloomy prospect, especially with a Conservative government in office. In 1975, the Conservatives were spectacularly disunited, and one of the main rallying cries for party unity was Margaret Thatcher's powerful anti-Soviet rhetoric and the steady attack on the Labour government's failure to raise military spending. This alone was indication enough that, back in office, the Conservatives could be expected to increase military spending, even if the Labour government had already committed itself to the target of annual increases of three per cent for five years. It implied new arms programmes and the possibility that in the early 1980s British military spending could consume a rising proportion of the national product. Of course, if the British economy slipped into a yet deeper trough, the Conservative government might be forced to trim its ambitions, as its predecessor in 1973 was. But in the discussion of British influence in reorganisation within NATO, a further reason has emerged for the Conservatives keeping military spending high. It is not simply a problem, as Conservative politicians argued on countless occasions between 1974 and 1979, that failing to increase Britain's military budget reduced British status in NATO; this was never a very convincing argument, particularly since the picture of Britain overspending itself would not be especially edifying to NATO allies. Rather, if the government wants to play the card of British military and military industrial capabilities, those capabilities must be nourished, and with equipment costs continuing to rise the only way to do that is to increase the military budget.

Britain's relation to NATO, then, will partly be expressed through increased military spending, because the basic preferences of the Conservative government will be strengthened by the need to have some area in which the British state can make its long-term preferences felt as international reorganisation and jockeying for position develop. British requirements in the current stage of rivalry and alliance in NATO will be reflected in the defence budget.

They may also be reflected in another way. In the discussion on NATO strategy in the 1980s I made no mention of the possibility of NATO military actions outside Europe, particularly in Africa. Belgian and French intervention in Zaire in 1978 may be thought to have been preliminaries to an extension of NATO's sphere of operations, although the two states mounted effectively separate operations. But were this extension to occur, and were West European states requested to participate or were they even to dominate action in an extended sphere, the Conservative government is ideologically equipped to play a leading role; that is, while one can envisage a fumbling half-apologetic explanation of its actions by a Labour government, one can equally easily conceive of the Conservatives announcing a small military adventure in Africa as a triumph. And, as I suggested while discussing the rationale for Britain's new anti-submarine warfare cruisers in Chapter 5, for certain types of intervention it is also militarily equipped. New British military interventions in Africa would be utterly distasteful, but if the British state emphasises its military cards in relations with other NATO states, and if NATO's operations were extended, the logic is that British forces would be prominent.

We must conclude by asking whether increasing the military budget will finally provide a resolution of the dilemma between available resources and desired military capabilities that is the theme of thirty years of British defence policy. Superficially, it would seem that if extra resources are to be made available, and especially if the logic of collaboration in weapons procurement is accepted, the dilemma should vanish. But the kind of scepticism which is bred by considering the history of British defence policy suggests that the dilemma will remain, but at a new level.

Towards the end of Chapter 5, I argued that if current force structures and military preferences were retained, and if ambitious programmes

such as replacing *Polaris* went ahead, then in view of the tenacity of
equipment cost increases, raising the military budget by as much as six
per cent a year in real terms for five years would be barely adequate to
sustain the current military posture on a proper footing. I suggested that
a sustained annual budget increase of ten per cent might meet the bill,
but that this would require a reformation of some of the basic assumptions of British politics, a change as radical in a different direction as
the social and political change implied by a policy of disengagement
from NATO. In the context of general upheavals in the international
capitalist system, such change may be possible, but one element of this
argument on the budget needs to be brought out: if the intention were
to go beyond repairing Britain's military posture and keeping it up to
date with new equipment, and instead to effect a major strengthening
of the armed forces, then annual spending increases in real terms of
from seven to ten per cent are the probable requirement.

Yet during their years in opposition, it was precisely this kind of
ambitious beefing up of the services that was implied in virtually every
statement on defence by the Conservatives. That is, Conservative defence
policy has consistently implied the need for military spending to absorb
a greater proportion of national resources and for basic political assumptions to be reshaped accordingly. Indeed, if military spending is increased,
and that must be the assumption, not least because it was already rising
under Labour, the forces, defence civil servants and Conservative opinion
will probably demand that increased spending has something to show
in terms of visibly increased capabilities, increasing the pressure for the
annual increases to go above the six per cent level. It should be noted
that setting out so ambitiously in the early 1980s will be too soon for
the effects of co-operative weapons programmes to make themselves felt
in terms of slower increases in equipment costs; however eagerly standardisation and collaboration might be pursued, they will not reduce the
budgetary burden the state would have to bear as the 1980s progressed.

Therefore, unless basic political assumptions can be reshaped, or
unless the temptation to provide greater military capabilities can be
resisted, the dilemma between capabilities and resources will re-emerge
in the 1980s to plague defence planners, but at a much higher level of
expenditure. The state's long failure to resolve this dilemma can be
eradicated only by a change in the state and therefore in society, in one
direction or another; the critical question is whether change will occur
and, if it does, what direction will it take.

Notes

1. Because much of this chapter summarises material and arguments already presented, substantiating references will be kept to a minimum.

2. *Strategic Survey 1976* (IISS, London, 1977), pp. 66-71, discusses and criticises French priorities in military planning.

3. *The Guardian*, 8 November 1978.

4. Useful comments on the FRG's economic policies and its ability to export unemployment by expelling the *gastarbeiter* were made by S. Holland, 'The High Risks of the New Money Game', *New Statesman*, 6 October 1978; on the FRG's repression of basic political freedoms, see S. Cobler, *Law, Order and Politics in West Germany* (Penguin, Harmondsworth, 1978).

5. B. Rowthorn, 'Imperialism in the Seventies — Unity or Rivalry', *New Left Review* 69, 1971.

In considering the range and possibility of choice in defence policy in the 1980s, we start from the fact that the British state has only one defence policy; for all its deficiencies and ambiguities, it exists on paper, expressed in concrete form in the deployment of forces and in industrial projects financed from the defence budget, buttressed by resilient assumptions about the importance of NATO to British security and deeply held, if often inexplicit, conceptions of world affairs. Starting from existing policy, it would be possible to outline an infinite range of changes, major or minor, radical or cosmetic: there is only one existing policy, but there is an unending range of choice theoretically available for the 1980s. This itself hampers debate about alternatives and choices, for confronting the solidity of current policy there is only the vagueness of what is possible.

But the unlimited range of choice available in the abstract is sharply pruned by political realities, by factors which much of the discussion in this book has been directed at identifying. Domestic and international conditions provide the constraining context within which choice about defence policy must be made, and while a large number of options could be outlined, only a much smaller number would be in any sense feasible. However, whether policy choices are made by deliberate consciousness or, as is more likely, emerge through force of circumstance and the compromise between intention and practicability, their meaning can only be understood through a sense of the broad alternatives, the alternatives which might be made feasible if a different political route were developed. The meaning of what is chosen can be clarified by considering what was discarded, or what did not even enter the debates of policy-makers. This chapter therefore discusses a limited range of options, but includes among them a policy of disengagement from NATO which, under the current Conservative administration and equally under its Labour predecessor, is a highly improbable path for defence policy to take.

In the context of rising equipment and personnel costs, the basic long-term structural choice concerns the principle of maintaining balanced forces.[1] If it is preserved, the next questions concern whether there is room for pruning within the services, whether there is space in the equipment budget for replacing *Polaris*, and the political and economic issues of how the resources are to be made available. These questions are particularly acute if the intention is also to ensure that military personnel are properly paid and living and working in adequate conditions with a support infrastructure improved from its current tattered shape. If balanced forces are not preserved, the questions concern what capabilities can be jettisoned and which of the services will thereby 'lose out', and the political implications of basic change in force structures.

In addressing, with varying degrees of explicitness, this complex of questions, most commentaries on the future of British defence policy leave aside the question of whether or not Britain should remain a full member of NATO, although some discuss the form of membership. For them, membership of NATO is the ever-present basic assumption of defence policy: they accept the valuation of NATO as the linchpin of British security.[2] In doing so, they establish their role as essentially technical discussions in which the basic political questions have already been answered. In contrast, the discussion of options for defence policy in this chapter will be essentially a political analysis of their meaning. The tactical operational details of defence policy are not unimportant, but in establishing the framework of policy options the first task must necessarily be to focus on the wider issues; only when political directions have been mapped out and evaluated is a technical discussion required. In fact, sharp change in tactical doctrines is unlikely in most of the options discussed; what can be expected is a process of relatively minor incremental changes to take account of the capabilities of new equipment, with the basic doctrines changing only slowly if at all.

The options outlined below are centred around the relation of the British state to NATO, for reasons discussed in the preceding chapter. Three basic options are discussed, each with variations: NATO membership, NATO integration and disengagement. When policies are formulated there is often a temptation to think that that is the end of the matter: the policy has been decided, and now the concern is simply to implement it. But things are never so clear-cut in practice. The processes of formulating policy themselves permit a considerable degree of ambiguity in policy: in considering the direction of arms procurement policies in Western Europe it became clear that the same state can lean in two directions at once, because the basic issues at stake in the further development of procurement policy have not been conclusively resolved and the states concerned have internalised conflicting tendencies. More than this, neither the domestic nor the international conditions in which policy is formulated and implemented are static; the state's responses to their constant changes lead to gradual erosion and evolution of policies, or to reconsideration and change. To try and take account of this, the options discussed below are open-ended: there are areas of overlap and blurred edges between them, reflecting the possibility of policy decisions failing to close off other options and changing over time.

Membership of NATO on Current Terms

We start with the possibility that the present relation to NATO will continue; there may be, indeed, must be changes, but the basic form of the relationship need not be affected. NATO could continue, and the British state could seek to encourage it to continue, as an association of states allied in defence policy as they are bound by other mutual interests, with the possibility and the desirability of closer integration discussed both in the strategic literature and by governments, yet without decisive progress being made towards a fuller pooling of defence resources throughout the 1980s.

The strategic and political assumptions underpinning this policy would be more or less as they are at present. The maintenance of sovereign statehood would be perceived to face its main challenge from the USSR and its WP allies, and therefore require military and political alliance in NATO. The essential cohesion of the alliance and the basis of its deterrence would continue to be provided by the USA; American strategic nuclear forces, American provision of tactical nuclear weapons under controls and American reinforcements in the event of war would remain central aspects of NATO strategy and political cohesion. Within this context, West European states would continue to make independent provision for their contribution to NATO's overall forces, with collaborative projects entered from time to time on a continuing *ad hoc* basis. The dichotomy between rivalry and alliance among NATO states would continue without leading to a reorganisation, a new equilibrium, a fundamentally changed balance of power.

Against such a background, the fundamental questions for British defence policy concern the dilemma between available resources and desired capabilities and, consequently, the principle of balanced forces. A context of unchanged strategic assumptions, a feature of this option for defence policy, would provide no room for a major reduction in any one of the armed services unless one of the other NATO states were prepared to replace the British contribution in a particular field. There are really only three candidates for increasing their own military contribution to NATO to compensate for a diminished British role.

The FRG might be able to increase its ground or naval forces to counterbalance the effects of Britain reducing its navy or the British

Army of the Rhine (BAOR), and might even welcome this chance to claim a greater share of senior NATO command positions and increased influence in NATO generally. On the other hand, BAOR is regarded as a concrete expression of British commitment to the defence of the FRG and its other West European allies; reducing it, let alone eliminating the deployment altogether, would be interpreted as a reduction or abandonment of that commitment. In the case of British naval reductions, with the introduction of the *Invincible* class of anti-submarine warfare cruisers, the British navy would be left with a 'top heavy' force structure in which the deployment of the cruisers could be hampered by lack of adequate support forces, a prospect which would certainly not appeal to the navy, would lack credibility in the eyes of NATO allies, and would make little sense from any perspective. Moreover, for the FRG to increase its forces, especially its navy which now maintains relatively limited capabilities compared to its land and air forces, would raise the question of West German leadership in Western Europe with all the discomfort that implies for the British state no less than for its NATO partners.

A slightly less likely candidate is the USA, but an increased American contribution to NATO in Europe or, in the case of naval forces, the eastern Atlantic would be likely to meet stiff Congressional resistance. Although the withdrawal of American forces from Europe seems far less likely than it did at the start of the 1970s when there was for a time a strong body of Congressional opinion in favour of it, Congress could be expected to refuse to countenance the USA 'bailing out' West European states which refused to make enough provision for their own defence. On the other hand, increasing American forces committed directly to NATO in Europe would strengthen the USA's hand in intra-NATO politics and might therefore be attractive to the administration and even to Congress. The willingness of the British state to pay this price is again open to question.

The third and least likely candidate is France, whose possible re-integration into the NATO military command system might validate reducing some British forces. Military reintegration in NATO, however, would be a difficult step for France to take, at least in the first half of the 1980s. The picture of Britain poised to reduce forces as soon as France re-entered the fold might be enough to dissuade the French state from taking the step. And even were the British state prepared to accept second place behind the FRG among West European NATO states, it would find it hard so openly to accept third place behind France.

Indeed, the prospect of reduced status in NATO would not only be a strong argument against cutting down forces on the expectation of some other state filling in, it is probably a genuine fear within the British state that its capacity to uphold and advance its interests within NATO is slipping; a policy which almost deliberately diminished its political capacities still further would certainly be resisted. It can, of course, be argued that the cost of sustaining these capacities through deploying strong armed forces is too great, that the political outlook such a fear derives from is anachronistic, and that a smart step down the NATO ladder is preferable to drifting down slowly yet inevitably. Such an argument, however, is unlikely to appeal within the state or to a Conservative government.

If these arguments suggest that the principle of balanced forces is likely to be maintained through the 1980s, various other options present themselves, amounting to making relatively small yet still important reductions within the services. For example, the provision of ground forces for the defence of Britain itself might be reduced; the air force might be persuaded to do away with the mission of long range bombing; adjustments of programmes within the navy might reduce submarine forces or support forces for the anti-submarine cruisers without completely undermining the force structure. All three steps would be resisted and are in any case difficult to contemplate. Reducing army forces in Britain would not only cause palpitations within the state, it would make the administration of the army more complex, particularly in view of the practice of rotating army units through BAOR and back to Home Forces. With *Tornado* being introduced into the air force, one can hardly believe that the mission it seems most suited for would be discarded. In a sense, the navy is the most vulnerable, but paring it down must be carried through in the face of considerable, even if exaggerated concern about Soviet naval strength. The principle of balanced forces severely limits defence planners; thoroughly restructuring the military posture will be almost impossible, and small numerical reductions here and there seem the most that is possible. Yet failure to discard the principle will lead defence policy straight back into the dilemma between resources and capabilities.

Taking office in 1979, the Conservative government inherited a commitment to increase military spending by three per cent annually in real terms for five years, and this is probably the lowest level of increases it will want. Retention of balanced forces raises the question of whether this three per cent will be enough both to maintain current force levels and to repair deficiencies in the forces in wages, conditions and the support infrastructure. Over the five year period of this programme of increased spending, the annual budget would rise by about sixteen per cent in real terms.

Arguments by David Greenwood that major reductions in force levels, of the kind necessary in the mid-to-late 1970s to cut spending by 20 to 25 per cent, would be required simply to keep the budget stable in the 1980s suggest that a real increase in spending of up to 25 per cent over five years would be required to keep force levels steady.[3] If we add further spending increases to make good infrastructural deficiencies, then it is clear that a programme of three per cent annual increases is well short of what is required simply to keep force levels steady and eliminate the effects of being over-stretched. If we add yet further increases to accomplish full mechanisation of the army and to cover British contributions to the costs of potential NATO programmes to improve communications and logistics or 'harden' bases to withstand nuclear attack, then it emerges that over the longer term a programme of relatively modest budget increases amounts to a programme of gradual reductions in forces. If force reductions cannot be accepted, the alternative is to watch British defence policy develop the same ailments in the mid-1980s that it had in the late 1970s and await the reappearance of the crisis of services' morale.

These arguments suggest that sensible budgeting on the basis of current force structures and levels requires a programme of budget increases of up to six per cent in real terms for at least five years. This would leave little room for increasing force levels or strengthening military capabilities beyond the continuing introductions of new equipment.

If greater ambitions are entertained, defence planning must be based on the assumption of budgets increasing by six per cent and upwards a year, for most of the 1980s. Such ambitions might include some permutation of extra army manpower and fuller mechanisation, strengthening British air defence by more than the 165 copies of the interceptor version of *Tornado*, increasing air transport capacity, replacing *Polaris* with a larger force, procuring a fourth anti-submarine cruiser and appropriate support vessels, bringing forward the date when the new battle tank, MBT-80, enters service, proceeding with the AST-403 aircraft project to replace *Harrier* and *Jaguar*, and redeploying forces to the Mediterranean and East of Suez.[4] Planning for all of these would almost certainly require increases in the budget of around ten per cent annually, in real terms, beginning some time in the early 1980s leading by the early 1990s to a doubling of the defence budget. A more modest combination of some of these possibilities would, even if we make charitable assumptions about the costs of the projects, require an increase over the whole decade of above 70 per cent in real terms.

Unless British economic performance picks up in the 1980s to an extent far greater than any reasonable forecast dare suggest, such a programme will mean defence consuming a rising share of government expenditure and, more importantly, a rising share of total economic resources. The planning assumptions for such a programme would therefore have to be predicated on changes in basic domestic political assumptions and expectations so that the resources could be freed from other demands. Comparative analysis of capitalist economies' perform-ances in the period since World War II leads to the conclusion that increasing military expenditure in this way would absorb resources which might otherwise go to civil industrial investment;[5] thus, such an ambitious military programme would actually hinder the performance of the domestic economy, and further strains would be imposed on national resources and on basic political assumptions and expectations.

It may be that the current form of conservatism can effect such a dramatic political change; it may be that defence planners will enter a veritable 'golden age' in the 1980s. If it happens, the consequences for British society will be decidedly unpleasant, and if it does not, the con-sequences for defence policy will be decidedly chaotic.

Thus, two variations of a defence policy in which the main theme is membership of NATO on continuing current terms – modest budget increases and major budget increases – provide disagreeable prospects. In the case of modest budget increases, it is only if the principle of balanced forces can be jettisoned that we can foresee some degree of sanity in defence policy in the 1980s, yet jettisoning that principle seems unlikely.

To accord with the principle of proposing alternatives even if their adoption seems unlikely, it is necessary to consider the prospects and consequences of a policy of reducing defence budgets while remaining a fully committed member of NATO. This, of course, is extremely improbable under a Conservative government; under the Labour govern-ment of 1974-9 it seemed possible initially, but the possibility slowly diminished and then disappeared entirely as the government prepared to raise spending from 1979. The major study of the possibilities with a reduced budget was conducted by a group established by the Labour Party's National Executive Committee, and to illustrate the options available this group adopted a framework laid out by David Green-wood.[6] With a target for budget reductions set by the Labour Party's 1974 election manifestoes, the illustrative options added up to sharp reductions in a choice of two out of the three services together with the abandonment of the *Polaris* force. The specific options discussed by the study group have now been overtaken by events, but the basic principle that real reductions in spending require major restructuring of the services still stands.

Adoption of the kind of defence policy illustrated by the study group would imply, indeed, necessitate a number of things. To begin with, the principle of balanced forces could no longer be sustained. The strategic assumptions on which such a policy would be based would include a very different analysis of Soviet military power and intentions than was subscribed to by the Labour government of the time and by most NATO states. The possibilities for radical change in military doctrines, especially to take advantage of the opportunities provided by precision guided munitions, would have to be examined and developed. The British state would have to swim against the tide of opinion among NATO states and be prepared to withstand their opposition, ready to accept isolation within NATO for a period.

At the time, I argued that a government that was determinedly set on such a course should be able to sustain it, that none of these factors need deter it.[7] In principle, that argument still holds, but it is likely that it will soon also be overtaken by events, if that has not already happened, for two main reasons. First, as costs rise so that modest budget increases could no longer hold the line against some level of reductions of forces, the changes in force structure and policy needed to implement major cuts in the budget become more and more radical. Secondly, with NATO states looking increasingly firmly set on boosting military spending, Britain's isolation in its independent course would be more profound. The consequences of these two factors are twofold: first, the determination needed to hold the course becomes enormously greater, requiring widespread political support within Britain; secondly, taking an independent course in defence policy casts the British state further adrift from the basic political and strategic assumptions underlying NATO. In other words, the passage of time is forcing the issue so that a policy of major cuts in defence spending increasingly tends in the direction of a policy of disengagement from NATO.

This is not to say that all arguments which oppose particular increases in military spending must conclude by proposing disengagement from NATO. But it is to say that proposals for major reductions in British military spending will, during the 1980s, have to propose such major changes in policy that they will amount to some form of partial disengagement from the alliance.

Of course, the stronger the tendencies towards integration in NATO,

the more emphatic that point must become. And here we must return
to the premises which underlie this option in defence policy for the
1980s, for the longevity of the option must be in doubt.

It is very unlikely that even the most ambitious defence plans of the
British state will rely completely on independent procurement policy;
indeed, the more ambitious the state is, the more likely it is to seek
collaboration with other NATO states as a way of possibly avoiding
some of the worst economic strains its defence policy would impose.
Moreover, one of the rationales for an ambitious defence programme
is that it can permit Britain to play an important role in NATO and in
Western Europe as changes occur in both. Defence policy, even if not
consciously planned to fit in with one scenario of NATO integration or
another, will almost certainly foster integrative tendencies within the
alliance. Even though the 1980s are entered with an independent defence
policy within the confines of membership of the alliance, it is likely
that by the end of the decade a process of greater integration will have
begun to unfold, and the general trajectory of the British state makes it
unlikely that defence policy will stand aloof from that process. If the
'reduced budget variant' of continued membership actually tends in the
direction of disengagement, the 'modest increases' and 'major increases'
variants both tend towards greater integration.

Towards NATO Integration

Moves towards greater integration of military preparations in NATO are
almost certain to be made up of small steps. Co-ordinating procurement
policies, logistic and other infrastructural arrangements, command
structures and doctrines will be a slow and difficult business, not only
because of the genuine complexities of administering the movement of
many states towards new arrangements but also, more importantly,
because of the continuing balance of rivalry with alliance, of competition
and conflict with the need for cohesion and unity. In any scenario of
greater integration, the decisive issue is whether West European states
are to integrate their defence policies more closely under American
leadership, or whether West European moves to military integration will
effectively diminish American influence on West European policies while
providing the West European states with more influence within NATO.

As the arguments in Chapters 7 and 9 suggested, the form in which
this issue will be resolved is as yet uncertain and will be affected by all
aspects of relations within Western Europe and between Western Europe
and the USA, while the process of resolution will be slow and intricate.
States will proceed through relatively short-term measures and the

exigencies of the present are, at each stage, likely to weigh as heavily as aspirations for the future. It is therefore possible to speculate that the development of NATO integration, whatever direction it takes, will have fairly limited effects on British defence policy through the 1980s; the time-scale for the emergence of new forms of organisation and a new political balance within NATO is probably greater than a decade. This also means that laying out grand designs for integration, as in the Klepsch report with its proposal to transform the European Programme Group into an international weapons procurement agency,[8] whether it is done for purposes of advocacy or illustration, is vulnerable to being overtaken by events. Indeed, grand designs are not particularly relevant, since even formal adherence to them by states means less than the contradictory impulses revealed in practical policy implementation. As David Greenwood suggests, it is more likely that NATO states will 'muddle through', and the most that can be expected is that this muddle will have some sense of direction to it (in Greenwood's argument, an essentially Europeanist direction).[9]

So if in the case of the option for British defence policy of continuing membership of NATO on current terms the problem we face is one of impermanence, in the case of a defence policy predicated on integration in NATO the problem is one of incompleteness and uncertain overall direction. Depending on whether the dominant tendency is ultimately Europeanist or Atlanticist, the basic strategic assumptions of British defence policy will be different in important respects.

The perception that the basic threat to security comes from the USSR will stand in either case, and it is almost certain that the strategic perspectives expressed in concern over WP conventional forces and the need for retaliatory nuclear deterrence will also stand. The Europeanist model of integration might, however, imply a departure in nuclear deterrence in which some of the sophistications of American strategy would be discarded in favour of emphasis upon massive retaliation against the USSR. Certainly, if the suppressed strategic crisis in NATO, discussed in Chapter 9, were to surface and lead to a West European nuclear force and strategy in the 1990s, strategic divergence along these lines would be implied. Although the West European states might retain an approach of flexible response, thereby emphasising the need for the full range of conventional and nuclear forces, the first stages of an in-dependent integrated West European military posture might well entail greater accentuation of nuclear retaliation against the USSR and a diminished role for limited nuclear warfare.

The fundamental strategic divergence between Europeanist and

Atlanticist models of integration, embodied in these possible developments in nuclear deterrence, naturally concerns West European
perceptions of the importance of American forces to West European
security. The threat may be perceived in essentially the same form, but
the response to it would be very different. In essence, the Atlanticist
model emphasises current perceptions that an intrinsic component of
West European security is the USA; these perceptions would be taken
further, with West European armed forces more thoroughly dove-tailing
around US forces and doctrines. West European dependence on US
policy, strategy and capabilities would be intensified, even if, paradoxically, West European forces were strengthened. On the other hand,
while it need not entirely exclude American forces from any role, the
Europeanist model must stress the capacity of West European states
co-operatively to provide adequate forces to meet a distinctively West
European policy and strategy. If West European states want, in the
context of a developing political unity, to supersede the risk of 'catching
pneumonia when Washington gets cold feet',[10] they must provide the
unified wherewithal with which to stand alone if need be. Only if they
can attain independence from the USA in this ultimate form can they
also express their independence in situations more likely and more
frequent. But an American contribution to West European security
need not mean West European dependence upon it.

Changed strategic assumptions underlying West European defence
policies, however, need not by themselves lead to dramatically altered
military postures, except in the possible development of a joint nuclear
force. New assumptions would be of fundamental political importance,
but the deployment and missions of, for example, the British navy need
not change significantly: while American sea-borne reinforcements
might be less emphasised, there could still be the intention to use them
to strengthen West European forces, so that the navy would still prepare
for anti-submarine warfare to protect the reinforcements and would,
no doubt, be a major component of a West European effort to retain
control of the surrounding seas.

The main route to integration lies in processes of joint weapons procurement, in the industrial collaboration, harmonisation of procurement
policies and time-tables and doctrinal standardisation needed to make
joint procurement work. The integration of defence policy would be
primarily in the higher echelons of strategic planning and in the administrative and largely non-uniformed sections. It is possible also to
conceive of integrative measures within the uniformed-military establishments of the various states. This could begin with communication

systems and logistic arrangements; the establishment of multinational forces, such as the one proposed to operate the Airborne Warning and Control System (AWACS), or such as might be created for a West European nuclear force, would take the process further. Proceeding along this path it might finally be possible to eliminate effective national distinctions in military command systems, bringing the integrated NATO command further down the hierarchy, although the mundane problem of different national languages probably provides a point below which integration would not proceed.

Within the same framework of integration in procurement and aspects of the military infrastructure, with the possibility of multinational forces retained in some missions, an alternative route is available which could diminish the need for uniformed-military integration. This is the route of national specialisation, where individual states would give priority to particular military missions and forces, leaving others to be met by other states. Specialisation could take place on the basis of particular security requirements, geographical situation, capabilities or national traditions.[11] For example, in the context of the Europeanist model, the FRG might give priority to land and air forces in Central Europe, Italy and France naval deployments in the Mediterranean, Britain naval deployments in the Eastern Atlantic, Channel and North Sea and air defence of North-western Europe. This, of course, implies discarding the principle of balanced forces, since it largely works on the principle of making all the states interdependent as a result of none deploying forces for the full spectrum of military missions.

In the Europeanist model of integration, specialisation would be an emphatic symbol of unity since it would mean no state providing completely for its own security. In the Atlanticist model, it would emphasise the dependence of the West European states on the USA. In either case its attraction is not only the symbolism of unity but also the possibility of budgetary relief that could come with the abandonment of balanced forces.

Yet the very degree of interdependence implied by specialisation reveals the difficulties. For example, were Britain to concentrate on maritime forces and on deploying air power above those maritime areas, the logic would be to withdraw forces from continental Europe, except that this might appear as a reduced commitment to the defence of continental Europe and especially the FRG, especially since Britain would presumably retain ground forces in its own territory. Warding off the spectre of diminished British commitment in continental Europe by, for example, deploying West German or other forces for defence of

Britain is of dubious political practicability. But if the spectre is warded off by keeping British ground forces in the FRG, the logic and advantages of specialisation are eroded.

British defence policy in the event of specialisation might show some resemblance to the posture resulting from the low-cost variation on membership of NATO on current terms, discussed in the preceding section of this chapter, which also revolved around the abandonment of the principle of balanced forces. The major difference would presumably be in terms of the size of the budget — if British military spending were to increase, as it could do in the context of specialisation, the policy would not tend in the direction of disengagement. The reduction in the budget, and the different reading of the strategic situation implied by that reduction, are crucial elements in the independent stance which could be enforced upon Britain if it decided to opt for a cheaper defence policy within NATO. But a whiff of disengagement is almost unavoidable in a policy of specialisation for Britain, unless ground forces in the FRG are granted highest priority at the expense of naval or air forces. If that were to happen, other states would have to fill in the air and naval gaps, possibly developing completely new military capabilities which would, again, somewhat erode the logic of specialisation. Resolving these difficulties and fears would require a process of bargaining at least as intense and intricate as the entire scenario of integration implies.

For British defence policy, the budgetary implication of integration is, or ought to be, evading the scale of increases which are possible if current terms of membership are maintained. Reduced spending, or even a stable level of spending, is unlikely for two main reasons. First, the pressure for integration will be maintained at least in part by reference to the Soviet threat, and it would therefore be inappropriate and self-defeating to reduce or stabilise spending and thereby imply that the threat was not growing. Second, as I argued in Chapter 9, if the British state wishes to play an active part in reorganisation within the alliance it must be equipped with bargaining counters which, in its present condition, it will find most easily to hand in defence policy and a military budget rising in real terms to compensate for increasing costs of weapon systems. While industrial collaboration might provide some relief from rising costs, and that is not certain, it is most unlikely to reduce costs: that is, collaboration in procurement may mean equipment costs less than it might otherwise have done because the expansion of industrial capacity should at least be slowed, but it does not mean that, for example, the next generation of tanks will cost less than the present generation. However, this limited degree of budgetary relief will probably be off-set by restrictions on the room for budgetary manoeuvre. The closer integration of defence policies will necessarily reduce the ability of each state independently to alter its planning assumptions and budget; not only will the pressure of other states be all the stronger, but the commitments entered into collaboratively with other states will be far harder to cancel or reduce.

As I argued in Chapter 7, the dominant tendency within NATO, as a result of the problems of rising weapon costs if nothing else, is towards a greater integration of defence planning by some or all of the member states. The political terms of the outcome of this tendency – whether Europeanist, Atlanticist or at some point between the two poles, and if predominantly Europeanist, whether under the leadership of the FRG or of a more diverse bloc – and the prospects of this tendency achieving effective institutional expression can only be settled by the unfolding of events in the 1980s. The future shape of defence policies within the alliance is equally unclear in terms of force structures – whether there will be a greater integration of the uniformed-military or greater national military specialisation. Yet whatever the political colours and forms of the final result, and a Europeanist tinge seems the more likely, the new internationalisation of the armament process poses profound problems for democracy in each state and for efforts at achieving solutions to international problems through measures of disarmament. If a defence policy based on continuing membership of NATO on current terms with either modest or major spending increases provides gloomy prospects, it is sadly the case that no relief is offered by turning instead towards a closer integration in NATO.

Disengagement from NATO

This, then, brings us to consider the basic alternative for British defence policy in the 1980s and beyond – a policy of one form or another of disengagement from NATO. The first question about this option concerns the extent to which it actually is a practical option in the 1980s. I have argued that for the British state in its current form, independence of the kind disengagement would imply is not a genuine option; to this it can be added that neither the Conservative nor the Labour Party have shown any sign of turning in the direction of disengagement, although within the Labour Party there has been a body of opinion, far short of a majority and looking unlikely to increase its strength, favouring some kind of disengagement. Two possible sources of the kind of radical change needed can be identified. The first is the fragmented socialist movement in Britain, which includes many members of the Labour Party but not the party as such; following the swing to the right in British politics in the second half of the 1970s, culminating in the election of the Conservatives with a comfortable parliamentary majority in 1979, it is clear that the conditions for major advances by the socialist movement do not yet exist. The second lies in the nationalist movements of Scotland and Wales, which might, if their aspirations were achieved, make disengagement possible for newly formed Scottish and Welsh states. But while Plaid Cymru appears committed to a non-aligned foreign and defence policy for an independent Wales, thinking within the Scottish National Party seems to lean towards continued membership of NATO and acceptance of its basic political and strategic assumptions.[12] In any case, the electoral advances registered by both parties in the mid-1970s had dissipated by 1979, and one must conclude that both are well short of attaining their objectives although an upturn in their electoral fortunes and influence is not out of the question.

In other words, a policy of disengagement from NATO is not in any effective sense on the political agenda in Britain. Any proposal or outline of such a policy must be made and read in the light of this basic qualification. Yet it is not inconceivable that, during the 1980s, the political agenda in Britain could be changed, and if that is to occur one element in it will have to be the formulation of alternatives to the directions in which the British state is travelling, in many aspects of its functioning including foreign and defence policy. It is in that spirit, as well as in order to understand the more likely options by comparing them with more desirable options, that the discussion in this section is included.

In Chapter 9 I argued that the kind of break which disengagement from NATO would constitute would create the space for new approaches and solutions to the problems of defence policy; indeed, since it is hard to conceive of a policy of disengagement except within the context of radical change more generally in Britain, it can be argued that new approaches and solutions are an integral and necessary part of the policy. A redefinition of 'national security' into perspectives and policy in which security could focus at once on more genuinely *national* concerns, rather than on the concerns of the ruling group, and on the necessary dimension of concern for the *international* context, together with the adoption and development of a strategy of defensive deterrence, form the political and strategic bases for these new approaches. But this still leaves an open question: placing the emphasis of deterrence on defence rather than retaliation and defining national security as indivisible from international security would change the basic terms of defence policy, but must still be predicated on the need to deter some threat which, whatever else it may also be directed at, menaces the safety and well-being of the people of a particular country, Britain. In other words, the perception of a threat to a single national political entity remains an important aspect of this approach, and the question which then arises concerns the identification of the threat.

In present defence policy there is no doubting the major threat: it is the USSR. But the perception of how the Soviet threat is constituted is surprisingly diffuse; the 1975 defence White Paper announced the government did not believe the WP would contemplate outright aggression against NATO in existing circumstances. What it feared was the use of military power to bring pressure to bear on NATO countries.[13] Yet it is difficult to see how military strength can be used to bring political pressure to bear, except as far as its relatively peaceful use serves as a reminder of the possibility of using it aggressively — and the British government had stated that it did not think the WP would embark upon outright aggression, so that, logically, it ought not to have feared the use of military power for imposing political pressure. The way out of this apparent *impasse* is twofold. Given an all too evident military factor in relations between NATO and the WP, the emphasis is placed less on short-term advantages the USSR might gain in this way and the direct utility of force, and more on the long-term effects which stem from 'the view of the *beholder* of military power' rather than the actions of the holder.[14] This feeds into the second argument, which is simply that as an intrinsically aggressive power, the USSR is not to be trusted; the evidence of its formidable military power together with the assumption of its basic, even if hidden, expansionist ambitions means that NATO states cannot afford to lower their guard.[15] This view often slides into the assessment of detente as, essentially, Soviet deception.

Against this it must be said that NATO is neither a passive nor a reluctant participant in the military relation between it and the WP. The tendency of NATO governments to imply that NATO is solely concerned with a *response* to the threat from the WP evades NATO's historic responsibility in constructing military confrontation; it cannot be too often recalled that NATO was formed before the WP, that it deployed nuclear weapons before the WP and that WP states are certainly justified in believing that NATO also threatens them. The system of inter-state relations in which NATO might fear the political impact of the WP's military forces was constructed by both sides.

Of course WP forces threaten NATO states, but it must equally emphatically be noted that NATO forces threaten WP states. Should

Britain disengage from NATO, the system of mutual threat would lose some of its relevance to Britain. Moreover, there are compelling reasons for arguing that, alongside the system of mutual threat, neither NATO nor the WP are likely to be tempted into aggression against the other in Europe, not only because of the scale of destruction which would then be unleashed upon both, but also because, unless the assumption of intrinsic aggressiveness on the part of either alliance is entertained, it is hard to identify the political benefits either side would gain. As I noted in Chapter 9, the case of Yugoslavia provides a dangerous potential qualification to this judgement, and a new Soviet leadership might be less cautious than the Brezhnev leadership, but stability and the *status quo* in Europe remain the USSR's basic interests.

It therefore becomes difficult to identify the threat to which British defence policy after disengagement from NATO might constitute a response. The diffuseness of current perceptions of threat is only prevented from undermining the basic assumptions of NATO by the system of confrontation which NATO helped create and the ideology which surrounds it. Opting out of the system and, necessarily, developing a new ideological basis for defence policy could diffuse perceptions of threat even further. Yet it is not clear that from this we can conclude that there would be no threat and that it would therefore be possible unilaterally to disarm Britain comprehensively, although there are respectable arguments that lead in that direction.

International politics provide both diffuse and specific challenges to states' policies, and a state undergoing political transformation and setting out on new paths, such as Britain would be with a policy of disengagement from NATO, might be thought especially vulnerable. The benefit of imposing a government on Britain by the use of military power might be hard to identify for any other state, although the use of military force in an attempt to bully an elected government may seem more likely; neither is inconceivable. It is not just the USSR one thinks of here: it is simply impossible to know what the reaction of other NATO states would be to a future social and political transformation of Britain which, among other things, opened cracks in NATO's military system. Too many factors, including the role of public opinion in other NATO states, would have to be accounted for in arriving at a conclusion. Perhaps more likely than a military intervention are other forms of pressure, particularly economic instruments. But it is in any event reasonable to argue that even if a specific military threat cannot be identified, British defence policy could have an important role in sustaining political independence in conditions of social and political transformation.

Whether disengagement from NATO were partial or complete, and for reasons outlined in Chapter 9 I favour partial disengagement, the focus of defence policy would therefore be on the protection of political independence against potentially hostile reactions. This could take the form of a strategy of defensive deterrence, based on demonstrating a capability to resist aggression against British territory.

Proceeding from the assumption that British defence policy is cheaper inside NATO than it would be facing the same threat outside the alliance, it is common to argue that territorial defence would mean increasing the annual military budget. The model often taken for this is Sweden which, though non-aligned and an active proponent of disarmament measures, also deploys strong military forces.[16] It is certainly possible that disengagement would result in higher military spending, but there is no reason why this should necessarily be so. British defence policy now includes territorial defence as well as the commitment to providing forces in continental Europe and other further-flung deployments. Concentrating on territorial defence would reduce the scope of British defence policy and a strategy of defensive deterrence would eliminate certain types of forces – long-range strike aircraft, nuclear weapons, ocean-going naval forces – with, one expects, consequent budgetary savings. In fact, I am not clear what the example of Sweden is supposed to prove. At present Sweden's population is about 15 per cent of Britain's, its armed forces about 21 per cent and its annual military spending about 23 per cent; consequently, *per capita* military expenditure is higher – $355 compared to $239 in 1978.[17] But this can hardly be taken to prove that British military spending would have to increase to the same level *per capita*; apart from any other consideration, Sweden's territory is a great deal larger than Britain's, and while *per capita* expenditure is one among several ways of measuring the economic burden of military preparations, it is no sort of a guide as to how much should be spent on defence policy.

It is therefore reasonable to argue that a disengaged military posture could be cheaper, and the reduction in the scope of defence policy provides a strong basis for believing it would be cheaper. Within the context of defensive deterrence and territorial defence, the emphasis would be upon being able to inflict heavy damage on air or naval forces attacking Britain and on any ground forces which managed to land. Consequently, the force posture would most likely stress relatively small naval craft (possibly frigate-size and down), surface-to-air missiles, a limited air force for air defence and possibly striking at naval targets, and a highly mobile infantry force supported by helicopters. In such a posture, there is less room for tank forces and for aircraft for striking at ground targets, one reason being that forces which would destroy large areas of Britain in defending it would neither make much sense nor, therefore, constitute a particularly convincing deterrent. In the restructuring of armed forces to provide this kind of posture, the opportunity to wean them away from allegiance to expensive weapon systems of low cost-effectiveness, such as tanks, could provide a very different appearance for armed forces.

Naturally, these brief remarks provide only the very barest outline of military posture in the context of disengagement from NATO; numerous variations on it are possible. But the principle, of a basic restructuring of forces to accompany a fundamental reworking of policy to provide effective forces of more limited scope and size than the present, should be clear. Alongside this restructuring, institutional change in military industry would be required, converting parts of it to other work, diversifying elements of it, breaking up development capacity and reconstructing it, releasing resources for other uses and ensuring that the most important of these resources, the skills of the workforce, were positively and rewardingly utilised.[18]

Some writers on alternative defence policies have been attracted by the possibility of non-violent methods which could replace the military role in defence.[19] Frankly, I have never been convinced by these arguments, not least because although non-violent techniques have been used to resist military *coups* and weaken the grip of colonial administrations, they have yet to withstand invasion. The crucial element in non-violence appears to be the social unity and determination required to present a single unco-operative and actively resistant front to the aggressor, in the face of attempts to divide the resistance and intimidate or buy off sections of its leadership.[20] Such a degree of unity would be virtually impossible to sustain for any period in a class-divided society, even one in which those divisions were changing under the impact of a process of social and political transformation. Moreover, reliance on non-violent means would be an upheaval in the terms of defence policy and strategy as usually understood to a degree where it is no longer clear that it would be perceived as a deterrent by potential aggressors; even were the policy successful when put to the test, the point is that an aggressor might not be put off by it beforehand. Despite these qualifications, a British government in conditions of transformation might back up its military preparations by training the population, or as much of it as could be persuaded to go through the training, in techniques of non-violent resistance. This might act as a further deterrent to aggression by suggesting that the chances of successfully occupying the country or installing an effective government were very low, and could be supplemented by preparation for physical and organisational sabotage with the same intention. The use of such methods to resist a military *coup* would be a further and important bonus, while the consequent capacity of the people to resist and undermine authoritarian rule might usefully pre-empt the government succumbing to any authoritarian temptations.

As these last points illustrate, the concerns of non-violence usefully highlight a further problem of a policy of disengagement: the resistance of the military to restructuring and to basic change in the underlying assumptions of defence policy. This is not a problem, however, which would be confronted in the limited context of defence policy, but rather in the broader context of the overall transformation I have argued is the only possible basis for disengagement from NATO. The solution which would have to be developed would also emerge in the context of the broader social changes, and it is in political support for the whole process that a counter to any military reaction would have to be found. Over the long-term, however, it is possible to speculate that precisely the restructuring which the forces could be expected to resist would, if successful, gradually erode any military threat to democratic processes. In this context, the separation of military from society entailed in professional armed forces constitutes a constant source of danger for democracy and thinking about defence policy should increasingly face up to this problem. I believe that it is in this connection rather than with regard to an external threat that non-violent and related techniques seem most promising and important.

The Politics of Choice

Adequate debate on defence policy is hampered by a variety of power-ful factors, to such an extent that the sense that there could be more than cosmetic alternatives to current policy is widely lacking. It is to help develop this sense of the possibility of alternatives, both sweeping and modest, and to contribute to creating the foundations for a sober and thorough debate on defence that this book has been written. There are groups who would prefer to see debate contained within an elite of experts, within which, perhaps, there may be room for the occasional individual with unorthodox views, but if there is to be any genuine process of choice in defence policy it is crucial that debate extends out-side this 'magic circle': the key to genuine choice is democracy, both in power and in information.

Despite the shakiness of British defence policy through the years, the consensus which supports it has been relatively stable. There have, of course, been important debates, often expressed in the most stinging terms, yet even when the participants have seen themselves as dealing with the most fundamental issues of defence the debate has usually been restricted. The evil intentions of the USSR, the superiority of WP forces in Europe, the absolute centrality of NATO to British security and the necessity of nuclear strategy have constituted the limits to debate. Only over the issue of nuclear weapons has the consensus been dented at all severely, and there the passage of time has permitted it to regain its hold. And the bulk of the mass media not only subscribes to but energetically promotes that consensus.

The grip of consensual opinion is strengthened by the presentation of policy, particularly by the blanket excuse of secrecy in the service of national security which obviates the need for a full presentation of policy. It is very unlikely that a little more openness by the Ministry of Defence would equip the British people with any more information than the USSR already possesses, but it might risk increasing public disenchantment with defence policy as its shortcomings became more widely and fully understood. Some secrecy restrictions are probably reasonable, but the obsessiveness of British restrictions is both a denial of democracy and often quite ludicrous. The 1974-9 Labour government's most miserable and farcical episode was undoubtedly the prosecution of two journalists and an ex-soldier in 1978 for offences under the Official Secrets Act; the trial of Crispin Aubrey, John Berry and Duncan Campbell included the nonsense of a government witness being ordered not to reveal his name while giving away the details which permitted him to be identified through recourse to public material, and, far more worryingly, the official vetting of potential jurors and appearance of an ex-member of the elite Special Air Services as foreman of the jury.[21] As the affair ground on into a second trial with a new jury and judge, the withdrawal of most of the charges, one suspended sentence and two conditional discharges with heavy costs, the government and state security services stood revealed as oppressive fools. But if their silliness is laughable, their anti-democratic instincts deserve another quite different reaction.

The stakes involved in defence policy are the greatest possible — survival. In such a context, the indiscriminate use of an obsessive secrecy is little less than criminally irresponsible. The response must be the attempt to open up the terms of debate through sceptical and thorough enquiry. This is made doubly necessary by the deep hold on political consciousness of the basic assumptions of defence policy: most people probably take on trust what the government presents as facts about defence and accept the basic judgements of the policy, even though they often refuse to let it get away so lightly in other fields. It is more useful to treat every government statement about defence as, at least potentially, incomplete, evasive, distorted, biased or downright lying; this may seem perverse, but it is actually a duty because of the immense stakes involved.

But it is not only the presentation of policy which hampers debate. Most people not only accept but reproduce the basic assumptions of policy, not only because the subject can be difficult to unravel, not only because the mind tends to flinch from the very immensity of the stakes, but because they actually and positively believe them.

In the face of this, the conditions for genuine choice in defence policy will not emerge simply through an exercise like the one in this chapter, comparing different possible options. The basic aim must be to redefine the concept of national security and generate thoroughly new approaches to international politics, but this must be argued for at every level. There is a need for those who oppose the current shape of policy to involve themselves in detailed debate about it.

British defence policy is in such bad shape that it contains a number of vulnerabilities where there is room to enter debate on short-term and limited aspects of policy in a way which is informed by a wider perspective. Not only the overall size of the budget, and the sense of social priorities which it may reveal, can be tackled in this way, but also individual weapons programmes − such as *Polaris*, *Tornado*, MBT-80 − and decisions on the deployment of forces. If choice in defence policy is going to have any real meaning, those who seek alternatives must engage at all levels of debate, tackling the small problems as well as the large; only as this process develops and involves more and more people will the possibility grow that British defence policy can be hauled out of its present mess.

Notes

1. See the analysis in D. Greenwood, *The United Kingdom's Current Defence Programme and Budget* (University of Aberdeen, 1978); see also Chapter 5, above.

2. See, for example, the very brief reference to non-NATO possibilities compared to the discussion on other possibilities in D. Hazel and P. Williams, *The British Defence Effort: Foundations and Alternatives* (Univeristy of Aberdeen, 1978); see also, G. Pattie, *Towards a New Defence Policy* (Conservative Political Centre, London, 1976); membership of NATO was also the basic assumption in The Labour Party Defence Study Group, *Sense About Defence* (Quartet, London, 1977); for an exception see R. Cook and D. Smith, *What Future in NATO?*,

Fabian Research Series 337 (Fabian Society, London, 1978); for discussions of the NATO context, see the series of Adelphi Papers, published in London by IISS, under the title, *The Alliance and Europe*, in six parts: W. Heisenberg, *Crisis Stability in Europe and Theatre Nuclear Weapons*, no 96, 1973; K. Hunt, *Defence with Fewer Men*, no. 98, 1973; R. Facer, *Weapons Procurement in Europe – Capabilities and Choices*, no. 108, 1975; S. Canby, *Military Doctrine and Technology*, no. 109, 1975; U. Nerlich, *Nuclear Weapons and East-West Negotiation*, no. 120, 1975/6; D.C.R. Heyhoe, *The European Programme Group*, no. 129, 1976/7.

3. D. Greenwood, 'Postscript' to 'Defence Programme Options to 1980-81', in M. Kaldor, D. Smith and S. Vines (eds), *Democratic Socialism and the Cost of Defence* (Croom Helm, London, 1979).

4. Plans for this were reportedly prepared under the Labour government during its last months in office: *State Research Bulletin* 12, June/July 1979.

5. See R. Smith, 'Military Expenditure and Capitalism', *Cambridge Journal of Economics*, vol. 1, no. 1, March 1977, and *idem*, 'Military Expenditure and Capitalism: a Reply', *Cambridge Journal of Economics*, vol. 2, no. 3, September 1978.

6. Greenwood, 'Defence Programme Options to 1980-81'.

7. D. Smith, 'Strategic and political implications of reduced defence programmes', in Kaldor, Smith and Vines (eds), *Democratic Socialism and the Cost of Defence*.

8. *Two-way Street* (Brassey's, London, 1979); see Chapter 7 and Figure 7.1 above.

9. D. Greenwood, 'Politics, Economics and European Defence', in *RUSI and Brassey's Defence Yearbook 1975/76* (Brassey's, London, 1975).

10. Ibid., pp. 122-3.

11. See the proposal that Britain should emphasise its naval traditions in force planning, in Pattie, *Towards a New Defence Policy*, p. 15.

12. G. Evans, 'Welsh Nationalists Reject Bomb', *Sanity*, December/January 1978, G. Kennedy, *The Defence Budget of an Independent Scotland* (Andrew Fletcher Society, 1975), and *idem*, 'Defence', in D. Mackay (ed.), *Scotland 1980* (Q Press, Edinburgh, 1977).

13. *Statement on the Defence Estimates 1975*, Cmnd 5976 (HMSO, London, 1975), p. 8; see also the following year's *Statement*, Cmnd 6432, p. 9.

14. R.J. Vincent, *Military Power and Political Influence: The Soviet Union and Western Europe*, Adelphi Paper 119 (IISS, London, 1975), p. 20; on American use of military power for political influence, see B.M. Blechman and S.S. Kaplan, *Force Without War* (Brookings Institution, Washington, DC, 1978).

15. The FRG has argued that people in the German Democratic Republic receive an 'upbringing to hatred' which endangers peace: *White Paper 1975/1976: The Security of the Federal Republic of Germany and the Development of the Federal Armed Forces* (trans) (Ministry of Defence, Bonn, 1976), pp. 10-11.

16. For example, Hazel and Williams, *The British Defence Effort: Foundations and Alternatives*, pp. 48-9.

17. *The Military Balance 1978-1979* (IISS, London, 1978), pp. 19, 31, 88 and

18. References on the conversion of military industry were given in Chapter 8 above, n7.

19. See for example the following: A. Boserup and A. Mack, *War Without Weapons* (Frances Pinter, London, 1974), S. King-Hall, *Defence in the Nuclear Age* (Victor Gollancz, London, 1958), and *idem*, *Power Politics in the Nuclear Age* (Victor Gollancz, London, 1962); A. Roberts (ed.), *Civilian Resistance as a National Defence* (Penguin, Harmondsworth, 1969); *Bulletin of Peace Proposals*, 1978, no. 4.

20. It could be argued that it was here, rather than in the tactics on the streets, that the decisive weakness of Czechoslovakian non-violent resistance to Soviet aggression in 1968 lay, heroic though the resistance was; see the account in J. Pelikan, *Socialist Opposition in Eastern Europe: The Czechoslovak Example* (Allison & Busby, London, 1976).

21. The events of the trial were summarised in *Time Out*, 24 November 1978.